8D $3⁰⁰N

Poetic Process

George Whalley

POETIC
PROCESS

Routledge & Kegan Paul Ltd

London

First published in 1953
by Routledge & Kegan Paul Ltd
Broadway House, 68-74 Carter Lane
London E.C.4
Printed in Great Britain
by Butler & Tanner Ltd
Frome and London

To my Mother
and to the memory of my Father
this essay is affectionately dedicated.

Per correr miglior acqua alza le vele
omai la navicella del mio ingegno,
che lascia retro a sè mar si crudele.

πᾶς γοῦν ποιητὴς γίγνεται, κἂν ἄμουσος ᾖ τὸ πρίν,
οὗ ἂν Ἔρως ἅψηται.

PLATO

No one can leap over his own shadow,
but poets leap over death.

S. T. COLERIDGE

Was ist Unendlichkeit?
Wie kannst du dich so quälen?
Geh' in dich selbst.
Entbehrst du drin Unendlichkeit in Sein und Sinn
So ist dir nicht zu helfen.

GOETHE

O the mind, mind has mountains; cliffs of fall
Frightful, sheer, no-man-fathomed. Hold them cheap
May who ne'er hung there.

GERARD MANLEY HOPKINS

Preface

*When I must shipwrack, I would do it in a Sea, where mine impotencie might have some excuse;
not in a sullen weedy lake, where I could not have so much as exercise for my swimming.*

JOHN DONNE

Now that this book is finished, the best thing of all is to look back and think of all the people who, one way and another, have helped to complete it. Dr W. O. Raymond and the late Dr A. H. McGreer encouraged the project when it was first getting under way. Professor R. D. Maclennan, Miss Dorothy Emmet, Dr H. A. Hodges, and Mr John Buxton at different times illuminated the subject with their conversation. Professor Louis Arnaud Reid did me the honour (when a complete stranger) of making forthright and astringent comments upon the text, made me the confidant of his mature reflections upon aesthetics, and gently rebuked me for philosophical rashness and incompetence. Professor Geoffrey Bullough, whose reputation as scholar and teacher does not wait upon my witness, gave encouragement at a crucial time; and his personal contempt for jargon and pedantry taught me to cultivate—even if I have not mastered—the good manners of a clear style of writing. The late G. H. Clarke offered advice and criticism upon an early draft of this essay. Professor A. R. C. Duncan came to the rescue when I was trying to make up my mind about Kant in my fourth chapter. In all matters to do with Samuel Taylor Coleridge—and this turns out to be a somewhat Coleridgean book—I owe a great deal to Miss Kathleen Coburn. I am grateful to my associates at Bishop's University and Queen's University for their encouragement. And it would be churlish not to thank those students whose amiable obtuseness has forced me to restate my case in a multitude of different forms. The Arts Research Committee of Queen's University generously provided a grant for typing the manuscript. My greatest debt is to my wife Elizabeth, who has attended patiently upon a hard birth.

I began this essay in sheer ignorance and was impelled by the arrogant isolation of one who imagines he is breaking new ground. As for the newness of the ground, I am now less certain than I was seven years ago. Whatever ignorance or arrogance remains in the following pages is no fault of any of the people I have mentioned.

An inquiry of this sort, like the prospect of the gallows, marvellously sharpens the wits. Everything one sees, hears, reads, thinks seems to reflect back upon the same centre; and one is all the time picking up hints and portents where they could least be expected to lurk. My debt to previous writers, alive and dead, is very extensive. Whenever I knew that I was borrowing—and what I was borrowing —I have recorded the details in the footnotes. Unfortunately it is not always possible to trace the exact nature, extent, or identity of one's borrowings—even the most important ones; and sometimes I have made discoveries for myself, only to find that somebody or other had feloniously anticipated me. If I have overlooked any of my debts, I hope that a general apology will exonerate me from all suspicion of flaunting feathers not my own.

G. W.

Kingston, February 1953.

Contents

Introduction

THIS essay first began to take shape in 1946 when I embarked upon a study of the growth and operation of Coleridge's mind. It seemed to me then—and still seems—that a task so delicate and susceptible of distortion might not be possible faithfully to complete; but at least I could explore the most likely causes of distortion and avoid them. Not a few books, I found, had been written about art both from the philosophical and critical points of view. But as I read through some of these and recalled others that I had read and tried to bring these into relation with Coleridge's mind, they seemed to be talking about something other than the experience and values of art. In some quarters there was a good deal of talk about Beauty and in others a tone of patronizing severity; many critics, in treating works of art as 'things', seemed to force alien preconceptions upon their subject-matter—some insisted upon common sense and others maintained fiercely that one must at all costs be scientific. A few artists, however, when they were writing about their own art, seemed to be talking about something that could be recognized as falling within the scope of an artist's experience; and these artists represented the root and core of criticism. Enraged that philosophers and critics could so disingenuously avoid the subjects they purported to illuminate, I wished to mend their ways. So my first shot at this essay was *A Critique of Criticism,* an attempt to determine the nature of the critical judgments we make in the presence of works of art.

This proved to be an evasion—precisely the evasion I wanted to drive out of aesthetics and criticism: one was assuming art and concentrating upon something else. I wished to know more about the way an artist's mind worked, what activities it shared with other minds, and how one could distinguish and compare different activities of mind. As soon as I started to ask direct questions about artistic experience, a number of other questions cropped up with them; the most searching questions, it seemed, that one could ask in ethics, psychology, philosophy, religion, and science. This would have been reason enough to lay the whole matter aside to await the attention of intellects more acute, sensibilities more refined, experience more profound, judgment more mature. Questions about knowledge, perception, vision, fact, truth, faith, symbolism, logic, imagination, moral judgment, had been asked from the beginning of recorded philosophy; and although some answers had been offered, the questions did not cease to clamour for attention. I could find no satisfactory attempt to integrate them into a single vision. Plato and Aristotle seemed to offer the greatest hope; Aquinas was not hostile; Bergson and Whitehead, though suspect in some quarters, seemed hospitable to the artist's attitude. Not until my work was well advanced did I come upon the fulfilment, in the work of Kierkegaard, Jaspers and Marcel, of much that Coleridge had striven for and of much that, in a tenuous and indistinct form, I had been led by my subject to adopt. Kierkegaard had noted in his journal in 1848, 'My whole life is an epigram calculated to make people aware'; but no such appropriate centre seemed to have been chosen for a study of art. And there was no single comprehensive philosophy that took its departure from the nature of artistic experience itself.[1]

It was necessary to ask why philosophers, even when writing aesthetics, failed to recognize some of the most rudimentary assumptions that an artist makes. Martin Turnell, for example, in an article on Jules Laforgue and the theory of *vers libre*, has observed that 'The foundations of modern art were laid in the period when the classical metaphysic was challenged by the rise of the idealist systems, by the change from a philosophy of *being* to a philosophy of *knowing*.' Descartes' *cogito ergo sum*, he suggests, is perhaps the turning-point— 'it marks the retreat of the thinker and the artist into the world

[1] Croce's *Estetica*, it is true, following somewhat in the steps of Vico's *Scienza Nuova*, had attempted to start from the 'facts' of art, but through an imperfect understanding of artistic experience broke its back over the central term, 'expression'. Professor H. A. Hodges' book, *The Philosophy of Wilhelm Dilthey* (1952), unfortunately did not come into my hands until after my manuscript was completed; there is much in that book that would have profited me.

within'. But why 'retreat'? Has not the artist's creative charter always been *patior ergo sum*—I suffer, therefore I am? And is it not in suffering that knowing and being meet luminously in value? And why were critics content to break off their discussions with an elegant gesture of evasion—as Eliot does at the end of his *Hamlet* essay: 'If it is complained that I have not defined truth and fact and reason I can only reply modestly that it was never my intention to do so'? Was there no relation between the philosopher's world and the artist's? That seemed unlikely. Had the practice of art no light to throw upon the graver questions of philosophy and psychology, of morality, value, behaviour? There were no signs that art was clearly enough understood to be dismissed without a hearing. Other questions crowded in. Was artistic experience somehow abnormal, pathological, parasitic? Was art (as I had found some maintaining) simply an escape from those 'facts of life' which (it was alleged) every sane person knows are hard, intractable, and perhaps hopeless? Was scientific method the sole and final judge of what was real? Must knowledge always be judged by the access it gave to power—and if so, what kind of power? Or was art a crude sort of groping which the refined methods of analytical logic and scientific technology had now rendered obsolete?

Certain similarities between artistic and mystical experience began to become clearer; there seemed to operate there a kind of knowing, valuable in its own right, which did not support itself either by logical or by sensory verification. Art and religion were not fighting a rearguard action against a new and self-sufficient development of the mind as revealed in science and certain kinds of philosophy; art was not a pterodactyl waging futile battle against Nature's latest masterpiece. I came to see that, whatever knowledge was, the end of knowledge was not material power but awareness; that whatever battle is going forward in the mental and spiritual spheres, it is not between rival avocations like science, art, religion, philosophy, big business, but between fundamentally different ways of mind. The ways of mind could, for my purposes and without over-simplification, be reduced to two. These I called 'contemplative' and 'technical'; the second term was to embrace both the practical way of mind that discharges in immediate action, and that state of suspended practicality which in defiance of Greek usage is commonly called 'theoretical'.

My purpose was to clarify to myself what may be called 'the facts of artistic experience'. It was now clear why this had not been undertaken more often or more vigorously: such an inquiry could not be confined within the limits of any recognized intellectual activity —not of aesthetics, art-criticism, history, psychology, metaphysics, ethics, or any other special department of philosophy. It lay at the intersection of all these special interests, and probably others. Art then might provide a fresh entry to many ancient problems and a novel attitude towards them; it might bring together into a single glance problems which had grown into unwholesome separation; it might supply some means of accurate inquiry into whatever experience is essentially moral, valuable, and individual.

But theories and systems and the solution of specific problems were something for a distant future. For a start it was a matter of seeing clearly what art and artistic experience were. Philosophy was to me a chilly and unfamiliar country, as vividly unreal as Paris or Los Angeles on a first visit; but if the trail led there too, one must try to avoid both bucolic vacuity and provincial intolerance; for there was no saying that philosophy might not be, in its own way, a holy city.

2

Philosophy, psychology, and criticism, I felt, had not notably succeeded in giving an adequate account of art. The most penetrating critics were inclined to gloss over the philosophical and moral implications of whatever they might conclude about art; the more busily the scientific critics analysed, the farther they moved away from art; philosophers were inclined to consider art as an afterthought, adding it as an appendix or footnote to a settled scheme, sometimes with a virtuoso's condescension.[1] In short—with a few exceptions—art was being 'explained' (sometimes explained away) in terms which had previously been established for other purposes but which were neither sensitive enough nor comprehensive enough to embrace art.

One could not fail to notice that the only philosophers who had made any particularly illuminating remarks upon art were those whose thought started from and constantly returned to the irreducibly moral character of human experience. It was clear that the philosophical problem for artistic experience was in certain respects identical

[1] R. G. Collingwood's influential and somewhat authoritarian writings in aesthetics are irredeemably hampered by his refusal to allow art to modify the philosophical position he had previously adopted. I suspect from the texture of his writing that he recognized how disrupting art could have been in his philosophy, but was not prepared to let that disruption occur.

with that of moral experience, and that neither could be understood without examining each for what it was. The reality for art and the reality for ethics intersected in value and knowledge. Aesthetic theory had been seriously hampered by attempting to introduce value and knowledge only when they could be shown to arise from certain conceptual processes and to rest upon logical tests of evidence. Samuel Alexander—particularly in *Beauty and Other Forms of Value*— placed the emphasis upon Value; but he simultaneously centred his attention upon Beauty. Even though he conceived Beauty to be value and not quality, Alexander seemed to envisage value, much as he envisaged space-time, as substance and not as relation. In Richards' 'psychological theory of value' (*The Principles of Literary Criticism*) the question of knowledge and value was evaded or disguised by arguing that everybody knew what knowledge was—that it was conceptual, and that value was only the psychological reconciliation of personal 'wants' or 'drives'. In seeking a scientific—that is, experimental and quantitative—basis for judging works of art, he had enjoined a wholesome respect for the complexities of art but had seriously mis-represented the nature of the creative act. It was necessary to return to artistic experience itself and settle the primary questions about art in the light of artistic facts and not on some other basis. For, as Herbert Read had written,

> Beauty has no other reason
> than the eye can indicate;
> Only the miraculous conception
> is immaculate.

Logic and conceptual verification could bear only upon propositions; but art was not basically propositional. Was the non-propositional character of art reason enough to deny that art arises from genuine knowledge? If fully developed artistic experience could be examined, would it be found that in art the situation of value was much the same as it is in instances of moral choice?

From a direct inquiry into artistic experience certain facts emerged with compelling force to dominate the whole investigation. (*a*) In art, fact and value are inseparable. (*b*) Value is not a term to be ascribed to certain classes of things or to events in general or in the abstract, but only to an individual event in which a person is actually, sensitively and comprehensively, involved. (*c*) Value and genuine knowledge are ineradicable features of artistic experience;

they are vital features of poetic process in its most rudimentary beginnings and are largely responsible for its distinctive character; they are not to be regarded as 'terminal products' that appear when aesthetic experience has passed over into conceptual and veridical activity. (*d*) The archetypes of the event of value, of knowing, of perception, of language are more readily to be discerned and more accessible to examination in art than anywhere else. (*e*) A work of art is not first conceived and then made; it is discovered and realizes itself in the making. (*f*) Art bodies forth reality.[1]

This final axiom had to be assimilated with caution. The term 'reality' had to be given a genuine meaning beyond a gesture of applause; it had to be shown as the intersection in time of the timeless, of value, and of the person. I therefore took art to be metaphysical in a sense not usually assigned: that is, art was concerned to express reality and being, in forms which were structurally faithful both within themselves and to reality. 'Being' was not to be regarded as involving a question about the abstract 'existence' of things; but was taken to affirm the quality of that experience which was at once personal, valuable, and responsible. The centre of emphasis for an inquiry into art must be at once moral and experiential. But Whitehead's caution was to be observed: 'There is a conventional view of experience . . . persistently lurking in tacit presuppositions. This view conceives experience as a clear-cut knowledge of clear-cut items, with clear-cut connections with each other. This is the conception of a trim, tidy, finite experience uniformly illuminated. No notion could be further from the truth. . . . The word "experience" is one of the most deceitful in philosophy.' Other methods of inquiry claim access to reality and means of revealing reality: these had to be considered in the light of a reality which was not so narrow as to be silly, nor so inclusive as to be meaningless.

3

Albert Schweitzer repeats with approval the questions by which Goethe always examined a new philosophy: 'Is it concerned with

[1] Some time after establishing these premises for myself I find the first three luminously set forth by A. E. Taylor in the second chapter of *The Faith of a Moralist* (1930) and in his essay 'Knowing and Believing' in the *Philosophical Studies* (1934). For further comparison Leone Vivante's *English Poetry and its contribution to the knowledge of a creative principle* (1950) may also be consulted. Gabriel Marcel's *The Mystery of Being* (1950-1) rests upon a similar position.

natural reality without preconceived theories, and does it bring man into direct relationship with nature? Is its conception of ethics profound and enlightened? When it has arrived at the final questions raised by research and reflection, has it the courage to admit that there remain unfathomable mysteries, or does it pretend to offer a system which explains everything?' If the pages that follow can satisfactorily survive questioning along those lines, I shall be content.

This is not primarily an essay in method; but in writing the essay a suitable method of inquiry had to be discovered for it. I did not feel entitled to make any presuppositions about the nature of the materials under inquiry, nor about the method proper to elucidate and correlate them. The inquiry was not to be an analysis of propositions or statements *about* art, but an inquiry into certain kinds of experience; the method therefore became suspensive and dialectical. No matter how useful the methods of logical analysis might be in refining terms in the approaches to the main inquiry, the integrity of the complex states exhibited in art had to be preserved under inquiry. To suppose that the subject could be exhausted by a succession of propositions, and that the worth of the inquiry could be determined by the logical correlation of those propositions, was an assumption that I could not accept. To demolish by analysis whatever meaning a statement might have been intended to have, is a common enough gambit in positivist argument; it usually shows that the statement did not mean something that it was never intended to mean. An artist recognizes clearly enough when he has got hold of a fruitful germ: why should not a philosopher single out certain accounts and statements which he recognizes as fruitful, accept them, and see what light the implications of that position would throw upon other established opinions, methods, and conclusions?

This way of working does not renounce analysis, nor does it seek to avoid criticism; it simply reserves the right to select starting points which it recognizes to be fruitful and relevant, and to examine them in a way that will fertilize rather than annihilate. In this way we arrive at an account of art by a process of dialectic—a dialectic in which the terms held in tension are contemplative entities and not propositions.[1] By means of analysis the contemplative terms are refined, clarified, and criticized before being brought into dialectical

---

[1] It seems to me that in Hegel's dialectic the terms are suppressed propositions couched in single words; the concealed technical character of his method makes it, as the Marxists have found, easily susceptible to disingenuous distortion.

tension with other terms. Analysis in this sense is Aristotle's *analusis* —a loosening of mental knots, an unravelling of what is dense, compact, germ-like, packed with implications not indicated by the outer structure. By this restricted use of analysis contemplative entities can be clarified, and gently detached from the narcotic obscurities that confuse their margins. The analysis does not, however, penetrate into or anatomize the contemplative entity itself; only in a state of passive concentration, of vision, can a person hold a contemplative entity within the range of attention. Purified, detached from parasitic accretions which are no more of their own nature than barnacles are of the nature of a ship, contemplative entities can then be brought into collision and tension with each other as a stage towards dialectical synthesis. This is synthesis in the true sense of the word; not an analytical diagram or *schema*, but an integral comprehension of the related entities in a single moment of vision. But this contemplative dialectic evidently belongs in the sphere of art rather than in the sphere of any technical discipline so far established. Total assertions are brought into collision to generate further total assertions.[1] But no technical method can provide assertions other than partial: even in the 'thinking' process there are always needed the successive leaps into the dark. But the leaps must be carefully prepared: 'There always comes a moment for the "thinker" when, at the limit of his elaboration, elimination, fractionizings—at the end of his analysis—it is the first idea now received that carries him forward, as all the skill of the tight-rope dancer finishes up just at the extremity of the rope. There always comes a moment when every thinker is the victim of the conclusion of his finished effort, and of his own transformation (from thinker into sufferer)' (Paul Valéry). The language of the sufferer, the language of total assertion, is the language not of science but of poetry. The appropriate language for revealing these contemplative entities and their dialectical relations cannot be formulated beforehand. To prescribe a way of language, a manner of exposition, is to prescribe a way of mind; and the history of aesthetics and criticism does not show that an appropriate way of mind can yet be prescribed for poetics. Valéry has indicated the delicacy of the task.

'To invent ought closely to resemble the recognizing of a tune in the monotonous fall of raindrops, in the throbbing of the train and the alternating strokes of a machine.

[1] For the meaning of the term 'total assertion', see my pp. 32–3 below.

'One must have, I believe, an object, or nucleus, or substance that is vague—and a disposition. . . .

'The general advance of inventions belongs to this general type: a sequence of successive deformations, almost continuous, of the given matter, and a threshold—a sudden perception of the *future* of one of the states.'

Looking back over the book I find that this is the method which has emerged by allowing the materials to discover their own coherence. I do not claim that this essay is a model of method. Only now at the end can I see at all clearly what the method was. If, with that in mind, I were to rewrite the whole book as a formal exposition or example of that method, clarifying and stylizing the procedure, the book would be an essay in method and not an essay in poetics. Poetry was what I wanted to write about, not method. But since poetry in particular, and art generally, impose peculiar difficulties for the inquirer, it seems not altogether presumptuous to set forth as clearly as may be a sketch of the method which seems to have been forced upon me in this case.

By putting on a particular pair of methodological spectacles it would seem that we could correct our aberrations of vision. But the analogy of spectacles does not apply to aesthetics and ethics; neither does it apply (I suspect) to any philosophy which is regarded in its ancient sense as the persistent search for wisdom and fullness of life. In these instances the observed and the observer are one and inseparable in several senses. In one sense the observer observes himself always, in that he can observe only what he can see; and what he can see is determined by what he is. Spectacles may clarify vision but they cannot create vision. They may, by limiting the field of vision, increase acuity; but at the same time they may act as blinkers or shutters occluding much of what must be seen at a single glance. I suspect that in studying poetic activities system and technique must be renounced; the method, the line of approach, wants to be heuristic, an alert way of open-minded seeking which does not prejudge either the nature of the materials or the final issue; an attitude of discovering, a rigorous and delicate sense of relevance; an embracing hospitality for all sorts of ideas and evidence which at first sight might seem to have nothing at all to do with art. If this essay gives a hint towards this method, it simply asserts the method that Socrates and Plato used, the method that Aristotle regarded as the crown of philosophical attainment although he left no writing of his own to illustrate this manner. This dialectical, heuristic method is (I believe) returning to the West, with encouraging force, chiefly under the name of existentialism.

Theory and system, and a neat box-hedged plan for poetry—these were never my intention. How to analyse without destroying the vitality and diversity; how to generalize without destroying the individual uniqueness; how to keep constantly in sight, as point of departure and test, the intricate and vigorous activity which terminates in works of art, and the arresting excitement and peace enjoyed in their presence—these were the problems in method. How such a method is to be classified I do not know; it is, I suppose, philosophy in the perennial sense. I have ventured to use the term *Poetics*, not simply in deference to Aristotle's fragmentary monument of that name, but because a name is needed for those inquiries which are neither aesthetics nor criticism but both at once; for it was necessary to claim the privilege of moving freely back and forth across whatever boundaries of method or subject those two more specialized studies might legitimately claim for themselves. The object is to see poetry and the poet in their full stature, in their full complexity, in the perspective of value and eternity: to see the poem as timelessly valuable, and the poet as a person who—through little virtue of his own—is transfigured by his art.

4

Whenever the attitude or method of science and positivism is mentioned in this essay, I observe that a note of asperity enters. This I should have liked to remove, if only to give my work an air of cool detachment, and to avoid the company of those cheerful partisans who insist upon dividing mankind into sheep and goats. An account of imagination, of the mind's ways of discovering and making, would be ridiculously narrow if it could not include every genuinely valuable event of making and discovering. There must be some way of thinking of Bach, Sherrington, and Beethoven, Matisse, Hindemith, and Einstein in one breath. John Livingston Lowes, in *The Road to Xanadu,* wrote about Newton in a way indistinguishable from his way of writing about a poet: 'Once more there was the long, slow storing of the Well of memory; once more the flash of amazing vision through a fortuitous suggestion; once more the exacting task of translating the Vision into actuality.' He continues: 'But it is of the utmost moment to more than poetry that instead of regarding the imagination as a bright but ineffectual faculty with which in some esoteric fashion poets and their kind are specially endowed, we recognize the essential oneness of its function and its ways with all the creative endeavours through which human brains, with dogged persistence, strive to discover and realize order in a chaotic world.'

When I try to discipline out of existence my acrimonious remarks upon science and the technical mind, I find that I am dealing with something more solid and serious than an 'emotional block' on my own part or a state of sublimated envy. The technical mind is undoubtedly a powerful instrument for analysis and specific application. Its refined operations have undermined many superstitious fears and given leisure and space—both physical and mental—in which the mind can seek the central peace and freedom it longs for. But the very success of the technical mind has bred other superstitions no less oppressive than the old ones. We are probably cleaner than our ancestors, and better fed; generally we live longer. But we have not mastered the terrors of space and time, nor do we bother much to heal the sick conscience. A 'rational' and materialist obscurantism is solidly in the air we breathe—more so, one supposes, in North America than in Europe but rapidly invading Europe under the guise of cultural and democratic insemination. It is difficult to cite actual instances, for obscurantism is nebulous and evasive; its power depends upon dispersal and the uncritical mind. It has no name or label, does not readily associate itself with single names or particular groups; and when one tries to pick out illustrations they sound like the excoriating jeremiads that envious men and social misfits, time out of mind, have screamed at their contemporaries. 'Science' is the prevailing superstition, subserving every form of materialism, distorting principles, motives, and 'facts', with the bold inconsequence of propaganda broadcasts, inducing a destructive futility and what somebody has called 'cosmic impertinence'. This is only partly to be laid to the charge of true scientists; it gathered full weight only when science came to be exploited by those who were in no sense scientists but were prepared, through ignorance or to serve material ends, to deify the technical mind, the expert view, the scientific method. For it thrives whenever belief has been debased into sophisticated gullibility, when curiosity grows blunt and inconsequent for lack of discipline.

Perhaps the most disastrous aspect of this superstition is the view—

endorsed by experts and fomented by enthusiasts—that the technical mind is man's most refined instrument of discovery and the final criterion of all knowledge. At all events the forces of (what may conveniently be called) 'positivism' and of a cerebral oversimplification disguised as common sense are not men of straw or Quixotic windmills. Bertrand Russell writes in his *History of Western Philosophy:* 'There remains a vast field, traditionally included in philosophy, where scientific methods are inadequate. This field includes ultimate questions of value; science alone, for example, cannot prove that it is bad to enjoy the infliction of cruelty. *Whatever can be known, can be known by means of science*; but things which are legitimately matters of feeling lie outside its province' (my italics). At first sight he seems handsomely to be conceding, as few positivists would be prepared to, that there are limits to science. But the concession is immediately withdrawn by asserting that knowledge and science are co-extensive, and (by implication) that outside science there is no knowledge. The word 'science' is the anglicized form of the Latin *scientia* = knowledge; but that meaning of the word 'science' has only slowly made headway, and it is not much more than a century since science has come to be regarded as a genuine form of knowledge. Whence then this arrogant appropriation of knowledge to science? That is a historical question with which I cannot at the moment be concerned; but it looks very much like that inversion of values which the Greeks called ὕβρις, the one-sidedness that makes a man spiritually blind and leads him to imagine that he is a law to himself. As long as science maintains speculative detachment within its own methodological limits, it is not much less useful than breathing and not much more reprehensible than chess-playing. But when the 'scientific attitude', in a vulgarized form, mistaking hardheadedness for wisdom, invades the moral basis of responsibility, then obscurantism is undermining the health of a civilization. And rather more than a century ago Coleridge had already noticed that 'We have purchased a few brilliant inventions at the loss of all communion with life and the spirit of nature.'

Here the central issue is that raised by Bertrand Russell—knowledge and the claim that knowledge is wholly embraced by science. A study of artistic experience, like a study of religious experience, brings one to recognize that there are other forms of knowing than the scientific kind, and that the immediacy and power of artistic knowing places scientific knowing in an ancillary and not a sovereign position. One of the results of this study has been to show that the technical mind, despite its brilliant triumphs, is a limited mental organization constructed in response to the circumstances of the human situation, and distorted into tyrannous oversimplification by an accident of emphasis.

But my essay has in this matter a more positive purpose. Whatever conflict this obscurantism implies, it is a conflict not between rival avocations—between scientists and artists and men of religion—but between two ways of mind: the technical and the contemplative. I wish to distinguish those two ways of mind and particularly to draw attention to the contemplative. Within the sphere of formal philosophy there is bitterness enough between those who would retain some connection between philosophy and life, and those who, by limiting philosophy to the narrow ambit of logic as we know it at present, deny the philosophical validity of value and of metaphysics. It may be that within philosophy the conflict of assertion and counter-assertion can never be satisfactorily resolved: there is no common meeting-ground between positivism and what the positivists with comprehensive scorn call 'idealism'. Yet it is difficult to see how the whole sphere of moral inquiry can be dismissed as an illogical muddle. The direct study of art, of artistic experience, of the activities of mind exhibited in art, and of the artistic use of language enjoy an especially powerful *point d'appui* for metaphysical, epistemological, and moral questions.

In accepting the facts of artistic experience one is obliged to recognize processes which are synthetic and integral, ringed about with mystery and darkness, infused at crucial moments by events which can only be regarded as fortuitous. In poetics a contemplative attitude is required; otherwise there is no poetry to examine, no poetic experience to be recognized. Poetics concentrates upon whatever is capable of conveying wisdom, of broadening our awareness for the values of being and the qualities of human experience:

> *And wisdom is a butterfly*
> *And not a gloomy bird of prey.*

Poetics asserts—to put the matter in a very rudimentary form—that faithful self-abandonment is more valuable than cerebral consent. It has been said that 'religion is what a man does with his solitude'. Poetics seeks to enter into the state of solitude, to discern value, to consider the implications of a categorical imperative, not of doing but of being. For poetics strives to reveal how in the artistic mind form and content become a unified entity which is neither form nor content but simply art. That such a unity is possible—and it proves to be a complex and extensive unity—suggests that there may lie here a clue to the quality of being which arises, neither from the contemplative mind alone, nor simply from the technical way of mind; but where both operate simultaneously, fusing purpose and vision, means and end, in that contemplative activity which is not merely action but value. Both ways of mind fall within the scope of artistic experience; singly neither can produce a work of art, yet when integrated in a delicately poised activity they can discharge in works which are timeless and inexhaustible.

The two ways of mind are neither mutually exclusive nor strictly antithetical; they are complementary, but at a level so radical that to integrate them is—and always has been—the most delicate and urgent practical problem for society and for the individual. They are not, however, of equal or interchangeable value, nor can we without peril choose one to the exclusion of the other: the human tragedy arises from our being endowed with both capacities; refusal or failure to integrate them is Death-in-Life. Poetics throws a peculiarly clear light, not only upon the distinction between the technical and the contemplative, but upon the relations between the two; for, in its critical function, poetics has power simultaneously to discriminate value and intention.

This essay then is not intended as another pamphlet in the strident logomachies between science and poetry, faith and reason. It is intended for a strong plea that the mind should be recognized for what it is; that mental creations should not be regarded too arrogantly on the one hand, nor too condescendingly on the other; that before any conception of reality is assumed, we should consider such apparent antitheses as ideal—real, actual—phenomenal to see whether some notions of reality widely current are not simply assumptions convenient for some activities but inappropriate if extended to others. In short, this is a plea that we should notice how from time to time, in those persons for whom we reserve the name of genius, the mind asserts itself by breaking through the opaque screens of cultivated custom, social formality, and intolerant professionalism, to achieve and embody acts of vision; and how those acts of vision, by bringing us suddenly and humbly back to earth, restore for us the memories of incandescent moments-in-time which are our only glimpses of eternity.

For it is always a salutary shock to find that the vision of God is reserved, not for the excessively clever, urbane, or cultivated, for the men of ponderous learning or for those who display sharp singleness of purpose in the world of affairs or research; but quite simply for 'the pure in heart'—not for the expert but for the initiate, and for the initiate in the discipline of humility, patience, and wholeness. This essay does not advocate one way of life and condemn all others. Purity of heart is not a trade specification and does not fall under any specialized category of function. It is a quality of intension.[1] Nothing can reveal the intension faithfully except the finished and realized work itself, and then only when the work is appropriately grasped. For the work is the intension embodied, the value arrested and made physical. Biography, personal statement, and reminiscence, throw at best a wavering light upon intension. The concept of motive involves a causal regress: it is as difficult to apply in philosophy as in a court of law, not because it lacks external criteria but because it implies a disguised attempt to explain the contemplative in terms of the technical. If we choose as fundamental criterion in art, not motive but intension, we are on much firmer ground; for each of the two ultimate intensions when embodied reveals itself in a distinct texture and rhythm. Once we can distinguish these two organizations—and the distinction has been asserted before in a variety of forms—it is possible to distinguish intension. Further, if in a particular case we can distinguish intension, we are in a fair way to adopt an appropriately receptive attitude; and this applies not only to works of art but to any kind of utterance or action whatsoever. But when we choose as our fundamental term intension rather than motives, emotional 'drives', and the like, we are renouncing the mechanistic determinism which scientific method seeks to assume even for human behaviour; we are asserting that will and value and moral judgment are of the irreducible essence of art and of all the higher forms of human experience and activity.

Whatever interest this essay may hold for the philosopher as distinct from the art critic will centre upon the distinction of these two

[1] By *intension* I mean something more comprehensive and internal, something less deliberate and 'conscious', than is implied by 'intention'. Intension may be defined as the impulsive orientation of the person in a moment of awareness. Part of the task of resolving intension into action is to externalize the impulse into an 'intention'; the Greek for intend being to 'have it in mind [to do] . . .' The word 'intension' belongs with Hopkins's words 'inscape' and 'instress'; although it has a technical application in logic it is not likely to lead to ambiguity.

attitudes of mind as exhibited in art. There may be some psychological interest in the suggestion that each intension does not simply arise from a special set of assumptions; each intension imposes—or simply *is*—a distinctive psychic and mental organization. In the long ascendancy of the technical way of mind, the contemplative mind has been recognized less and less clearly for what it is, and has seldom in recent years been submitted to patient scrutiny. On the other hand, the technical way of mind has been misrepresented; it has been described as though it were wholly distinct from—and had outmoded—the contemplative; consequently the speculative meeting-point of the two—in inference, discovery, vision, invention—has not been clearly understood. Yet 'recognition', a certain quality of insight, has recently come to dominate the philosophical scene. In this essay I am concerned primarily to examine the contemplative way of mind as exhibited in art; not because it occurs only in artistic activity, but because in art intension, activity, and product are so closely related in their modes of overt expression that they can, within the compass of poetics, be compared and examined without distorting their pristine character.

The contemplative mind in art relies upon and manifests in its physical products a primitive prelogical mode of knowing. The value and status of this mode of knowing is to be judged in individual events of value, not by its logical relations with generalized events, but by the structure and inner coherence of the individual cognitive act itself. Prelogical knowing does not preclude analytical thinking, but it is not propositional and does not arise from analytical thinking, nor does it return to it for verification: it bears its own argument within its body. This mode of knowing I believe is far more prominent and potent in human experience—even of the most humble and earthy sort—than is generally recognized. There can be no doubt that not all effective technical action is valuable. It may well come to be recognized that the contemplative prelogical mode of knowing exhibited so forcibly in art, the knowing that terminates in recognitions and not in 'conclusions', is the source from which all valuable action flows. For my own part, I am convinced that prelogical knowing is not only more reliable and comprehensive than the intellectual knowing of analysis, abstraction, generalization, and verification, but that it is in fact—in its directness and vividness—the prototype to which all human knowledge is referred in action, in actual events of reality.

Throughout this essay I have assumed and asserted the unity of art: that is, that there is no essential difference between the different arts if a correct adjustment is made for differences in medium and if the inquiry be carried to an appropriate level. The account here offered, however, concentrates upon poetry; the other arts have been used for illustration and to avoid the misunderstandings that occur when general statements about art are drawn from some special feature of a particular art. In most passages of this essay the words 'poetry', 'poem', and 'poet' can be taken to stand for 'art', 'work of art', and 'artist'; for I have tried to consider all general statements about poetry in the light of the other arts.   I have used the phrase 'poetic process', not so much to indicate that the essay is concerned principally with poetry, but to recall the word 'poetic' to its original Greek meaning of 'creative'. There are however at least two strong objections to using the word 'creative'. It has been too much used 'for ritual terror and adornment', for mystification, and for evasion—particularly in the phrases 'creative imagination', 'creative artist', and 'creative writing'. It is well that artistic activity be regarded as different in kind from the practical and technical activities which seem 'normal'. But there is nothing gained by placing the matter beyond inquiry either by re-tiring into a cloud, or by presupposing a partial view of 'making'.

The second objection is fundamental. The word *creative* can only be applied analogically and not actually to human activity. An artist's experience is integrative; he selects and arranges in order to produce a translucent entity which is of value and which had not existed before in precisely that quality and character. But is that in the fullest sense creation? I believe that we cannot claim—even for the highest human achievement—a greater power of creation than Coleridge claims for the artist's imagination—'a repetition in the finite mind of the eternal act of creation in the infinite I AM'. Some years ago Ivor Richards, in his *Principles of Literary Criticism*, was infuriated beyond measure by this phrase of Coleridge's, and asserted that an account of Imagination must be 'devoid of theological im-plications'. Richards at that time was anxious to establish a scientific criticism; that perhaps explains his impatience fully enough. Perhaps art should be devoid of *theological*—that is, dogmatic and apologetic—implications; but I cannot see how any honest inquiry into art can be devoid of religious implications. The highest artistic creativity in man arises from a state of humility which is in truth not merely self-abasement, but self-annihilation. The great artist is not omnipotent: he is at best omni-viable, a perfectly translucent medium, ideally a conductor free of resistance or distortion. To call this 'creative' is either honorific nonsense or hybristic blindness; a poet no more *creates* a poem than a mother *creates* a child. Most literary critics and writers on aesthetics contrive to pretend that no moral or religious issues should enter the realm of art; but it is not until we examine the implications of art in the sphere of moral value that we can understand why art proceeds perpetually upon a knife-edge, not only of achievement but also of damnation.

'Works of art', Rilke once remarked, 'are of an infinite loneliness and with nothing so little to be reached as with criticism.' In respect of judgment the artist is also of an infinite loneliness; the complete work of art, the artist in creation, is always right, is always unassailable; and as far as the range of the work extends, each work of art stands impregnable and timeless. To regard the artist as creator is more than a polite analogy; it represents the acute menace that the artist is to himself and to society. The artist is always right; he asserts, and his affirmations are beyond proof and disproof. Yet in his humility and irony he does not much care whether the world thinks him right or not. What he has made is not entirely or even primarily his own; nor has he fashioned it out of his own power and knowledge, rather he has allowed it to happen through him. He has adjusted himself to a state of translucence, of medium-like conduction; he has co-operated in a minute moment of the universal and eternal process of coming-to-birth, the self-bodying of reality. In that activity he has realized himself; but that realization is a marginal product of the making, and the making is not the product of the realized self. In some sense the artist's function is priest-like; through the laying on of hands, by the ritual *ordonnance* of the sensory materials, a state of grace may be induced in the reader—but only if the reader, abasing and abandoning himself, is prepared to allow the vision to complete itself in him. A work of art, in the manner of a sacrament, offers perpetual access to reality. But between the work of art and the potential reality there is no *necessary* relation; to be in the presence of a work of art is not enough—its influence must fall (as in a sacrament) like rain upon the humble and thirsty heart. When the priest regards himself as exerting power in his own person, he becomes a dictator; when the sacrament becomes a formal benison, a documentary dispensation which disregards the recipient's attitude of mind, religion has degenerated into superstition.

Yet a complete work of art is timeless, a rendering and arrest of the luminous instant of reality, the perpetual now. So to arrest time is at once godlike and treasonable; or rather it becomes treasonable when the artist feels that of his own power he can arrest and annihilate time. Jacques Maritain, in his *Art and Scholasticism,* says that 'Rimbaud's *silence* denotes perhaps the end of an age-old apostasy. At all events it clearly indicates that it is folly to try to find in art the words of eternal life and rest for the human heart: and that the artist, if he is not to shatter his art or his soul, must simply be, as artist, what art would have him be—a good workman.' Here there seems to me to be some confusion. If the 'words of eternal life' can be uttered they can only be uttered in poetry: if there is to be found any 'rest for the human heart' it will be found in a vivid and courageous apprehension of the present, perpetually novel and the sole source of value. Certainly the artist will probably 'shatter his art or his soul' if his attitude towards his work is not the matter-of-fact attitude of the skilled craftsman. Yet if it is folly to try to find in art eternal truth, that is a circumscribed notion of art; for only in art can eternal truth ever be expressed. In the perfect state of man it will be all art, or no art. Not all art is secular; and not all secular art—including Rimbaud's—is irreligious. If art is not confined to 'Beauty' but can embrace, in its embodiments of reality, 'the horror, and the ugliness, and the glory', why then should the religious mind depart from the infinite pity and wisdom that would find the seeds of eternal life in the secular and non-ecclesiastical, in the horror and emptiness of an ascetic discipline of evil? [1] Could it not be said, as Eliot has said

---

[1] Jacques Maritain describes this well in *Art and Poetry*. 'There is a *speculative* sincerity, I mean with respect to the self and in the very order of the interior life; a straightforward gaze before which the heart spreads like a deployed campaign; for which the shames, the opprobriums, the social prohibitions and all the rules concerning the dialogue with others, do not enter in, transferred to the secret colloquy in which God alone takes part, to dissimulate aught of what is. If such a sincerity is not frequent, this is because it requires courage.

'The saints possess it, lighted as they are by the gift of knowledge, illumination of tears, and upheld by the gift of strength, which prevents them from dying of grief in seeing themselves. On another level certain gifts of the artistic order procure this kind of sincerity in their manner. Such appeared in profane literature, at the price of what ransom, of what redoubtable availability, the privilege of Proust. Such is also, in the

in his introduction to Kipling, that 'it is not a Christian vision, but it is at least a pagan vision—a contradiction of the materialistic view: it is the insight into a harmony with nature which must be re-established if the truly Christian imagination is to be recovered by Christians'? Some connection between the artistic and the religious there certainly is, and it meets in the vivid integrity of the inner life. Henry James observes, in the Preface of his *Portrait of a Lady*, that 'There is, I think, no more nutritive or suggestive truth . . . than that of the perfect dependence of the "moral" sense of a work of art on the amount of felt life concerned in producing it. The question comes back thus, obviously, to the kind and degree of the artist's prime sensibility, which is the soil out of which his subject springs.' This, being the root of the glory, is also the root of the apostasy.

We know how reluctantly Matthew Arnold brought himself to the view that religion had decayed, that if civilization was not to degenerate into an apathetic materialism, art—as the 'criticism of life' —must for the time being take the place of religion. Arnold's vision of art, and particularly his view that criticism must make the best ideas prevail, has tended to settle into a kind of literary fundamentalism. Art never can be a substitute for religion; but of the many (including Eliot) who have used Arnold as a whipping-post, few have shown respect for his penetrating insight. The connections between art and religion (but not theology) are neither slight nor accidental. Art has its heresies; these are not dogmatic divergences so much as the truncations of awareness, the rejections of responsibility, the wilful assertions that are all comprehended within the single sin of pride, the desolating game of playing at being God; these end in despair by a process of apostasy that Kierkegaard has described.

'Every human existence which is not conscious of itself as spirit, or conscious of itself before God as spirit, every human existence which is not thus grounded transparently in God but obscurely reposes or terminates in some abstract universality (state, nation, &c.), or which, in obscurity about itself, takes its faculties merely as active powers, without in a deeper sense being conscious whence it has them, which regards itself as an inexplicable something which is to be understood *per se*—every such existence, whatever it accomplishes, though it be the most amazing exploit, whatever it explains, though

mystical description of the most singular religious itinerary, the marvellous gift that we find in René Schwob.'

it were the whole of existence, however it enjoys life aesthetically—
every such existence is after all despair.'

The crisis of self-consciousness in an artist's life is a microcosmic
sketch of his always being under threat of a capital charge for treason.
Herbert Read has indicated how self-consciousness may undermine
a system of myth: 'A religion like Christianity is built up largely of
unconscious symbols: it find its most powerful forces in unconscious
processes like faith, prayer, grace. The effect of experimental sciences
has been to destroy the unconsciousness of these symbols: it under-
stands them and therefore equates them with conscious equivalents,
which are no longer symbols and which on that account no longer
compel the imagination.' Once an artist notices that he can make a
work of art whenever he wishes, he is in danger of never making another. If he continues to make, he may easily fall into the position of
Eliot's Thomas à Becket, desiring to find eternal power in the ultimate self-sacrifice of martyrdom. It is a shadow of emphasis that
stands between the priest and the ruthless man of power—both in
their own ways sincere, devoted to the point of self-destruction, convinced to the point of destroying others. The artist's position can be
very similar.

Thomas Mann has rendered the mature form of this crisis with
appalling directness in his portrait of Goethe in *Lotte in Weimar*.[1]
The artist, he says, may be illumined, but not inspired. 'Can you
imagine', he continues, 'the Lord God being inspired?' 'One ascribes
to Him a peculiar coldness, a destructive equanimity. For what
should He feel enthusiasm, on whose side should he stand? For He
is the whole, He is His own side. He stands on His side, His attitude
is one of all-embracing irony.' Goethe's God here is the projection
of Goethe, of Goethe's conception of the artist, the man who exerts
'the gaze of absolute art, which is at once absolute love and absolute
nihilism and indifference and implies that horrifying approach to the
godlike-diabolic which we call genius.' The 'neutrality of absolute
art' is a unity of allness and nihilism 'having nothing to do with
gentleness, and amounting to a most peculiar coldness, a crushing
indifference'. That neutrality arises from the artist's double nature, at
once willing and suffering. 'What I am after is the productive, male-
female force, conceiving and procreating, susceptible in the highest
degree. I am the Lindheymer [female ancestor] in male form, womb

[1] Whether it is an accurate portrait of Goethe is not the question at issue here. I
take it to be a faithful account: it is shockingly repeated in Rilke's life.

and seed, androgynous art, quick to receive, yet myself begetting, enriching the world with that I have received.' Androgynous the great artist certainly is, but in respect of consciousness and not of creativity. When Goethe conceives the double nature of the artist as concentrating in one person the double function of creation, he justi- fies his shocking cruelty to Lotte, his crushing insensitiveness, by supposing himself God, omnipotent, amoral, impervious. This is the pinnacle of temptation that the artist is led to: he can create, he knows he can create, he is God. Goethe is not an isolated instance: any powerful heresy is at least half true. But between this attitude and the attitude of a brutal and self-deceiving autocrat there is no difference. The difference, it might seem, is that the one attitude pro- duces abiding works of art, and the other manifests itself in mass graves and the shattered conscience. The paradox is only verbal; for no abiding work of art can grow out of a lust for power, but only out of the humility of the craftsman who can be perpetually surprised that his work can at times transcend and redeem the limits of his own power and his own weakness. The artist is not absolved from the moral order of man's universe of value; only his position is more hazardous, more solitary, more desolating.

There is a profound difference between the way art is created and the way it is recreated. Art can never be morally neutral, and it can never be separated from profound (if sometimes only momentary) beliefs. Although it is now fashionable to reject with scorn the principle of '*l'art pour l'art*', it is difficult to see how any other attitude in the artist can preserve him from the sin of pride and the lust for power. So intricate, and delicate, and impossible is the making in art that it absorbs the whole of the artist's energy and attention; the virtues of humility and disinterestedness are forced upon him by the nature of his activity. But that does not mean that his work is amoral or powerless to communicate and influence. Only when criticism regards art as an isolated end-in-itself does the notion of art for art's sake become vicious and sterile. Criticism has been enriched by re- garding art in the perspective of morality rather than in the light of a Puritan or Philistine moralism; it has increased its stature and power by going beyond the tests of Beauty and naughtiness to take serious account of qualities of intelligence and sensibility. It has been whole- some for a time to say with Rémy de Gourmont that '*La vérité est tyrannique; le doute est libérateur*'; and to cry with Gide, 'Let us drop the word *Truth*, which might lead one to believe that the despotism of

certain ideas is legitimate.' It was well perhaps for our time to concentrate upon fidelity to inner experience, to find means of rendering
the luminous envelope of the individual sensitive life, to assert—even
with brutal force—the artist's privilege to cultivate his private universe of vivid being regardless of social custom and convention. But
when one considers the sedulous cultivation of sensibility and intellect *in vacuo*, in the padded satin room pervaded with nostalgic per-
fumes; when one regards the universe of Proust or Gide or Joyce or at
large the world of the Pre-Raphaelites and the Symbolists; one
recognizes self-abnegation, a particular asceticism in the inner discipline of suspension, avoiding every formulation which might mar
the nacreous evanescence of the naked sensibility. Yet about it all
there is an air of death; for all the vaunted integrity, so much is
narrowly circumscribed, private, narcissistic, unashamedly self-ex-
hibitory. One marvels at the cool-headed criticism that can do full
justice to the qualities of intelligence and sensibility in this work
without noticing its moral vacuity. So to suspend moral discrimination is not a true scepticism but an evasion of judgment, an evasion
of the responsibility to judge wholly of art in all its implications.

It does not follow from what I have just said that I am advocating
an exclusively rosy-cheeked jumper-and-gym-shoes school of art.
But I am frankly puzzled by the self-gratulatory onanism exhibited in
some of the literature of this century, and, behind the unquestionable
originality and brilliance of some of its achievements, by the inconsequence and emptiness of the world it reveals. Even this I am prepared to accept in the all-embracing name of art, and in the hope of
finding illumination there and some correction for my personal
cranks of taste and response. It is less easy to accept the irresponsibility of those critics who have arrogated to themselves a 'creative'
role in order to add professional dignity and paedagogic authority to
the unassuming chore of carrying literary slop-pails and pruning-
hooks. Plato banished much poetry from his state, not for philosophical convenience, but because—being a poet—he recognized and
was appalled by the power of poetry; a power which could bemuse
and pervert as well as liberate. Yeats was to suffer some afterthoughts:

> *Did that play of mine send out*
> *Certain men the English shot?* . . .
> *Could my spoken words have checked*
> *That whereby a house lay wrecked?*

The youthful Shelley withdrew from Ireland frightened lest his writing might stir up civil war and end in the spilling of blood. It is easier—and altogether more comfortable—to dismiss these facts with laughter than to recognize the truth they point to. Most of the art criticism of this century is guilty of renouncing moral judgment. And this has usually been done, not designedly, but absent-mindedly: by limiting critical judgment to the order of scientific judgment and 'aesthetic' propriety. In art, however, judgment is a direct grasp of value, intention, integrity—in short, of morality. Such judgments are not purely aesthetic any more than they can be purely scientific. If one supposes that poetry is the utterance of wisdom and being, and that philosophy is the criticism and correlation of statements about wisdom and being, then poetry and philosophy go hand in hand. Criticism, in trying to become more philosophical, has merely tended to become more positivist; it has thereby tended to fragment poetry as well as criticism and has helped to drive a wedge of 'humanist' materialism between the two great centres of contemplative wisdom —poetry and philosophy.

For several years the New Criticism has divided its allegiance between the School of Value as represented by T. S. Eliot and the scientific or Manifesto School as represented by the early Richards. For many years Eliot's poetry and criticism have served as host for much clever and parasitic journalism. During the last year or so, however, former admirers and scholiasts of Eliot's work have started to show their teeth. One would not be surprised if the revulsion were an elementary gesture of surfeit; but there is a note of terror in it. In all conscience Mr Eliot has been evasive enough behind his erudite dogmatism; he has not been easy to label—not even with his own labels. But now he has stepped forward, unabashed, in the role of heresy-hunter. 'Aesthetic sensibility', he asserted in his *Notes towards a Definition of Culture,* 'must be extended into spiritual perception, and spiritual perception must be extended into aesthetic sensibility and disciplined taste before we are qualified to pass judgment upon decadence or diabolism or nihilism in art. To judge a work of art by artistic or by religious standards, to judge a religion by religious or artistic standards should come in the end to the same thing: it is an end at which no individual can arrive.' This is an unnerving statement. It destroys—or ought to destroy—at a single stroke the comfortable and defensive fiction that in art nothing counts beyond intelligence and naked sensibility.

This is not the place fully to examine these issues. I simply wish to indicate at one extreme some of the issues forced upon us by inquiring into artistic process and the experience of artists. Art, being an integrated activity of the person, cannot be separated from the most serious and persistent crises that man in his angelic obtuseness is called upon to survive with honour. But in the pages that follow there will be no plentiful use of words like 'death', 'God', 'life', and 'love'—I have tried as far as possible (following Paul Valéry) to eschew these trombones.

6

In the body of the essay, and in notes upon the text, I have introduced parallel and supporting quotations from other writers. There may exist an account of artistic experience similar to mine: if there is, I have not seen it. In reading and in discussion I have found numerous anticipations of details of my own position, and a gratifying quantity of support. The only claim I can make is not for originality, but for singleness of conception. I have striven to work persistently from the facts of artistic experience and aesthetic facts, as far as I was able to grasp them for myself in the presence of works of art. The method is neither eclectic nor deductive; no doubt it has most of the classical defects of an inquiry primarily introspective. Yet because I wished to examine artistic experience and not something else, I was determined that the inquiry must constantly be referred to and tested by artistic experience. How far my introspection has been modified by reading and discussion, how deeply germinal debts and borrowings may be submerged, I cannot possibly say: I know that my debts are numerous and heavy. The essay was first drafted after very little specific reading, and has not substantially altered its premisses or conclusions since then. During the five years that that draft has lain fallow I have been encouraged to bring the work to completion, not by finding numerous disagreements, but by finding in later reading a quantity of fragmentary agreements. The original draft was almost completely bare of illustrative material; the parallels and particular illustrations now included have been drawn very largely from reading carried on while the final draft was being written. Whatever authority the essay may have will arise, I suggest, from the fact that it was conceived existentially with the single critical test of my own experience; it is encouraging that an account so conceived should coincide at some points with the statements of artists whose work and reminiscences were not known to me until the work was virtually finished.

When I speak of a poem or a work of art I do not include everything that might conceivably be called a poem, but only the few greatest poems which are unquestionably entitled to that name. But I do not offer a list of these few greatest poems, nor can such a list be inferred from my essay. Great poetry is at once too widely dispersed and too severely localized to be comprehended within any one person's critical grasp. My view of poetic process has not been, and could not have been, deduced or evolved from any specific group of works of art; it has grown out of meditations upon the experience of the artist and upon whatever other 'inner goings-on' clustered around that experience. Nor do I believe that my view could have been deduced or inferred from any specific collection of statements made by artists themselves: the evidence there is too confused, and by its very nature it resists most attempts to reduce it to a datum for comparison.

A writer skilled in philosophical exposition would have made a tidier job of this essay. For myself, I did not hold clear philosophical exposition as a principal aim. If I have been able to delineate in some wise the arch and movement, the urgency and mystery, of artistic activity; if I have been able to strike a blow against the gross oversimplifications of art that have gathered weight in this century; if I have been able to indicate that the complexities, delicacies, happy accidents, the tensions, collisions, and illogicalities of art present a fruitful and almost virgin field of inquiry for the philosopher who would extend philosophy, to the psychologist who would make his study at once more sensitive and more personal; I shall be content. Clarity is difficult to achieve; words—inscrutable, fertile, unbiddable as they are—always stand between the force of the felt thought and the marks on the page. To avoid the ambiguity of using eroded terms I have reluctantly introduced two or three special terms. These are not 'technical' terms so much as unavoidable, if somewhat clumsy, devices to prevent the reader from crossing over to somebody else's tramlines of thought. If I am correct in believing that the study of poetic process will be fruitful for philosophy, psychology, and logic, a clear break with some earlier ways of thinking about art will be necessary at some points. Until a fresh mode of thought is established in poetics, until a new way of thinking about art becomes natural, the mind will tend to follow more familiar and comfortable highways. To start with, we need a few one-way words. When usage has turned a blazed trail into a paved road, the road-signs can be less numerous, the police force smaller; we shall enjoy the luxury of regarding every word as a four-cross-roads because we shall know in what direction home lies if we want to get there. If I am mistaken in this, there will be a little more terminological wreckage lying in the ditches of scholarship: that risk seemed worth taking. But here I hope will be no undue 'abusing of God's patience and the King's English'.

Somewhere between the excitement of discovery and the discouragements of 'trying to use words', between the sudden brilliance of vision and the successive desolations of striving to render the vision—somewhere in that middle land of ordered and accidental communication the words rest when the pen is put aside. 'In the beginning of important things,' André Gide has said, '—in the beginning of love, in the beginning of the day, in the beginning of any work—there is a moment when we understand more perfectly than we understand again until all is finished.' But perhaps when all is finished there will be no art and no language; and then all the anguished struggles towards clarity in words will be redeemed when the mind falls upon the simple enterprise of going naked.

I

What is Art?

How in its naked self
Reason wer powerless showeth when philosophers
wil treat of Art, the which they are ful ready to do,
having good intuition that their master-key
may lie therein: but since they must lack vision of Art
(for elsewise they had been artists, not philosophers)
they miss the way.

ROBERT BRIDGES

A START must be made somewhere; let us begin with John
Ruskin's statement that art is universal language. If the
question 'What is Art?' is taken to be a legitimate question, it would seem to require a definition as an answer. Ruskin's
dictum proves not to be a definition at all; or at best a partial and
equivocal one. Yet if we examine it we can see what sort of difficulties arise when we attempt to construct a definition in answer to such
a question. The definition may illuminate the question even though
it cannot satisfactorily answer it.

The verb 'to be' is one of the most treacherous words a philosopher
can use. A convenient mark for indicating subtle relationships best
left unexamined, the verb 'to be' is seldom a mark of precise equivalence. And the relation indicated by the verb 'to be' will seldom work
in more than one direction: if, for example, we say 'universal
language is art' we are saying something very different from what
Ruskin said.

What is Ruskin describing here? what is he attempting to define? The function of art? the nature of art? or are function and nature indistinguishable? If we examine the terms of the statement closely they yield surprisingly little clear or concrete meaning. Some pulses will quicken instantly at the words 'universal language'; and no doubt Ruskin (who could be provocative enough to bring Whistler to court) intended that they should. They seem to promise within the sphere of art a democratic equality, the promise of treasure accessible to the uncultivated: art is a language which can be understood by anybody regardless of race, tongue, period, or education. But what is language? What do we expect language to do? At very least we expect it to communicate intelligibly. But the word 'intelligibly' conceals some further questions. If an utterance cannot be translated precisely into another language, or into other terms in the same language, are we entitled to say that it is intelligible? If exact translatability is an essential feature of language, then art is not language. For nobody seriously believes that a work of art can be translated into another mode of language without irretrievable loss: nobody seriously doubts that a poem ceases to be a poem when translated into scientific prose. And most people will recognize that—attractive though the fancy may be—it is impossible to translate without distortion from one art to another. To talk of a symphony in colour, a lyrical painting, or even an intelligible poem is an amiable, because not totally worthless, use of metaphors. That they are metaphors at all suggests, however, that they indicate a relation not otherwise to be expressed.

When Ruskin coined his phrase he was evidently referring to painting. What happens if the statement is extended to include other arts—poetry, music, and sculpture as well as painting? Would this obliterate differences between the separate arts which cannot be overlooked? I think not. Indeed it is not until we examine the definition in a broader application that we can see what is good about it and what is misleading. The most prominent difference between the various arts is that some arts use a language which is also used in, or closely related with, other activities than art. Poetry uses words, and words are the primary means of communication in all human affairs; painting and sculpture use shapes, colours, lines, arrangements, which we also sometimes see in our natural surroundings. Music would seem to assume a special position among the arts—more abstract, more pure, more spiritual; and so Paul Valéry would have

it, though his supporting argument will not stand up to analysis.
Schopenhauer and others have asserted that all art strives towards the
condition of music. But that conviction destroys the unity of art,
unless we take him to mean that we must not expect poetry or painting to be any more accessible or intelligible than music; that we find
the highest condition of an art when we experience it in its own
terms, when we do not attempt to interpret it in terms of another
activity which happens to share the same language. The unmixed
'language of sound' is not recognizably used for any other coherent
mode of expression except music; yet music, far from being 'abstract',
is the least abstract of the arts in that it is the most direct means of
communicating feeling of an intricate and ordered kind. Music is
not generically different from the other arts: it is in some sense—but
not in all senses—the prototype of them all. And the different arts are
included in the single term Art because each, in its own medium
and in the way proper to that medium, fulfils the same function.

But what is that function? To communicate? To please? Yes;
both—and more. But how to communicate, and to communicate
what? In what way to please? Ruskin implies that art communicates
in the same way that 'language' communicates, that it pleases by
making utterances which are 'universal' (whether in appeal or application is not clear). But the language of poetry is not intelligible or
translatable in any usual sense of those words; or rather, it is intelligible or translatable only at a level which is not the level of poetry.
To put it in another way, poetry has an inner coherence which
cannot be generalized into a set of external rules; but that coherence is
not arbitrary—it will play no tricks with the reader if the reader does
not try to play any tricks with it. And perhaps that is an essential
feature of all language—a much more characteristic feature of
language than the practical test of whether it can be translated into
another mode of thought or expression, or whether its meaning can
be supported by other evidence or by behaviour. And as for the
universality that Ruskin claims for art, he surely cannot mean generality; for the function of art is to convey, not generalities, but unique-
nesses. If art does sometimes—or even often—convey matters of
general interest or validity, the generality may be incidental and not
essential. Art communicates something: there can be no doubt of
that. But the something—except when the art is contaminated by
didactic purpose—is not a description, nor a proposition, nor a
conclusion; art never assumes the propositional form which is the

indispensable requirement for logical analysis. Here for the moment our probing must cease. We are confronted with the central 'Mystery of Art', the crux which is usually evaded by introducing some convenient term like Beauty or Imagination. The absence of a logical starting-point places philosophical exposition at a severe disadvantage, and makes a writer fret against the inadequacies of a language which has fashioned itself inflexibly around the principle of causality and syllogistic sequence.

By examining Ruskin's assertion we find that no precise meaning is to be distilled from the words themselves, beyond the suggestion that art has something to do with language and is universal in its appeal. The statement looks definite enough, and most—if not all —of the statements that can be made about art assume this same characteristic and misleading form. 'Art is communication'; 'Art is expression'; 'Art is language'; 'Art is irrational'. All these statements suggest an equation of the form $x = z$, where x is to be determined and z is known. Actually the known quantity in such pseudo-equations is not fully enough known to permit of direct solution. We may modify the statement to the form 'Art is *a kind of* expression', suggesting an equation of the form $x = yz$, where z is known and y is a modifier to be determined. But this will not do either; for if art is in fact a kind of expression, the term 'expression' cannot be fully known until it includes 'art-expression'. The equation—if equation it be in any sense—is always of the form $X_z = Z_x$, where X is a function of Z and Z is a function of X. And the solution lies, not in seeking fuller knowledge of a Z independent of X, or fuller knowledge of an X independent of Z, but in a series of simultaneous dynamic approximations to both. For the philosopher then the problem is, not to illuminate the independent 'nature' of an X and a Z, but to extricate more and more clearly the relationship between X and Z, the relation so approximately and crudely indicated by the mark $=$, by the word 'function', or by a part of the verb 'to be'.[1]

---

[1] Cf. Gabriel Marcel, *The Mystery of Being*, I, 12–13: 'Could we say that the philosopher is a kind of locksmith to whom we turn when we want to open some particular door? Even this is much too simple. In this case door, keyhole, lock, are not given. The task of philosophy, to my mind, consists precisely in this sort of reciprocal clarification of two unknowns, and it may well be that, in order to pose the true questions, it is actually necessary to have an intuition, in advance, about what the true answers might be. It might be said that the true questions are those which point, not to anything resembling the solution of an enigma, but rather to a line of direction along which we move.'

The relationship is sometimes indicated by a more vigorous verb: 'Art gives pleasure'; 'Art transcends and creates the artist'; 'Art grows out of wholeness of mind'. These propositions are as ambivalent as the others and assume the same form; but they attempt, by the metaphorical implications of the verb, to indicate—and sometimes to render—the relation between the two terms of the proposition. This use of analogy and metaphor is not peculiar to theories of art and ethics; all 'natural laws' are analogies inasmuch as they are means of expressing a number of diverse phenomena in terms of a single reference: and 'natural law' was a very bold metaphor when Bacon introduced it. But since art is concerned with rendering unique events of experience and not with generalizing upon groups of phenomena or events, the analogies and metaphors of art are constantly changing, becoming obliterated or eroded, being discovered, refreshed, reworked; they must always be unique not general; discovered or 'made', not carried over uncritically from convention or applied in a prejudicial manner. In the same way the metaphors and analogies which may be used when we try to describe artistic experience and activity cannot be reduced to any single metaphor or analogy. To inquire into artistic experience one needs, not only to use language delicately and precisely, but to use language as the artist uses it; each single metaphor must be exactly rendered, for if the relation can already be explained in unmetaphorical terms there is no need for the metaphor. Many metaphors and many analogies will be used, and they will all be needed in various ways at once; but here, as in poetry, metaphors are not contradictory—not even 'mixed metaphors' are contradictory. When one metaphor illuminates one aspect of a problem it is used; when it ceases to illuminate it is abandoned and another metaphor sought. The same procedure occurs in the successive revisions of scientific 'laws'; the only difference is that in science a metaphor once found inadequate is discarded or retained for subsidiary uses—in aesthetics they are all retained. For the purpose of aesthetics and criticism—I take it—is, not to establish a single basis of description or explanation, but first to discover and see clearly what art and works of art and artistic experience are.

Communication is evidently a definite feature of art. But it is only one feature; and even in tracking down that single feature we are obliged to recognize that we do not know beforehand everything there is to know about communication. We cannot assume that the prototype of communication is known, otherwise we may confine the term to a meaning which has little to do with art. Does the word 'communication' mean much more than 'getting into touch with'? When communication occurs, does that imply that there was a conscious desire or design to communicate? Is communication limited to the transfer of 'meanings'—of whatever is intelligible, descriptive, indicative, or translatable? Or does communication establish (as the word itself suggests) some relation of unity between two people; a relation, not merely instrumental, in which two persons not only exchange information but come to 'know' each other more or less completely and permanently? Can it be that communication is characterized by such a mental identification rather than by the transfer of 'meanings'? Can it be that to transfer intelligible 'meaning' to another person, as though one were passing a bag of nuts, is an extension of that social equivocation by which we prevent ourselves from losing identity and protect ourselves from being too clearly known?

The genesis of works of art and statements made by artists themselves cannot entirely resolve these questions. We require also the convinced and carefully clarified statements of those who receive communication from works of art. We shall come to recognize that the creation and recreation of works of art is not an automatic mechanical response to stimuli, that the dynamic triad poet-poem-reader is always the irreducible unit for inquiry, that the element of 'concern' can never be eliminated, and that consequently we cannot proceed along scientific lines in any current sense of the word 'scientific'. Communication in art cannot occur unless there is a desire—or at very least a willingness—to be communicated with. The willingness need not be conscious at first, but in its most refined form it will be so. It is not enough that the reader or listener be physiologically capable of seeing or hearing: he must also want to look and be prepared to listen, and he must be prepared to look and listen in an appropriate way and to discover in each instance what is an appropriate way. And the way that will be appropriate is determined by the work of art itself and by the fact that it is a work of art.

Ruskin's statement that art is universal language should not be dismissed merely because it is not a true definition. Art is in any case indefinable; and Ruskin knew that as well as anybody. What we can do however is (as it were) to draw a ring around art, to mark out its boundaries; and this, rather than finding verbal equivalents for unknowns, is the function of definition. And if those boundaries include some familiar territory which may have been thought to belong to somebody else, there is no need for alarm or surprise; for we are dealing with what Coleridge called 'inner goings-on', and not with property; with what occurs and is experienced and not with what can be possessed.

Ruskin could at times be both wilful and hermetic in his statements, but in this case he is neither. If, instead of attempting to analyse his words, we meditate upon them and seek to recover what attitude towards art the statement implies, we come upon some important considerations of which the words themselves give little hint. This much is clear: he is uttering his belief that art has something to say, and that art is of value in human life; and with a bland gesture of didactic encouragement he promises that art is accessible to everybody. He engages the listener's attention by talking in what seems to be common language, and by suggesting that art can be placed upon a familiar practical footing. But when we pay attention to what he wants to say, when we shift the emphasis from the language to the art, he seems to have played a confidence trick: he has led us into conversation about language only to talk about a peculiar if not unique use of language. Perhaps nobody has any business to use language in a unique way. But Ruskin—whether he intended it or not—has brought us to a wholesome state of scepticism. Perhaps it is Ruskin and not his listeners who knows what language is. Is the 'normal' everyday use of language the type towards which all language should aspire? Is a divergence from 'normal' usage reprehensible, inadmissible, even bad, language? Or does it in the case of poetry merely mark a departure from practicality, arising from a purpose which is not that of everyday? If a poet is taxed with an 'irrational' use of language, with not sticking to the rules of grammar, he will probably answer in much the same offhand manner that Eliot adopts in *Sweeney Agonistes*:

> *I gotta use words when I talk to you*
> *But if you understand or if you don't*
> *That's nothing to me and nothing to you*
> *We all gotta do what we gotta do*

And after all, whose business is it to tell a poet how he should use language? It is the poet's business to use language superlatively. The language of art may seem unique to those who insist upon generalizing upon language and leave the language of poetry out of account. But is it the case that the language of poetry is abnormal, inaccessible, strange? Paul Valéry has said that 'there are no names for those things amongst which one is completely alone'. Yet that state of aloneness is the typical state for art and for moral choice: and it is that state of aloneness that the 'normal' use of language seeks to shatter, and which the social use of language strives to ignore or to destroy.

But Ruskin is talking about art, and not primarily about language; and by art he is thinking first of all about painting. Working in the medium of prose exposition it is fatally easy to 'explain' some aspects of painting by drawing illustrations from poetry; but the words once taken out of their poetic context shift out of the sphere of art into the abstractions of scientific prose where they can have no bearing upon painting. There is a classic instance of this in Ruskin's two essays on the 'Pathetic Fallacy'. And frequently some feature of poetry is 'explained' in terms of painting or sculpture on the assumption that because painting and sculpture are 'visual' they supply an external test for accurate sense-perception. But it is by no means clear what connection there is between the thing seen and the thing painted, in spite of all that painters themselves have said on this apparently straightforward subject. Ruskin got himself into difficulties when he tried to use art as though it were a universal language, whenever he sought to explain the 'meaning' of a picture or ventured to translate from one art to another. But these failures occur when he indulges his consuming desire to teach; as long as he concentrates on art and is content to look at it without wishing to foster, correct, or promulgate, he is on firm and familiar ground.

Two points then emerge from Ruskin's dictum—one which he intended, and one which may not have crossed his mind. Works of art are (in Herbert Read's phrase) entities of direct appeal: and this is the most important thing Ruskin is saying here. He also implies that, if we take the term 'art' in its broader meaning, the attitude of mind to which art can successfully appeal is the same or very similar for all the arts. This receptive attitude, he feels, is not the prerogative of a select few, but (theoretically at least) can be adopted by anybody; so he applies the adjective 'universal' to the language of art. But that word does not promise that the appeal can be made successfully without suitable preparation: Ruskin knew that too well from his frantic efforts to train a large number of people to appreciate art. And the preparation, far from being a training in adroit technical analysis, is an initiation—an initiation, not into the 'Mysteries of

Art', but into purity of heart and innocence of perception. The initiation induces us to discipline our fractious longing to 'understand', to discover 'meaning' in, works of art; and the end of that discipline is a receptive state of mind dynamically engaged with the work of art. In some periods of society art seems to have been widely accessible without such a preparation: in our own time the currents of the technical and practical have for most people silted up the simple naked state of belief—by which I do not mean make-believe —in which alone works of art can be created and recreated. That is why so much of the critic's energy must be directed against the uncritical.

The most impressive claim that is made for art—and it is made very persistently—is that art bodies forth reality; that art is metaphysical in virtue of its special capacity to penetrate below the surfaces of things; that art illuminates reality and the nature of Being. From whatever angle we approach art there is no avoiding the element of personal engagement, of what the Quakers vividly call 'concern'. If art does not matter to a person, for that person there can be no artistic experience. Any inquiry into art which neglects the elements of concern and value finds the back door locked. Even perception—that crux in artistic experience which also plays a vital role in all ordinary experience—is not to be understood in its bearings upon art until the element of concern is included; and no amount of scientific inquiry into perception can alter that condition unless the scientific method itself be altered.

> *In measure and in marksmanship*
> *lies the exactitude of death.*

It might appear that the two questions 'What is real?' and 'What matters?' were two different questions; many would jump to answer the first, but would hesitate over the second. Yet once we recognize that what we 'want' is not always either real or valuable, we can see that from the human point of view the two questions are the same and can scarcely be answered (short of a completely integrated theological system) except by the words 'Reality matters'. The phrase 'God is love' is no doubt a statement of the same sort, ultimate and compact, but expressed with greater personal warmth in terms of a particular belief.

If art does not bear witness to reality it is not much worth bothering about; if art does not express genuine knowing, if it is not in some important sense true, it can at best be an enervating fantasy detrimental to the soul's health. The terms 'reality', 'knowing', 'truth' have been so variously applied and interpreted that they easily become emblems of splendour, empty of meaning. But that is no reason to abandon them and to stop asking what of importance lies behind them. Art is not an apologetic poor relation, waving the time-worn credentials of truth, reality, and knowledge in the hope of securing a last place of honour. It may be the assured permanence of art that makes newcomers so inclined to take it for granted or to treat it with condescension when not actually trying to get rid of it. Art is inconvenient in any logical system: it refuses to fit neatly into any formula. But that may mean that there is something wrong, not only about the formula, but about the way formulae are framed. If art is true, not for what it says, but for what it is; if a work of art is inexhaustible to analysis because the forms of art grow from within, and embody themselves in a manner not repeated in any other objects constructed by man; then these will be facts to be reckoned with, even if they uproot all previous systems of formulation. Artistic experience forces us to recognize that the mind can operate in more delicate and comprehensive ways than scientific fact can either suggest or tolerate. If we can appreciate at all clearly the conditions and assumptions which make an artist's work possible, we may see reality, knowledge, and truth in a fresh—even an alarming—perspective. As we seek more clearly to grasp the conditions of art, we discover more about art itself, and more about experience in all its most heightened and valuable forms. For art claims to start from a peculiarly powerful kind of knowing; art claims to engage the whole person and to make the person whole; when all practicality is laid aside and the mind falls upon contemplation, art is the only possible utterance. It may be that in the activities which end in a great work of art we may find the prototype of reality and of the way reality is grasped and known and made known.

II

Artists on Art

What is a poet? A poet is an unhappy being whose heart is torn by secret sufferings, but whose lips are so strangely formed that when the sighs and cries escape them, they sound like beautiful music. His fate is like that of the unfortunate victims whom the tyrant Phalaris imprisoned in a brazen bull and slowly tortured over a steady fire; their cries could not reach the tyrant's ears so as to strike terror into his heart; when they reached his ears they sounded like sweet music. And men crowd about the poet and say to him: 'Sing for us soon again'; that is as much as to say: 'May new sufferings torment your soul, but may your lips be formed as before; for the cries would only frighten us, but the music is delicious.' And the critics come too, and say: 'Quite correct, and so it ought to be according to the rules of aesthetics.' Now it is understood that a critic resembles a poet to a hair; he only lacks the suffering in his heart and the music upon his lips. Lo, therefore, I would rather be a swineherd from Amagar, and be understood by the swine, than be a poet and be misunderstood by men.—KIERKEGAARD.

THE process which ends in a work of art is at once an act of discovery and self-discovery; it is an act of self-realization which at the same time makes the world more real. A work of art is, as it were, an extension of some valuable experience of the artist's—and it is an extension, not simply in mental, spiritual, or experiential terms, but also in physical terms. The artists' experience has somehow been embodied, incarnated, made physical while still preserving its spiritual identity. As a physical entity it is accessible to others; with due preparation others can engage themselves with the work of art (both physically and mentally), and so enter into the experience which the artist has embodied in his work. The irreducible unit for art then is not simply the work of art but the 'aesthetic triad'—the poet, the poem, and the reader. When these three come into relation through the physical focus of the work of art, we may expect that there will be some similarity between the momentary experience of poet and reader, and between the process by which the poem has been created and the process which recreates it. These two processes are not identical; nor are they mirror-images of each other; consequently the aesthetic triad cannot be reduced to two terms. And since this triad is the irreducible unit, and the work of art in isolation is not sufficient basis either for a theory of art or for a theory of criticism, it is advisable to inquire into the processes as well as into the persons and things. For the relations within the triad are dynamic relations. The more fully we understand the process, the more fully we shall come to understand both the nature of the artist and the nature of the work of art.

Perhaps artists themselves will throw some light upon these questions, either in their definitions of art or in their accounts of their experience of making works of art.

Of all the 'definitions' of poetry advanced by poets themselves very few can properly be regarded as definitions—they seldom define the limits that poetry operates within, and they can never offer a verbal equivalent into which the term 'poetry' can be satisfactorily translated. Many of these statements assert the dignity, value, truth, or reality of poetry; others are more or less veiled accounts of the experience of making poems; others are charms, formulae, or gnomic fragments of advice which help the individual poet keep his own personal problems and ideals in view; some appear to describe the function of poetry. Little would be gained by attempting to classify under such inexact headings all the statements that have been made about poetry: but it is interesting to notice that what appear to be definitions display such diverse functions, and that a single poet writing about his art will frequently embrace more than one of these purposes in a single statement. When Horace, for example, says that a poet should keep his manuscript by him for nine years and vigorously apply the file of criticism, he assumes the role of an old hand offering a craftsman's counsel; but he is also recognizing an important feature of the poet's inner experience—the period of gestation and silent assimilation. When Aristotle says that 'All species of Poetry are in their general conception modes of *Mimesis* [Imitation?]', he offers a succinctly condensed equation which, on inquiry, needs a whole universe of interpretation if we are to understand the term Mimesis. When Milton describes poetry as 'simple, sensuous, and impassioned' he is keeping in sight the qualities he wished to achieve in his work, but he also implies much that is essential to the nature of poetry. Coleridge's statement that poetry is 'the best words in the best order' is of the same sort; and in the same way, with its vivid, humble language, it strikes to the very heart of poetry. Dr Samuel Johnson, who in all sobriety could not be accused of making high-flown claims for the transcendental quality of poetry, announces that 'the end of poetry is to instruct by pleasing'; and this proves to be an inexhaustible statement, less narrowly limited to the 'rational' attitude of the eighteenth century than would at first appear. Mr T. S. Eliot waives definition: 'Poetry is a superior amusement: I do not mean an amusement for superior people. I call it an amusement, an amusement *pour distraire les honêtes gens*, not because that is a true definition, but because if you call it anything else you are likely to call it something still more false.' But elsewhere he produces a modified version of Coleridge's rule-of-thumb: 'Poetry is excellent words in excellent order and excellent rhythm.'

Most of these 'definitions', if fully extricated, arise from some complex insight into the nature of poetry: each holds in focus certain aspects of the whole intricate matter. And the more carefully one attempts to disengage what these statements imply, the more one is impressed by the intricacy of the problem of definition; the more one is likely to say with Herbert Read that 'Poetry is properly speaking a transcendental quality—a sudden transformation which words assume under a particular influence—and we can no more define this quality than we can define a state of grace.'

One very prominent group of 'definitions' asserts—often with intense honorific colouring—that poetry is an important matter, that somehow in its own right it embodies reality and utters truth. Aristotle has never been regarded as 'the poet's philosopher', yet he claims that 'Poetry is a more philosophical and higher thing than history; for poetry tends to express the universal.' Wordsworth, who admits modestly to have heard of Aristotle, gives more enthusiastic utterance to this same conviction: 'Poetry is the image of Man and Nature. Poetry is the breath and finer spirit of all knowledge; it is the impassioned expression which is in the countenance of all Science. Poetry is the first and last of all knowledge—it is as immortal as the heart of man.' Shelley similarly maintains that 'Poetry is indeed something divine. It is at once the centre and circumference of knowledge. Poetry is the record of the best and happiest moments of the happiest and best minds. Poetry makes immortal all that is best and most beautiful in the world. . . . Poetry redeems from decay the visitations of the divinity in man.' Other instances of this view—from Plato onwards—could readily be accumulated.

On the one hand, then, we have some hard kernels of truth about the nature of poetry; on the other a number of assertions about the high standing of poetry in the whole range of human endeavour. A third group, equally valuable but much less often submitted to inquiry, comprises accounts of how poems are made. Few artists before this century have left any detailed account of their experience of making poems. Chaucer in *The House of Fame* allows an owl to chide him for his bookishness:

> *In stede of reste and newe thynges,*
> *Thou goost hom to thy hous anoon,*
> *And, also domb as any stoon,*
> *Thou sittest at another book*
> *Tyl fully daswed ys thy look,*
> *And lyvest thus an heremyte.*

But Chaucer is no man for expansive confidences; and neither is Shakespeare. We catch a glimpse of Milton reducing his fifty loose lines of the morning to ten finished lines by evening—and Vergil gives much the same report; Mozart, Brahms, and Goethe tell us a little, and we can guess a certain amount about Beethoven; there are numerous hints about the exhausting labour of discovery and self-criticism and patience; Poincaré gives some details about mental processes in mathematical thinking; and there is plenty of evidence that most works of art are *made* and don't just happen. In a few instances we know what released the creative energy—long walks, ill-health, wine, opium, personal or vicarious emotion, tradition, hard work. Signor Vivante has shown how often the creative principle has been described in poems; and those descriptions have generally escaped notice. And still there is no way of telling what it felt like to write *Samson Agonistes,* or *A Valediction, forbidding Mourning,* or *The Hind and the Panther,* or the *Ode on a Grecian Urn,* or *Felix Randal.* We know practically nothing about the experience of composing *The Ancient Mariner,* yet the genesis of no other poem has been submitted to such minute examination. The genesis of *Kubla Khan* was described long after the event, and has been preserved because that birth was an exceptional one.

From about the middle of the nineteenth century, and particularly in Europe, poets began to record their creative experience. The theme became so persistent among the Imagists that they seemed in danger of being distracted from their practice of poetry by writing verses about what it feels like to write poems—or more often about what it feels like *not* to be able to write poems. Paul Valéry was a most persistent inquirer into these matters. In the late twenties John Livingston Lowes, in *The Road to Xanadu*, gave a fresh impulse and a more factual direction to such inquiries. A renewed interest in the psychology of poets and the genesis of poems has, however, induced a serious self-consciousness among poets as well as among the critics and scholars. A separate library has been founded to house drafts and manuscripts of the work of all contemporary poets—an admirable scheme, even though there are no signs yet that anybody knows what to do with the materials.[1] Fortified by this semi-technical enthusiasm, compendious volumes have been appearing (usually with titles like *Artists on Art*) and these have generally been compiled in the guileless belief that sheer bulk of evidence—no matter how uncritically collected and arranged—will force some reluctant theorist to make up his mind about the nature of art.

To this particular branch of autobiography the inquirer must bring an especially sensitive discrimination. Even when the words in two accounts are the same or similar, they may refer to quite different kinds of thought and experience. Then there is the question of veracity. Artists tell the story of their work for a variety of reasons; and the reasons are not always self-evident because not always conscious, and by no means are they always 'artistic'. Some do it because they are genuinely interested in their inner goings-on and have acute powers of introspective observation; others do it for fun, or to clear their heads, or to prove a theory, or to disprove a theory and denigrate their rivals, or to take a hand in the exhilarating sport of gulling journalists. In short, the evidence is confused and confusing. Yet poets often tell us what it feels like to make a poem, when they appear to be talking about something else. Not many poets of the first order have given a clear direct account of their experience in composition; but practically none has failed to say what he believes

[1] See for example *Poets at Work: Essays based on the Modern Poetry Collection at the Lockwood Memorial Library, University of Buffalo*, by Rudolf Arnheim, W. H. Auden, Karl Shapiro, D. A. Stauffer (1948). Miss Phyllis Bartlett has recently published a more compendious, but not more satisfactory, study entitled *Poems in Process* (1951).

poetry is—or should be. More often than not, a definition of poetry is a statement by the poet of the kind of poetry he is writing or hopes to write; and a theory of poetry constructed by a poet is often a generalized account of his own way of making poetry.[1] Wordsworth's celebrated, but often misrepresented, 'definition' of poetry as the spontaneous overflow of powerful feelings, taking its origin from emotion recollected in tranquillity, must be interpreted as an account of personal experience. He is not saying: 'This is what poetry *is*' nor 'This is how poetry *ought* to be composed.' By implication, he says: 'This is what happens to me when I make a poem: perhaps you will recognize a similar process in your own experience, and from that endorse the truth of my poems.' There are many luminous accounts of this sort widely scattered—in Coleridge's work, in Shelley's *Defence of Poetry* and even in his neglected *Speculations on Metaphysics,* in Keats's *Letters,* and (as Signor Vivante has shown) broadcast through the whole poetry of the language.

*　　　*　　　*

It has often been said that Wordsworth, Coleridge, Shelley, and Keats describe only one kind of poetry, that they are incorrigibly 'Romantic'—whatever that may mean—and that their remarks upon their art can be accepted only with reservation.[2] The self-styled Classicists, from Pope to T. E. Hulme and T. S. Eliot, have placed great emphasis upon the qualities of imperviousness, irony, distinctness, coldness, impersonality: and these qualities are frequently to be found in the work of the great 'Romantics'. For the moment the Classical-Romantic distinction may be left unexamined, for we are concerned with graver matters. The central question is: 'What processes in the artist and the critic (reader) end in the creation and re-creation of works of art?' As the first piece of evidence I choose the theories of James Joyce and William Butler Yeats. If these two should, in the light of some genuine distinction between 'classical' and 'romantic', turn out to be 'romantics', their evidence is not invalidated. When the creative process occurs it is subject, one supposes, to as slight individual variation as the physical processes of digestion and gestation—even though poetic process is not entirely a

[1] Cf. T. S. Eliot, *The Music of Poetry,* p. 9: '... when [the poet] theorizes about poetic creation, he is likely to be generalizing one type of experience'.

[2] But see Mario Praz, *The Romantic Agony,* and Herbert Read, *The True Voice of Feeling.*

physical process and is not a mechanism. I have chosen Joyce and Yeats because they were contemporaries with each other and with us. Their language and intentions should not, then, need much archaeological reconstruction; yet at the same time their differences of personal opinion and the differences between two strikingly similar theories should help to control any generalizations we may wish to draw.

In choosing James Joyce to represent a poet I am thinking not of the verses collected in *Chamber Music* and *Pomes Pennyeach* but of Joyce's novels. As early as 1914, in his *Portrait of the Artist as a Young Man*, he had given a coherent statement of his theory of art. In *Ulysses* and *Finnegan's Wake* he refined and amplified that statement, delineating himself and the poet at large under the name of Stephen Daedalus—poet, maker of words, maker of myths, the winged one; but the earlier statement, compressed and single as it is, is complete enough to stand by itself.

The dialogue between Joyce as undergraduate and his friend Lynch, in the seventh chapter of the *Portrait*, makes curious reading. His aesthetic theory is centred upon 'beauty' and apparently upon the sanction of Aquinas. But although his language and the form of exposition seem at first to have the crabbed detachment of the Schoolmen, his argument reaches out from and returns to a centre which is not the text of Aquinas but the core of his own creative experience.

Joyce takes his departure from Aristotle's definition of tragedy, by defining (as Aristotle had neglected to do) the terms 'pity' and 'terror'. 'Pity is the feeling which arrests the mind in the presence of whatever is grave and constant in human sufferings and unites it with the human sufferer. Terror is the feeling which arrests the mind in the presence of whatsoever is grave and constant in human sufferings and unites it with the secret cause.' The tragic emotion, looking towards both pity and terror, is static—it *arrests* the mind. He generalizes from this to state that the 'esthetic emotion' is static ('the mind is arrested above desire and loathing') whereas 'improper art' (pornographical or didactic) arouses 'kinetic emotion'—urges us to possess or to shrink away. Desire and loathing are aesthetically improper, not only because they are kinetic, but also because they are simply physical. Beauty as expressed by the artist ought to induce 'an ideal pity or an ideal terror, a stasis called forth, prolonged and at last dissolved by . . . the rhythm of beauty'. Art, he continues, is 'the

17

human disposition of sensible or intelligible matter for an esthetic end'—'to try slowly and humbly and constantly to express, to press out again, from the gross earth or what it brings forth, from sound and shape and colour which are the prison gates of our soul, an image of the beauty we have come to understand—that is art'.

John Donne has it that 'this ecstasy doth unperplex'. And we now find Joyce moving from this hard knot of compact definitions towards the more glowing figurative language of this last passage: he is turning towards home, where he started from—his personal experience as an artist. Aristotle and Aquinas are named; an illustration is drawn from physiology; Croce is in the background but only to be improved upon. This is Joyce on Joyce's experience of art. He complains of Aristotle's psychology as being too exclusive; and, having dispatched to his satisfaction 'the act itself of esthetic apprehension', Joyce sets off in a fresh direction. 'When we come to the phenomena of artistic conception, artistic reproduction, I require a new terminology and a new personal experience.'

The new terminology however is not a new coinage; he has shifted from the previous terms (stasis-kinesis, esthetic-physical) to the three terms in which Aquinas described universal beauty—*integritas, consonantia, claritas.* (Joyce translates these as 'wholeness', 'harmony', and 'radiance'). He now considers each of these in the light of his own experience. In the luminous apprehension of the aesthetic image, the thing is apprehended in its *integritas,* as single and whole, 'as self-bounded and self-contained upon the immeasurable background of space or time which is not it'.[1] The synthesis of immediate perception is followed by analysis, the apprehension of the thing 'as complex, multiple, divisible, separable, made up of its parts, the result of its parts and their sum, harmonious'—the *consonantia* of the thing is now discerned. *Claritas* is less easy to grasp. Joyce dismisses as 'literary talk' the notion that Aquinas may mean either 'a light from some other world, the idea of which the matter is but the shadow, the reality of which it is but the symbol', or that it is 'the artistic discovery and representation of the divine purpose in anything or a force of generalization which would make the esthetic image a

[1] Cf. a statement of Picasso's: 'It would be very interesting to preserve photographically, not the stages, but the metamorphoses of a picture. Possibly one might then discover the path followed by the brain in materializing the dream. But there is one very odd thing—to notice that basically a picture doesn't change, that the first "vision" remains almost intact, in spite of appearances.'

universal one, [and so] make it outshine its proper conditions'. *Claritas* is 'the scholastic *quidditas*, the *whatness* of a thing'. This supreme quality is felt only when the aesthetic image is conceived in the imagination. And that instant, when the mind has been arrested by the wholeness of the image and fascinated by its harmony, is 'the luminous silent stasis of esthetic pleasure, a spiritual state very like to that cardiac condition which the Italian physiologist Luigi Galvani . . . called the enchantment of the heart'.

The most noticeable features of this account are the artist's 'luminous apprehension' and the 'luminous silent stasis'; elsewhere Joyce comprehends these two in the single term 'epiphany'.[1] He also implies that the act of aesthetic apprehension is a process of integration, moving towards its consummation *through the solidity of the image*. That this should be similar to mystical experience does not escape Joyce's attention, and the connection is not accidental. Again, his third and most elusive term—*claritas*—does not apply simply to a quality of the 'thing', or even to the 'image': it is a state of the whole person, arising out of his manner of apprehending and constructing his images. (I therefore prefer the word *incandescence* to Joyce's word 'radiance'.)

Does that mean that the poet's experience is differentiated at the most radical level, in the act of perception itself? Is it not a function of all perception to be somehow 'luminous'? Or does Joyce require some special kind of perception? And how exclusive and precise is his division between 'esthetic' and 'physical'? And does the wide difference between 'esthetic' and 'physical' experience, as Joyce draws it, imply that aesthetic experience diverges from the normal, is a parasite upon a more wholesome ordering of life? Or does he mean that the same psychic components take their part in both kinds or experience, but are differently ordered?

Joyce does not discuss these problems here, but goes on to engage the question of artistic communication. All poetry exhibits an historical movement from lyric, to epic, then to narrative, and finally to dramatic forms; and this, he maintains, is a progression from 'the simplest verbal vesture of an instant of emotion' to the fully developed and enriched aesthetic image which is 'life purified in and projected from the human imagination'. The progression is one of wider and wider engagement, of deepening integration—and at the same time,

[1] In the same way Paul Nash's name for an imaginative experience was an 'event'. Whether the term owes anything to Whitehead I am not informed.

of increasing impersonality. We have now come full circle; the starting-point and conclusion meet in the arrest of the mind in pity and terror, the stasis purified at once of self and of the 'physical', the stasis generated and sustained by the 'rhythm of beauty' which at last dissolves it. And 'The mystery of esthetic, like that of material creation, is accomplished. The artist, like the God of creation, remains within or behind or beyond or above his handiwork, invisible, refined out of existence, indifferent, paring his fingernails.'

The traces of Homer, Bruno, Vico, and the Tristan legend in Joyce's later work do not seriously distress the intelligent reader in our time. But Joyce's unabashed use of Thomist terms in his theory of art can be expected to arouse a prejudice—whether of attraction or repulsion—violent enough to upset a cool apprehension of his doctrine. Yeats presents us with an even more difficult problem in interpretation. Poet, poseur, national revivalist, dabbler in politics and theatre management, lifelong practitioner in the occult, writer of static inhuman drama and of lyric with something of the force and complexity of tragic drama, moving in a long life of poetical activity from the shimmering indistinctness of the Celtic Twilight to the stubborn immediacy, the obtuse clarity of those poems which his critics have been obliged to call 'metaphysical'—Yeats is too complex to fit into any pigeon-hole but his own. 'In after time,' he wrote, 'they will speak much of me/And speak but fantasy.' The temptation to respond towards or away from some single feature of the man or of his work is almost irresistible. For this reason I have chosen him for the second part of this chapter.

Again my purpose is not fully to expound or to vindicate his theory, but to catch a glimpse of what, in his speculative inquiries into his own art, mattered most to him. Though studies of Yeats are not few, Yeats (like Keats) is still his own best interpreter. I shall be content to outline some of his convictions, accepting the partial and disconnected form in which they appear in his writings. Extracts from his critical prose—chosen without any nice regard for chronological sequence—will allow him to speak for himself in revealing the central principles of his theory of art.

Joyce's theory is a firmly-knit system sweetened by some brilliant *aperçus*: Yeats's theory is a congeries of brilliant *aperçus* occasionally subjected to some shadow of order by his wide-ranging but immethodical intellect. When allowance is made for a different use of terms and different religious beliefs, Joyce and Yeats are not so different in poetic belief as their early enmity and common Irish origin might suggest. Harry Levin, by an unexpected inversion, contrives to interpret Joyce through Yeats: and this is possible, not simply because in the two men certain temperamental, racial and theoretical factors intersect, but because both were great poets. It is possible to show that where the two theories are not similar they are complementary—that, approaching from widely separated points of view, they combine to form a broad contemporary sketch of the poetic character of art.[1]

Yeats, like Joyce, asserts the primacy of the imagination as having 'some way of lighting on the truth that the reason has not'; he also insists that art must have firm physical roots: 'All my art theories depend upon just this—rooting of mythology in the earth.' Whatever is artistically conceived must be 'conceived not in the brain but in the whole body'; and since poetry can be made 'only by looking into that little, infinite, faltering, eternal flame we call ourselves', nothing matters so much as 'Unity of Being'. But, he says elsewhere, 'if we become interested in ourselves, in our own lives, we pass out of the vision'.

The theme of integration and reconciliation moves at different levels. There is the problem of reconciling the secret and unique inner self with the world in which it is placed; there is the problem of transcending the self, of achieving the 'stasis' which is the mark of integration and abiding value; there is the problem of reconciling the longing and impulse towards joy with the acute suffering which lies at the heart of the artist's making.

[1] Yeats, like Joyce, was preoccupied with 'making', with 'the love of what is difficult', with intricate handiwork shored against the erosion and oblivion of time. This desire for the marmoreal perfection and permanence of the work of art is rather different from the Renaissance desire for personal immortality—and very different from the *exegi monimentum* vein in Shakespeare's sonnets. Perhaps it projects that schism between the artist and society which has pressed so heavily upon even the greatest artists of this century. That separation tends to produce a schism in the artist himself, by fostering the wrong kind of self-consciousness, a concentration upon craft and technique, which (when poetic energy flags) may destroy the direct and simple flow of utterance which characterizes all the greatest works of genius. Henry James (as Leavis has shown in *The Great Tradition*) succumbed in his later work to the dead-weight of critical indifference. Yeats—refreshed by the Metaphysical tradition—escaped this form of debility. Joyce, I believe, was less fortunate. And Pound, having squandered much of his gifts in a frustrated and aridly academic anti-academic violence, lived to write a sombre epitaph upon two minor poets: 'The artist has no business to break.'

. . . only an aching heart
Conceives a changeless work of art.

'There is in the creative joy an acceptance of what joy brings, because we have understood the beauty of what it brings, or a hatred of death for what it takes away, which arouses within us, through some sympathy perhaps with all other men, an energy so noble, so powerful, that we laugh aloud and mock, in the terror or the sweetness of our exaltation, at death and oblivion.'

This is a variant on Keats's Negative Capability—more daemonic, arrogant even, less patient, less pure, with a disconcerting sense of the beauty of violence.[1] But in the course of his mercurial gropings, Yeats redresses the balance: 'Does not all art come when a nature, that never ceases to judge itself, exhausts personal emotion in action or desire so completely that something impersonal, something that has nothing to do with action or desire, suddenly starts into its place.' The theme of 'stasis'—for which Yeats prefers another Greek word, 'ecstasy'—is frequently developed both in his prose and his verse. 'The end of art is the ecstasy awakened by the presence before an ever changing mind of what is permanent in the world, or by the arousing of that mind itself into the very delicate and fastidious mood habitual with it when it is seeking those permanent and recurring things.' 'The passions,' he says, 'when we know that they cannot find fulfilment, become vision'; and in a different context:

> *Nothing but stillness can remain when hearts are full*
> *Of their own sweetness, bodies of their own loveliness.*

That the poetic ecstasy is not essentially the bliss of the lover's ecstasy emerges in the bleak rhythms of his later poems, and especially in one of the 'Supernatural Songs'.

> *Civilization is hooped together, brought*
> *Under a rule, under the semblance of peace*
> *By manifold illusion; but man's life is thought,*

[1] In *Per Amica Silentia Lunae* (1917) he writes: 'Neither must we create, by hiding ugliness, a false beauty as our offering to the world. He only can create the greatest imaginable beauty who has endured all imaginable pangs, for only when we have seen and foreseen what we dread shall we be rewarded by that dazzling unforeseen wing-footed wanderer.' And again: 'It is not permitted to a man, who takes up pen or chisel, to seek originality, for . . . he cannot but mould or sing after a new fashion because no disaster is like another.'

And he, despite his terror, cannot cease
Ravening through century after century,
Ravening, raging, and uprooting that he may come
Into the desolation of reality.

The intricate and sorrowful paradox of the poetic vision leads him to regard artists as 'the servants not of any cause but of mere naked life in its nobler forms, where joy and sorrow are one, Artificers of the Great Moment'. The 'luminous apprehension of the present'—to use Joyce's words—is seen by Yeats as the artist's cross:

'The nobleness of the Arts is in the mingling of contraries, the extremity of sorrow, the extremity of joy, perfection of personality, the perfection of its surrender, overflowing turbulent energy, and marmorean stillness; and its red rose opens at the meeting of the two beams of the cross, and at the trysting-place of mortal and immortal, time and eternity.'

'I think that we who are poets and artists, not being permitted to shoot beyond the tangible, must go from desire to weariness and so to desire again, and live but for the moment when vision comes to our weariness like terrible lightning, in the humility of the brutes. I do not doubt . . . that every movement, in feeling or in thought, prepares in the dark by its own increasing clarity and confidence its own executioner. We seek reality with the slow tide of our weakness and are smitten from the boundless and the unforeseen.'

And the tragic paradox of the timeless instant of vision, the momentary present in the flux of time which it is the agony and delight of the poet to embody and so to make permanent, is caught in a single simple cry:

But is there any comfort to be found?
Man is in love and loves what vanishes,
What more is there to say?

For which reason he can state quietly his desire as a poet: 'I take pleasure alone in those verses where it seems to me that I have found something hard and cold, some articulation of the Image, which is the opposite of all that I am in my daily life, and all that my country is.'

Renouncing all established religion and relying not at all upon the clear-cut distinctions that scholasticism offered to Joyce, Yeats is more concerned with the intermingling of the physical and spiritual in art. With Joyce, he declares that 'All art is sensuous'; and as for the poet, 'passion is his only business'. Yeats perhaps confuses occult experience with what is more properly speaking religious experience; Joyce's 'epiphanies', his moments of incandescence, are not so readily confused with states of dream, reverie, and trance as Yeats's 'visions' are: probably Joyce with his more rigorous intellectual training was better able to discern the mechanism that underlies the state of dream, a state of inconsequent association for which surrealism has speciously claimed the highest freedom. Yet those are minor discriminations when we bring together Yeats's scattered remarks upon the nature of symbols and the construction and articulation of images. For Yeats considered that the poet's life is 'an experiment in living', and that 'We begin to live when we have conceived life as tragedy.' And his theory completes itself where Joyce's had started and ended: in his conception of tragedy and the instant of poetic stasis. 'Tragic art, passionate art, the drowner of dykes, the confounder of under-standing, moves us by setting us to reverie, by alluring us almost to the intensity of trance. . . . We feel our minds expand convulsively or spread out slowly like some moon-brightened image-crowded sea.' This is that dolphin-torn, that gong-tormented sea of *Byzantium,* the sea which both he and Joyce so perilously traversed in the supreme role of the artist—as myth-makers. Art for them was not an escape from life and reality, but a discovery and clarification of both. For them rhythm, image, and symbol were organic extensions of the mind in creation; image and symbol were the essential and element-ary (though complex) materials of poetry, the physical vehicles for those passions aroused by the impact of reality; the myth was the pattern—no matter how elusive—of reality grasped fearlessly, com-prehensively, luminously. 'I think profound philosophy must come from terror,' Yeats wrote in one of his last essays. 'An abyss opens under our feet; inherited convictions, the pre-suppositions of our thoughts, those Fathers of the Church Lionel Johnson expounded, drop into the abyss. Whether we will or no we must ask the ancient questions: Is there reality anywhere? Is there a God? Is there a Soul?' If Yeats was intoxicated with life, and Joyce haunted by death, both courted the terror of the abyss, knowing that where the tragedy of life and the ecstasy of vision meet, fuse, and illuminate each other we discover 'the best that art—perhaps that life—can give'. And when the poet has suffered this creative self-annihilation, what comes of it?

—such a form as Grecian goldsmiths make
Of hammered gold and gold enamelling
To keep a drowsy Emperor awake;
Or set upon a golden bough to sing
To ladies of Byzantium
Of what is past, or passing, or to come.

. . . .

Miracle, bird or golden handiwork,
More miracle than bird or handiwork,
Planted on the star-lit golden bough,
Can like the cocks of Hades crow,
Or, by the moon embittered, scorn aloud
In glory of changeless metal
Common bird or petal
And all complexities of mire or blood.

'It is the timber of poetry that wears most surely, and there is no timber that has not strong roots among the clay & worms'—this was John Synge's doctrine of poetry. 'Even if we grant', he continues, 'that exalted poetry can be kept successful by itself, the strong things of life are needed in poetry also, to show that what is exalted, or tender, is not made by feeble blood. It may almost be said that before verse can be human it must learn to be brutal.' When Grierson sent a copy of his edition of Donne to Yeats, Yeats replied: 'The intricacy and subtlety of his [Donne's] imagination are the length and breadth of the furrow made by his passion. His pedantry and the obscenity, the rock and loam of his Eden, but make us the more certain that one who is but a man like us has seen God.'[1] It is so easy to emphasize the spiritual character of art that one of its most profound paradoxes is often overlooked—its intensely physical character:

The commonness of thought and images
That have the frenzy of our western sea.

From what humble roots in the common earth the miracles of art grow to tragic impersonality and marmoreal stillness, a few lines from Shakespeare can show.

How sweet the moonlight sleeps upon this bank!
Here will we sit, and let the sounds of music

[1] Both these passages are quoted by T. R. Henn in *The Lonely Tower* (1950).

Creep in our ears: soft stillness and the night
Become the touches of sweet harmony.
Sit, Jessica. Look, how the floor of heaven
Is thick inlaid with patines of bright gold:
There's not the smallest orb which thou behold'st
But in his motion like an angel sings,
Still quiring to the young-eyed cherubins,—
Such harmony is in immortal souls;
But whilst this muddy vesture of decay
Doth grossly close it in, we cannot hear it.

And Jessica replies: 'I am never merry when I hear sweet music.'
Yeats however proposes a harder paradox and one that lies at the
heart of poetic.

Those masterful images because complete
Grew in pure mind, but out of what began?
A mound of refuse or the sweepings of a street,
Old kettles, old bottles, and a broken can,
Old iron, old bones, old rags, that raving slut
Who keeps the till. Now that my ladder's gone,
I must lie down where all the ladders start,
In the foul rag-and-bone shop of the heart.

III

Reality and the Artist

THE word 'reality' has been turning up more and more insistently and we shall have to deal with it. Before attempting to explain what might conceivably be meant by reality I should like to introduce an analogy or parable, to illustrate the various attitudes towards reality adopted by a poet, a mystic, a scientist, and an 'ordinary man'. One reservation must be made at once: the poet, mystic, and the rest are properly so called only when engaged in some activity that entitles them to that name. No system of classification is sensitive enough to accommodate the variations in attitude and activity of a single individual; an individual may well be—and most individuals are—a poet for an hour, a scientist for a week, and an 'ordinary man' for the rest of his life.

Let us imagine that man and nature (or 'subject' and 'object') meet and embrace each other at an interface, the interface being a

pliable and permeable membrane extending infinitely both upwards
and on either hand.[1] This membrane is to be regarded as a medium
joining, not separating, subject and object; as I conceive it the interface
has depth, some spatial characteristics—one can 'move about in' the
interface. In actual life, subject and object interpenetrate each other
but since for purposeful action we must pretend that subject and
object can be separated, the interface also represents this assumed
separation. Let us then suppose that life, naked living, occurs at this
interface—that it is here that man meets and shapes 'nature' and is
himself shaped by nature. Let us imagine further that living consists
in plunging the hands into the interface in order both to control
nature and to become real. The type of this action is to be seen in the
way a painter handles his brushes, or the way a gardener breaks soil
with his hands. Man's zest to live and his longing for freedom make
his living an aggressive action, plunging his hands through the
interface as though to assault the objective sphere. But the image of a
conquering hero or an advancing army will not serve, because there
is nothing in terms of life and value to be gained on the other side
of the interface. At the interface and within it everything is in continual flux, in a complicated involute movement of mutual adjustment. All values cluster at the interface and are not to be found
elsewhere. (Ranke must have had such a conception in mind when
he proposed as a first principle of historical interpretation that 'Every
age is equidistant from eternity'.) The situation at the interface, if we
attempted to analyse it, is infinitely complicated; but our experience
of it is simple and direct, almost as though it were tactile in quality
rather than visual. To be 'involved' at the interface is to be 'real', to
engage in reality; and somehow any contact with the interface con-
vinces that nothing else is of such supreme value.

[1] The image of the interface is suggested by a passage in Sir Charles Sherrington'
Man on his Nature (1946), pp. 141–2: 'Physics shows that where phases, for instance
liquid and solid and gaseous meet, special opportunities for interaction occur. Our
planet offers such a place. What we call its surface is a great interface where phase
solid, liquid, and gaseous meet. They meet as rock and tide and air. At this interfac
many new systems could be formed and must have been. There it was that the new
systems we are thinking of [the first manifestations of "life"] will have arisen at tha
particular stage of the earth's cooling. They were complex, delicate, and individuall
short-lived as against many of the old systems of the field around them.' I understand
that the word 'interface' was first used by Sherrington in neurology to refer to non
membranous junctions at which energy is transferred or transmuted. The term
had previously been used in a less arresting sense to refer to the internal angles in
crystals.

The mystic and the poet remain—or try to remain—involved at the interface. The mystic, using the interface as though it were some sort of optical instrument, looks *through* rather than *at* the interface; what by this means he sees is transmundate, being of neither the objective nor the subjective sphere. When he gains the sort of information he seeks, he is able to shape his conduct at the interface in accordance with the information. But his attitude is at once fastidious and detached, and he will turn the fruits of his contemplation to no other end than to ensure continuous contact with the interface, for his life is arrested in contemplation: he is attentively lost and absorbed into his reality.[1] The poet, on the other hand, looks *at and along* the interface; for his purpose is to reveal 'what it is like' at the interface.

The scientist's activity is of a different kind. He pretends that the objective sphere is worth conquering and proceeds as though he were an invading army. An act of intuition carries him deep beyond the interface. He then establishes, by means of logical manipulation, a line of communications with the subjective sphere. In this way the scientist's conclusions are cumulative and mutually coherent. The scientist's movement is not, however, the steady advance of an army, but rather a succession of raids into the objective sphere to bring back captured equipment with which others may (if they will) conduct purposeful action at the interface; but it is not perfectly certain that purposeful action is especially relevant at the interface. The line of communications established between the object of intuition and the interface insures that the scientist can return to the interface when he wishes. Since the interface is the instant creation of value and is an affair of bare hands, there is no guarantee that the equipment picked up on scientific raids will be of any use at the interface. And there is

---

[1] In *A Vision* Yeats says of the Saint: 'His joy is to be nothing, to think nothing; but to permit the total life, expressed in its humanity, to flow in upon him and to express itself through his acts and thoughts.' Graham Hough writes arrestingly in *The Last Romantics* (1949): 'The saint seeks the anti-self of the whole world, and renounces the world while it still has power to attract. But the hero finds his mask in defeat, and loves the world until it breaks him; and the poet finds his in disappointment and loves the world until it breaks faith with him. The saint assumes his mask for ever, and puts away the world and reduces his life to a round of customary duties. But the poet only assumes his mask while he is in the act of creation, and when it is all over Dante returns to his chambering; and as for Yeats himself, had he not written years before:

All things can tempt me from this craft of verse,
One time it was a woman's face, or worse.'

29

always a possibility that the pure fun of raiding will so engross him that, neglecting to come home, he will become—as far as spiritual matters go—a Don Quixote.

Philosophers and theoretical inquirers may be represented as flying in aircraft, trying to understand the whole situation better by examining it from a great height. The aircraft may fly either on the subjective or objective side of the interface, and may even pass through the interface. But their interest will tend to draw them definitely to one side or the other, and the speed of their passage tends to make their encounters with the interface brief and rare.

The 'ordinary man' does not much like the interface. Through incapacity or distaste, he withdraws into a carapace at a safe distance from the interface. If there should be any holes in his shell through which he might catch a distressing glimpse of the interface and of what goes forward there, he will patch these up with various clichés —of thought, feeling, action, even of perception. These clichés, unlike the interface, are opaque; once useful equipment for living, they have been rejected at the interface as too rigid to meet the essential requirement of plasticity. Those people who are not in any professional sense to be grouped with the poets, mystics, or scientists and yet are capable of conducting a vivid and valuable life are to be grouped rather with the poets. The 'ordinary man' in this parable is the average man in the twentieth-century democracies: by no means 'simple'—for that is a quality of the mystics and poets—but rather, sophisticated, partly instructed but not educated, the inert and apathetic product of social, commercial, and political propaganda.[1]

To 'be real' is presumably the purpose of living; that is what gives such force to the word 'reality', and what makes it such a difficult notion to render into words. It is extremely difficult to think of 'reality' other than as a group of external things with which we collide, or as an area of experience into which we may move; and in order to conduct the discussion at all it will be necessary to use sometimes one picture and sometimes the other. But we are particularly concerned with kinds of expression, especially those kinds called art.

---

[1] Cf. Paul Valéry, Note-Book B 1910: 'The civilized person in immense cities reverts to a savage—that is, isolated—state, because the social mechanism allows him to forget the necessity for common measures and allows him to lose the sense of bonds between individuals, which was formerly kept alive by need. Every improvement of the social mechanism renders useless acts, manners of feeling, aptitudes for the common life.'

If we consider what different kinds of expression are proper to the different people in the parable we may then be able to see whether different relations with the interface manifest themselves as different patterns of experience and different organizations of mind.

The poet and the mystic were represented as being—or wishing to be—in steady contact with reality. The other figures—the scientist, the philosopher, the theoretical inquirer—are represented as not being steadily in contact with the interface. Indeed, in order to fulfil their special interests these prefer to keep the interface in view without actually becoming engaged—it is in some way a condition of their purpose that they should not become involved. Whatever expression is proper to the poet and the mystic springs from the interface; all other expression is abstractive, uttered from an assumed position outside or away from the interface. The first distinction in expression can then be made in terms of relation with the interface: depending upon whether or not the person speaks out of 'involvement'.

The difference between involvement in reality and non-involvement must now be described. To be involved at the interface is to experience, to engage in, (in some sense) to construct, an event of reality; and this event I call *paradeigmatic*. This term has two implications: (*a*) the form or archetype of human experience is to be found in paradeigmatic experience and not in the experience of everyday man in a workaday world; and (*b*) that this order of experience is its own argument, carries its own proof within itself, is at once an event of value and of knowing. Mannheim, in his *Diagnosis of Our Time* (1943), applies this term to the source of all theological thinking, and describes it as 'a peculiarly vivid kind of awareness and responsiveness to reality beyond ourselves which seems to give insight into its nature'.[1] In the terms of the analogy of the interface, paradeigmatic experience is the responsive feeling of naked collision with reality; an intimate penetration into, or immersion in, reality. Not to be involved or immersed in reality is to be abstracted from reality; and abstraction is a feature of all experience which is not paradeigmatic. Lacking the internal self-evident argument of the

---

[1] Miss Bodkin, in *Studies of Type-Images* (1951), follows Oldham in substituting the word 'commanding' for Mannheim's 'repellent coinage' of 'paradeigmatic'. I prefer Mannheim's term, however, because it is self-evident.

Baudelaire remarks in *Fusées*: 'Dans certains états de l'âme presque surnaturels, la profondeur de la vie se révèle tout entière dans le spectacle, si ordinaire qu'il soit, qu'on a sous les yeux. Il en devient le Symbole.'

event of reality, experience which is not paradeigmatic must seek support and verification outside itself—if possible in reality. And since contact with reality is always paradeigmatic, all abstractive experience must be transmuted into paradeigmatic experience before it can claim the sanction of reality.

This claim that the artist's and mystic's experience is closer to reality and more 'knowledgeable' than the philosopher's or the scientist's probably seems excessive; it would be excessive only if it insisted that art and philosophy were permanent avocations, that reality was permanently inaccessible to the bulk of men. But reality, in the terms described, is inaccessible to most men most of the time—artists and mystics included. In speaking of 'reality' and 'abstraction' I mean only the moments of actual engagement or disengagement; all thinking *about* such moments must of course be abstraction. Each avocation claims for itself a peculiar power to understand reality; but that is a methodological postulate rather than a considered inquiry into the nature of reality.[1] And at the moment we are not concerned to set one avocation at another's throat, but to distinguish different ways of mind.

What are the two modes of expression corresponding to the paradeigmatic and the abstract experience? Miss Dorothy Emmet, in a suggestive passage of *The Nature of Metaphysical Thinking* (1945), draws a distinction between total and partial assertions—a distinction previously used by J. L. Stocks to elucidate the nature and grounds of religious beliefs. The terms match our present account very exactly; and Miss Emmet in her summary account points specifically to the facts of artistic experience.

'A partial assertion is either a proposition stating matter of fact, verifiable in sense experience, or a logical proposition which can be brought into a coherent system with other logical propositions of the same type. . . . But a total assertion . . . cannot be exhaustively analysed into any number of partial assertions of matter of fact. . . . Whereas the judgments of probability would be "partial assertions",

---

[1] Cf. A. C. Bradley's observation in his *Ideals of Religion* (1907): 'Art, religion, philosophy are perhaps rather three ways in which the infinite reveals itself in finite mind; but three specifically different ways, parallel to one another, all necessary and not mutually replaceable, so that in each way something comes which cannot come in any other way. Naturally, from its own point of view, each appears the highest, and so, intellectually, philosophy is the highest, and is bound to claim jurisdiction on questions of truth; but that does not show that it is the manner in which man comes most completely into union with the infinite.'

judgments of faith appear to be of the nature of "total assertions". They are *our conscious responses to the character of something as a whole.* They can be partly analysed into partial assertions; a literary critic may give his reasons for judging a poem or play good or bad; but the power of a poem or play to hold us, to arouse a conviction of inevitability, so that we say "Yes" to it, seems to be something more than the sum total of the reasons we may give for thinking it a good poem or play. In fact this positive response may be elicited before we have begun to analyse reasons.' [1]

A total assertion, however, is not simply a cry of acceptance or rejection: it is generally both at once. For it is the cry that arises from the knowledge of reality; and reality is intolerable as well as desirable. When that knowledge is sustained as vision, contemplated, ordered, transmuted into connected utterance, that utterance is art; the language that bodies forth individual events of reality, the language of the poet, the language of the mystic when he chooses to break silence. The utterance that arises from abstract experience is—very roughly speaking—the language of description, the prose of science, our delineations of the character of things when apprehended part by part and not as a whole. This language is always *about* experience; or more correctly, it is about propositions about experience, for it is always and characteristically propositional. The two uses of language are associated with two distinct organizations of mind, each exhibiting its own distinctive pattern. At the inner end of the process each pattern is associated with a particular attitude; at the outer end each pattern is associated with a particular use of language.

*　　　*　　　*

At this point it is convenient to confine the discussion to poetry and to speak for the time being only of different uses of verbal language. The 'normal' use of language in the present Western cultures is the 'prose' use, and the way of mind associated with that use of language is generally regarded as 'normal'. If poetry, as I have claimed, is of the order of total assertions, if it alone springs directly from reality and alone can embody experience, how comes it to be regarded as 'abnormal' or unusual? This is an historical consideration and not a matter of accident; but it is worth considering for the light it can throw upon the character of poetry.

[1] My italics. Bergson, in his *Introduction to Metaphysics*, had drawn a similar distinction between 'relative' (external) and 'absolute' (internal, 'intuitive') knowing.

There is this peculiar about man: whereas other organisms have been content simply to live, man desires to live better. This upward impulse in man (matched and balanced by the downward material impulse expressed in the second law of thermodynamics) has been called by various names: let us choose Whitehead's term Creativity.[1] Creativity is the pure activity underlying the nature of things. The most general statement that can be made about it is that it is the urge towards individuation and towards unification. By itself, Creativity is pure formless activity, implying no 'creatures' which in particular will reveal it. Creativity can achieve form only when limits are interposed. Creativity, in this general sense, is not particularly the prerogative of man. But the particular development of it in man, towards individuation and unification of the person, is represented by man's ability to choose and impose limitations—consciously and unconsciously—so that forms are permitted and stimulated to grow internally, according to self-causative and self-determining principles. This is to be seen in art and in moral action.[2] By recognizing that certain kinds of human activity are genuinely creative, man has (as it were) projected the principle of Creativity backwards into unhuman organic and cosmic processes. This upward reaching of man —at once tentative and aggressive—has in the course of several thousands of years shaped the human mind and human responses into certain definite patterns. It is man's tragedy that he must formulate patterns, and his glory that he can sometimes—when he needs to— break out of them.

Primitive man's experience must have been extremely complicated and confused; the primitive consciousness is not an elementary, crude, or simpler form of human consciousness as we now know it. This we know partly from historical and anthropological research: we know it more directly from the fact that in the course of time man may have lost some of his barbaric characteristics, but he has never lost his primitive mentality. Primitive man is not simply a man beset by dangers and threats without benefit of firearms, police, county council, or clergy: he is caught up in, immersed, inextricably mixed

[1] Since Whitehead's conception of Creativity appears in a philosophy of organism, it is interesting to notice the terms used by philosophers who have placed personality in a more central position: 'élan vital' (Bergson), 'zest for life' (Sherrington), and—in a somewhat different sense—'reverence for life' (Schweitzer).

[2] This passage is paraphrased from Miss Emmet's *Whitehead's Philosophy of Organism* (1932).

with, an ineluctable vortex. Reality for him is the sense of being immersed in a flux as central and immediate as the pulse of his heart. What forces and motives were engaged to extricate man from such a situation we can only infer, on the assumption that hope is permanently to be valued above despair. The story of man's development is very largely the story of his discovering, establishing, and refining a habit of abstraction and generalization—a habit forced upon him by his need to determine rather than to be determined.

The first fruitful response to the intolerable primitive situation must have been a miraculous trick, a subtle shift of view-point (like looking at a pair of photographs through a stereo-viewer) so that things suddenly jumped into perspective. The trick became a habit, and the habit has become so deeply rooted as to represent itself as something like a technique. The trick provided a lever for purposive action, a sort of sky-hook. For man, as an integral part of reality, could only change reality by changing himself, by adopting a different attitude.

The first step in abstraction was to distinguish between subject and object, between man and nature, or (more specifically) between oneself-as-subject and object-as-one's-environment—the environment including other people, both friends and enemies. To abstract is to raise something out of its setting, to see it as separate, bounded by a distinct outline. The ability to abstract brought with it an apparent increase in perception—a sharpening of visual perception particularly. Some responsive vitality was thereby lost, but the transaction was undoubtedly a profitable one; for inscrutable powers and events could be regarded as though they were made up of components and relations which, once isolated, could be tackled piecemeal. Once man had passed beyond single jets of appropriate reflex action, and began to learn how to consolidate that action by communicating within social groups, the situation rapidly became a matter of man against the animals, man against the jungle and the sea, man against other men. The purpose—to drive back the cloud of uncontrolled and ominous forces. The method—exterminate whatever threatens, placate what cannot be exterminated, and work out uncertain alliances *faute de mieux* with fire and 'power' and other men. And the trick of abstraction, originally contrived to gain control over an intolerable situation, ends in the paradox of man against the world—although man seems originally to have been an integral part of that world.

But the trick of abstraction works, and satisfies the clamorous need for action; for it allows man to act purposively—or at least with a self-deceptive air of purpose. Abstraction is practical; it is the only way of getting a handle on the outside world. And the habit of abstraction has stamped its image and mechanism upon the human mind, so that whenever we adopt a practical attitude towards a situation, whenever we decide to act in such a way that we can predict the result of our action with some confidence, we long-circuit our response into a pattern of abstraction and analytical thinking. And logic, as a basis for considered action and a means of relating one action with another, bears the indelible stamp of practicality, of systematically distorting reality by simplification.[1] The primitive simplicity was different: it involved a totality of response which was intolerable. The practical attitude, by seeing things simpler than they really are, achieves a measure of control by separating man from the reality by which his life is at once nourished and threatened.

The abstractive way of mind has specialized into a second mode of mental activity. Not only is it possible abstractively to analyse and so to gain control of a particular situation, but it has become possible to recall series of situations or events, to generalize upon them when they are not actually occurring, and to draw up general 'laws' both of abstractive analysis and considered action. In this way refined mental activity can be exerted upon data which are not actual events of experience; mental activity need no longer occur in response to external events while they are actually taking place. There is, in short, a way of setting the mind to 'think about' things, events, persons with a view to controlling or 'understanding' them. Although this way of mind does not necessarily discharge in overt action, it terminates in communicable propositions in the light of which individual events can be 'understood' and controlled. This way of mind I call 'technical', because this attitude of suspended practicality is characterized by those rules for coherent discursive thinking about abstracts which Aristotle formulated under the title of Logic—the craft or technique of thinking.[2]

[1] The most common feature of this distortion by oversimplification is to regard time, not as a real non-reversible flux, but as a pure succession of points of time: Whitehead reserves for it the title of the Fallacy of Misplaced Location. The annihilation of time by abstraction is the clue to some elegant Greek sophistries about arrows never reaching their mark and hares never catching up with tortoises; it is also the starting-point and basis for any disingenuous or 'ideological' interpretation of history.

[2] This way of mind is now more commonly termed 'theoretical'; but since that word derives from the Greek word for 'contemplation'—θεωρία—I prefer to draw attention to a word clearly enough used in our own time and submerged in the present

Since the purpose of this essay is to distinguish poetic process and the contemplative way of mind, there is no need to retain the distinction between practical and technical activity. The practical and technical ways of mind are both directed towards specific or potential practical ends, and differ in their distance from actual events but not in mental process; I shall therefore comprehend both in the single term 'technical'.

* * *

Logic may represent certain immutable laws of mind, but it need not be—and evidently is not—a comprehensive projection of the total activity of mind. Logic is a first approximation in the *science* of mind; based upon observation, Logic is an anology in terms of which single mental events of certain kinds can be 'understood' and criticized. But logical principles, required for a science and therefore evolved in the technical way of mind, project only that technical way of mind. This is the sort of thing Yeats had in mind when he wrote:

> *Empty eyeballs knew*
> *That knowledge increases unreality, that*
> *Mirror on mirror mirrored is all the show.*

If we are to gain a more comprehensive understanding of mind, we must allow to emerge into sight the dynamic patterns of integral mind, of mind in its totality and complexity. The clinical psychology of this century has not succeeded in doing this because it has been preoccupied with classifying and generalizing in order to effect cures. Illuminating though their researches may have been, impressive though some of the methods and practical results, experimental psychology remains incorrigibly technical; and being technical it is limited to certain scientific postulates about cause and effect. For practical purposes that method perhaps serves well enough; but it will not serve for ours. We wish to contemplate the mind, to know the mind; to think *about* the mind, or even to know *about* the mind,

use of the term 'Logic'. Our word Logic comes from the Hellenistic phrase ἡ λογική τεχνή—the craft of thinking. By τεχνή the Greeks did not mean 'art': all the words for art come from the root ποιεῖν, to create, to make. 'Science' and 'technique' are probably the more accurate words in present use for rendering what Aristotle meant by τεχνή. The distinction between the technical and contemplative uses of language is drawn in detail in Chapter VII (pp. 119 ff.).

is not enough. For our purpose a different method is required—a contemplative method. Herbert Read clearly outlines the psychological problem.

'All art originates in an act of intuition, or vision. But such *intuition* or vision must be identified with *knowledge*, being fully present only when consciously objectified. This act of vision or intuition is, physically, a state of concentration or tension in the mind. The *process* of poetry consists firstly in maintaining this vision in its integrity, and secondly in expressing this vision in words.'

Paul Valéry contributes a salutary caution:

'All criticism is dominated by the outworn theory that the man is the cause of the work as in the eyes of the law the criminal is the *cause* of the crime. Far rather are they both the effects. The pragmatic principle lightens the task of the judge and the critic. Biography is simpler than analysis. But of what interests us most, it teaches absolutely nothing.' [1]

As for the method—we need not go beyond a note in one of Coleridge's memorandum books: 'And yet what ample materials exist for a true & nobly-minded Psychologist—for in order to make fit use of these materials he must love and honor as well as understand, human nature—rather, he must love in order to understand it.'

*   *   *

Since 'reality' is closely connected in our minds with what 'matters', it is not surprising that we find a variety of meanings

[1] Cf. Jacques Maritain, *Art and Poetry* (1943): 'But then, let us beware, in trying to disentangle his thoughts, of misjudging the admirable complexity of the creative synthesis, of attributing to the artist in too brutal a manner, as issuing directly from *him*, what is not his except through and in the matter that he animates, what does not manifest his thought save by the rays of a thousand-times-refracted light, and by the total distribution of the light, and by the portions of shadow as much as by the light.' Yeats gives a more intimate account in *The Bounty of Sweden* (1923): 'When I begin to write I have no object but to find for them [my soliloquies] some natural speech, rhythm and syntax, and to set it out in some pattern, so seeming old that it may seem all men's speech, and though the labour is very great, I seemed to have used no faculty peculiar to myself, certainly no special gift. I print the poem and never hear of it again, until I find the book years after with a page dog-eared by some young man, or marked by some young girl with a violet, and when I have seen that I am slightly ashamed, as though somebody were to attribute to me a delicacy of feeling I should but do not possess. What came so easily at first and amidst so much drama, and was written so laboriously at the last cannot be counted among my possessions.'

attached to the word, or that many different things and events come to be called 'real'. From time to time, from profession to profession, from discipline to discipline, from individual to individual, from moment to moment in a single person's life, the concept of reality varies—as far as it becomes a concept at all. Very roughly, however, we may distinguish two kinds of reality. There is the 'physical reality', comprising all that is 'outside' us, whatever will be there when we get back, whatever cannot be avoided; physical reality usually suggests permanence and genuineness—somehow it just *is*. This is the way most common-sense people would describe reality, especially if they did not think about it too long. Then there is the 'psychic reality' which (without either asserting or denying the existence of the physical reality) refers to whatever occurs 'inside' us— thoughts, pains, feelings, self-consciousness, the sense of being a self, the 'feel' of acting and being acted upon, of being the focus of one's personal experience. This psychic reality is characterized by insubstantiality and peculiar importance; it is marked by a subtle fluency, a 'terrible fluidity'; it is constantly changing in content, emphasis, and vividness. It is this psychic reality that artists are particularly concerned with; this is the reality of which they bring the richest evidence. We might follow A. C. Bradley in regarding it as 'the whole of experience conceived completely harmoniously'. For the integral nature of the person supplies the first centre from which the physical reality is apprehended. Yet the physical reality is for the artist indispensable: it is in terms of physical reality alone that the integral and personal reality can be embodied.

One would prefer to be quite simple and specific and think of reality as 'outside' us, immutable or at very least predictable, subject to precise test. For some purposes it is convenient—even rewarding— to regard reality as a group of things or events outside us which can be located, examined, and analysed at will on the assumption that a person can be an impersonal recording instrument. No scientist can proceed far without some such assumption. But a thing or event which is (in the strictest sense) *outside* us, with which we have no contact and which we do not know, cannot possibly be of any concern. As soon as anything is of concern, we are in relationship with it, it is part of us, even though our apprehension of it may be indistinct and tenuous. When Dr Johnson, with portentous common sense, refuted Berkeley by kicking a stone, he made a good point for his argument but did not show himself a very profound metaphysician.

What concerned him was, not that it was a stone or that the stone existed, but that when he kicked the stone it hurt his foot. The one thing metaphysicians are sure of is that we do not know, and cannot know, anything about the nature of existence of 'things-in-themselves', of things as they exist apart from the human consciousness. The thing itself—the stone—did not matter, and from the human point of view cannot matter; but the relation between the thing and the person does. That the stone hurts or frustrates or delights; or in a more practical way, if it be part of a protective wall or a weapon to kill a man with—that is the sort of thing that does matter.

But what is the test of this reality? How does a poet *know*? And how do we know that he knows better than a scientist what a thing 'really is'? How can we support the position that the poet sustains a closer contact with reality than the scientist does—that the mystic is more *realistic* than the philosopher?

Each person constructs his own reality, more or less harmoniously, out of his experience. It would seem then that the varieties of reality are infinite, that possibly each personal reality is as valid as another. But reality is not so completely chaotic and individual as that. We must make sure that in attempting to resolve the variety of reality, we do not remove the basis of variety. For the basis of that variety is the essentially moral nature of human experience; and moral experience finds its unification, not in 'substance', but in value. When we say that something is real we are saying something about its value, about our concern for that thing or for the values it engages; we are not saying anything about the self-subsistence or the solidity of the thing. Our concern for a single person or thing may persist and deepen or vanish, even though in the physical sense that person or thing remains. (Indeed, when something persists we generally find some means of ignoring it—or of circumventing it by understanding or explaining it.) The depth and strength of our concern for a thing depends upon the vividness and clarity of our apprehension of the thing: we need apprehend it only once if we grasp it vividly; the more vivid the apprehension the more persistent the concern. This is what Robert Frost had in mind when he said: 'The right reader of a good poem can tell the moment it strikes him that he has taken an immortal wound and knows that he will never get over it.'

Deep concern is conjoined with vivid apprehension; and at the same time, deep concern clarifies and sharpens vision. If we see

apathetically, we cannot 'feel for' what we see; if we do not 'feel for'
a thing, we do not see it clearly.

* * *

Some prominent features of artistic experience now begin to
emerge. The artist has an exceptional capacity for sympathy, for
getting the 'feel' of persons and events; he also has an acute feeling
for 'inorganic things'. He has an exceptional clarity of vision; and
this clear insight is one aspect of his flair for 'getting inside' things,
of *knowing* what it feels like to be this person, this thing, involved in
this situation. Concern, sympathy, feeling—when these intersect in
any event of actual experience, they are the indelible marks of reality
and value; these are the intimate relationships which art most persistently embodies. But these relationships manifest themselves in
experience primarily as feeling. The artist differs from other people,
not so much in his capacity for seeing, feeling, and sympathizing—
for we all share that to some extent—but in his ability to organize his
feelings, and to organize them in their primal complexity.

'Certainly the poet must try "to see things as they really are"; but
nothing *really is* in isolation, pure and self-sufficient; reality involves
relationship, and as soon as you have relationship you have, for
human beings, emotion; so that the poet cannot see things as they
really are, cannot be precise about them, unless he is also precise
about the feelings which attach him to them.' [1]

The artist's reality is a universe of feeling.

* * *

Events can influence us without our knowing either the source or
extent of the influence; but we are only profoundly influenced by
what we apprehend vividly, by what we value. Human beings are
much more opaque, more impatient of influence, than they are commonly prepared to believe; and so arises a whole range of obtuseness,
and fear and evil. For there is no law that inescapably *makes* us seek

[1] C. Day Lewis, *The Poetic Image* (1947), pp. 24–5. I do not much like his
identification of 'emotions' and 'feelings' in this passage. A distinction is drawn
between these in Chapter V following. Meanwhile it may serve to quote Alexander's
remark in *Beauty and Other Forms of Value* (1933): 'Emotion is a poor and improbable
way of describing the meaning of a Mass of Bach, the Eroica or the Fifth Symphony,
a concerto, even less a minuet of Mozart.'

out the real, there is no power but one's own that can make us grasp
reality. But when we grasp reality, we also become real. The man
who is not aware can only know a limited, crude, and inhuman
reality; and he will not himself be real. The fullest and deepest
reality is achieved through love. This is clearly the case for love of
persons; but it applies also to the 'inorganic' world. Only when a
thing is grasped in the closest conceivable relationship—the relationship of love—do we begin to know that we are penetrating into the
inner nature of that thing. Only in love can we give ourselves out
fully enough to lose ourselves and so make real both the world and
ourselves.[1] It is the function of the artist with his capacity for loving
things, and not of the scientist in his bloodless and impartial detachment, to see things 'as they really are'. That is what Gerard Manley
Hopkins meant when, in the terms of his own mystical position, he
said: 'All things are charged with love, are charged with God and
if we know how to touch them give off sparks and take fire, yield
drops and flow, ring and tell of him.' But most of us are at best 'dull
sublunary lovers'. It is the gift and privilege of mystics and poets to
'know how to touch' things into life, to grasp the 'inscapes' of the
world. 'It is an uneasy lot at best,' George Eliot writes memorably
in *Middlemarch*, 'to be what we call highly taught and yet not to
enjoy: to be present at this great spectacle of life and never to be
liberated from a small hungry shivering self—never to be fully possessed by the glory we behold, never to have our consciousness
rapturously transformed into the vividness of a thought, the ardour
of a passion, the energy of an action, but always to be scholarly and
uninspired, ambitious, and timid, scrupulous and dim-sighted.'

*   *   *

True knowledge, then, arises in contemplation, in events of reality
in paradeigmatic experience. The theoretical or speculative state
of mind, being a state of suspended practicality, is also abstractive and
differs in kind from contemplation. There can be no question that
theoretical activity does terminate in knowledge of some sort; but it
is always a knowledge arising from an abstract world, from a partial
not a total universe. Theoretical (or technical) expression is a series

[1] Cf. Jacques Maritain, *Art and Poetry* (1943): 'Let us not confound the union of
love and the union of complicity. *Amor extasim faciens*: It is by love, not by an obscure
collusion, that the novelist is in his characters.'

of partial assertions; and those assertions, being partial, are particularly relevant to the practical sphere. The end of true knowledge then is not material power but spiritual awareness, a capacity for love of an increasingly sensitive and all-embracing kind. And it is in this aspect of knowledge that theoretical activities are redeemed from a self-circling paralysis and futility; for science and philosophy must be—and from time to time are—transfused by the blinding vision of contemplation. Spinoza has commented upon this feature of knowledge: 'He that would seriously set upon the search of truth ought in the first place to prepare his mind with a love of truth. . . . Whoever goes beyond this measure of assent, it is plain, receives not truth for the love of it, loves not truth for truth-sake, but for some by-end.'

The human consciousness is not a mechanism which responds only in set ways to impulses from without. The patterns of response are commanded by the patterns of selection and emphasis which we present to the flux of experience; the intensity and richness of response is a function of the capacity—the need even—for vivid apprehension and deep concern. We can see everything or nothing; we can 'see' everything *and* nothing: for we can formulate our responses so that we see only what we wish to see or what we find it convenient to see. The desire for what is predictable in experience can become so powerful as to lift a person out of the flux of unique experience into a static lifeless world of abstractions in which there is no reality and in which he ceases to be real. And such a state of affairs—as we see in our own time—can be misrepresented as reality, not only by individuals, but by families, societies, even whole nations. It is of no such world that the poets and mystics bring us news.[1]

Since reality is a matter of relationships and not a congeries of self-subsisting 'things', the smallest unit of reality is an *event*. It may be of theoretical interest to consider whether individual things exist in themselves; but nothing is of concern or value unless regarded as an occasion (actual or possible) for relationship. 'Existence' is an extremely abstract notion—it is not reality, but merely an abstract possibility of reality. Nothing is real until included in an event of value. If we recognize degrees of value, if we acknowledge that one experience is 'better' than another, that it is better to die for one's friends than to cheat one's enemies, then we also recognize degrees

[1] Cf. C. G. Jung, *Modern Man in Search of a Soul*: 'Any reaction to stimulus may be causally explained; but the creative act, which is the absolute antithesis of mere reaction, will for ever elude the human understanding.'

of reality. And the term 'real', which we are inclined to reserve as a measure of solidity, genuineness, and importance, also becomes a measure of the range of individual awareness and the capacity for response. But the sheer extent and richness of response to events is not, in itself, the test of value;[1] the response must also have some relevance on the one hand to the particular event and, on the other, to the person as an historical entity. When this unity embraces at once the event-constructed-by-the-person and the person-constructed-in-the-event an event of reality has occurred.

The fullest reality is accessible only to those who have a wide range and depth of awareness; and this reality is consistently accessible only to those who are capable of organizing complex responses. 'Sensitiveness without impulse spells decadence, and impulse without sensitiveness spells brutality.' The artist's characteristic impulse is to sustain, organize, and contemplate, and so to embody his events of reality. A hazardous occupation; for (as Kierkegaard observes) 'it takes more courage to suffer than to act, more courage to forget than to remember'. The ordinary man is prudent when he limits his awareness and responses: every surge of response, every occasion of reality, is an upheaval, a new birth, a destruction of much that has gone before, the threat of chaos, a threat to the foreseeable future. It is safer to avoid a succession of such shocks, for it takes inconceivable strength and faith to support the full and continuous weight of reality. But 'it is the business of the future to be dangerous'. Value—and so reality—inheres only in the present, in the minute window of awareness that moves across the river of time like a shaft of moonlight moving across a dark estuary. Perpetually novel, the luminous instant of value and reality has also the character of eternity: and eternity, in Boethius's arresting phrase, is 'the whole, simultaneous, and complete fruition of a life without bounds'. The event of reality constructs the person; it makes the person integral, and endows him with integrity. For the event of reality is instantaneous and timeless, striking dark roots of simultaneity into the history of the person, of the race, of mankind.

By retiring from the luminous present we can avoid the crushing burden of reality and all its astonishing novelty and consistency; we

---

[1] I. A. Richards, in *Principles of Literary Criticism*, is inclined to suggest that the *number* of components in a psychic event is a measure of a value. Although there appears to be some relation between 'richness' of response and value, value is essentially a *qualitative* feature of experience and can never be assessed quantitatively.

can avoid the stress of change and the responsibility of growing up. Yet the art of living is to discover how one may constantly change without loss of integrity; that is, to change without losing touch with reality. In renouncing the present—and with it the fullest responsibility that falls to man—we let slip the treasure which is of all treasures the richest: it is a treasure which can never be possessed because it is always slipping away; it can only be possessed by renouncing ownership, by recreating it afresh from moment to moment. And that is not the creation and recreation of a succession of 'things', but the creation and recreation of the self in the context of reality.

That such a life is possible and that it is the crown of human endeavour is a conviction supported intuitively by religious men and discursively by philosophers. Such a life is not the prerogative of artists and mystics: one supposes that, with due preparation, it is accessible to everybody. Yet few attain to such a life; and only those who can endure

> The backward look behind the assurance
> Of recorded history, the backward half-look
> Over the shoulder, towards the primitive terror.

We have direct evidence of it only through works of art. This is so, not simply because the materials of art are relatively permanent, not subject to the vertiginous evanescence of human events. It is so because the artist can discover to himself his reality only by making a work of art. By embodying in physical material his feeling of reality, by incarnating his feeling for reality, the artist discovers and realizes both himself and the world. And this discovery is of supreme value because it can communicate itself to others.

IV

Two Views of Imagination

It has been already hinted, that metaphysics and psychology have long been my hobby-horse. But to have a hobby-horse, and to be vain of it, are so commonly found together, that they pass almost for the same. I trust, therefore, that there will be more good-humor than contempt, in the smile with which the reader chastises my self-complacency, if I confess myself uncertain, whether the satisfaction from the perception of a truth new to myself may not have been rendered more poignant by the conceit, that it would be equally so to the public.—S. T. COLERIDGE.

Art begins with the mind and the will to select. The spontaneous welling up of images, without which there can be no poetry, precedes and nourishes the activity of the poet: and doubtless it is never the result of premeditation and calculation: this must be emphasized. As a general rule, however, the mind not only regulates but invites such an activity and gives it a direction. It then waits for the results, stops them as they issue, makes a selection and forms a judgment.

JACQUES MARITAIN

THROUGH the device of abstraction man has secured some measure of control over his environment, and has achieved some kinds of cohesive—though admittedly unstable—social organizations. In the course of time men have become more 'civilized'; but man cannot outgrow his past, he has not altered the fundamentally primitive nature of reality, he has not outgrown 'the primitive terror', he cannot dispense with the reality which is accessible only to the primitive prelogical mentality. This mentality persists in civilized man, but submerged; in poetry and through poets this mentality is invoked and perpetuated.

The only full reality for man is naked living, a rhythmic movement between contemplation and action. Certain actions are real

46

because they flow from events of reality; but reality is only grasped in contemplation, in an attitude of passivity, a total awareness which permits of total response. The action that flows from contemplative states has a special moral vividness, a peculiar human relevance; only in such action do we attain reality, become real. But social and considered action in Western civilization in the last few centuries has not consistently exhibited those qualities; one can only suppose that social action (as we now know it) is begotten on abstraction by the technical mind. So powerfully has the technical mind dominated Western civilization that it has represented its own theoretical and speculative activities as contemplative; it has maintained that knowledge is genuine only when proved by external evidence, and only when applicable as power to achieve predictable results in action. The contemplative way of mind seeks other ends than these, operates in a different manner, and terminates in action and expression of a different kind.

Science attempts to show what things are and how they work; by describing, prescribing, and predicting, science indicates how we may secure control over our environment and (to a certain extent) over ourselves. Science attains to its precision by successive stages of abstraction, by criticizing and relating generalities which, being no longer individual, must be abstract. Scientific action manifests its abstractness in an absence of responsibility and moral quality; scientific expression manifests its abstractness by the absence of feeling. The value and quality of different actions is difficult to determine because it is difficult to establish why an action occurred as it did. But the action that flows out of an artist's contemplative experience is his fashioning of a work of art. Provided we examine the work of art as an extension of the artist's mind and not as an abstracted 'thing', we may expect to find traces, not only of a certain kind of mental activity, but also of his basic beliefs and particular degrees of value. Yet all kinds of expression—the artist's as well as the scientist's—are in a sense abstract: they are not life, they are not reality. Although all kinds of expression are complementary, they form when combined not a synthesis of reality but a complete hollow world. But that is true only of the 'written things', the physical expression regarded as an unrelated entity not recreated in another mind. Edith Sitwell writes that 'with Yeats poetry meant no escape from life, poetry *was* life—it was action as much as dream—and dream was a part of life, a refreshment, and a reflowering'. When the artist claims to embody

47

reality, it remains to inquire how it is that an artist can endow his physical work of art with a vitality and value not to be found in the products of a different mental attitude.

Works of art can convey to us the *feeling* of things; they can tell us what things feel like. But how does the artist transfer that feeling into his words and tunes and rhythms, into his colours and lines—a feeling *for,* as well as a feeling *of,* things, persons, and events? Philosophical and scientific inquiries into art have seldom asked a question of this kind. They have generally been content to ascribe a special quality to artistic expression and account for that quality by invoking the term 'Imagination'. If the term Imagination seemed too wobbly, it was propped up with the word 'creative' and was then felt to serve as source and sanction for all the transcendent values in art—and even in 'life'. In a later chapter I shall examine the characteristic stamp given to language by the technical and the contemplative ways of mind; in this chapter I wish to show how each of these ways of mind also shows its true character when describing Imagination.

The 'ordinary man' at present has a somewhat tenuous grasp of reality; consequently he is inclined to assume that there is a clear-cut distinction between 'appearance' and 'reality'. This assumption colours his view of imagination. Imagination, he will say (in Lord Kames's phrase), is a faculty which can 'fabricate images without any foundation in reality', a faculty which can call up 'things not present to sense' and construct things that never were on sea or land. If art arises from imagination, the argument runs, then it must be a tissue of unreal fantasies; and even Plato, the poet's philosopher, reluctantly allowed himself to be steered into this conclusion. This view of imagination is not *wrong*; but it gives too much importance to an aspect of image-making that is not of primary importance to the artist and is too indistinct for a theory of art. It is interesting to notice what prominence this view assumes in the *New English Dictionary*; and even though the word 'imagination' can now be held to a different meaning, the cognate words 'imagine', 'imaginary', 'imaginative' all point towards this 'ordinary' view.[1] Shakespeare in

---

[1] Even such an accomplished philosopher as R. G. Collingwood could be misled by them: see his *Outlines of a Philosophy of Art* (1925), pp. 11–13. 'What the subject does [in the case of art] is to imagine: the object is an imaginary object, and the relation between them is that the individual or empirical act of imagining creates the object. In knowledge, on the other hand, the object is real; and the relation between them is that the empirical act of knowing presupposes the object and does not create

one of his rare comments upon imagination is evidently writing with his tongue in his cheek; but he gives three instances of the same view.

> The lunatic, the lover, and the poet
> Are of imagination all compact:—
> One sees more devils than vast hell can hold,—
> That is, the madman: the lover, all as frantic,
> Sees Helen's beauty in a brow of Egypt:
> The poet's eye, in a fine frenzy rolling,
> Doth glance from heaven to earth, from earth to heaven;
> And, as imagination bodies forth
> The forms of things unknown, the poet's pen
> Turns them to shapes, and gives to airy nothing
> A local habitation and a name.

In the same scene of *A Midsummer Night's Dream* he touches upon a more grave and paradoxical feature of imagination.

> Lovers and madmen have such seething brains,
> Such shaping fantasies, that apprehend
> More than cool reason ever comprehends.

But the claim seems in its context ambiguous, if not frankly playful. Until the end of the eighteenth century the word Imagination remained vague and confused; like 'imitation' and 'Nature' in eighteenth-century criticism, and 'ether' and 'instinct' in nineteenth-century science and psychology, it was too often postulated as a vehicle or faculty to embrace values and processes of which no connected account could be given.

One is inclined to agree with Herbert Read that the understanding of aesthetic consciousness 'has not advanced much beyond the level it reached with Wordsworth and Coleridge and their German contemporaries'.[1] But it is to Coleridge rather than to Wordsworth or to their German contemporaries that modern aesthetic theories of

it. . . . The object, in the case of art, is an imaginary object. . . . We certainly do use the word imaginary with a definite implication of unreality. . . . We are quite right to oppose the imaginary to the real. For the real is only real as it stands in the real world.'

[1] *Education through Art* (1944), p. 30. Herbert Read actually says that 'the scientific analysis of aesthetic consciousness has not advanced much . . .'; but I do not much like the phrase 'scientific analysis' here, any more than I like the term 'intuition' in the passage quoted in my previous chapter (p. 38). Herbert Read's later book, *Coleridge as Critic* (1950), which shows Coleridge as a forerunner of existentialism, suggests that he would be prepared to modify this introductory phrase.

imagination are to be traced. And it must be admitted that Coleridge accorded to imagination an intense honorific regard which, for some time, has arrested rather than stimulated further inquiry.[1]

Coleridge maintained that imagination was not the unique property of the artist, but that it underlay all knowledge even of the most prosaic kind. He sought to establish the claim that poetry be considered as a serious mode of revelation; he wished to show that poetry and 'life' were not divorced, that poetry is a window opening upon reality. The poet's activity, exceptional though it might be, was in his view an extension of ordinary cognitive experience; poetry and any other form of knowledge were to be judged by the same criteria.[2] Kant—to whom Coleridge owes something for the terms and articulation of his theory—had similarly grounded cognition in the synthesizing activity of imagination. But Kant, concerned by temperament to establish the primacy of conceptual knowing, takes little account of artistic activity. Though Coleridge's exposition of his theory of imagination is partial and scattered, the theory itself is supple and luminous in a way that less fragmentary and more dogmatic theories are not: for it grows out of his own experience of a rare creative faculty, is enriched by an acute and sensitive psychological insight, and refined by his capacity for sustained philosophical inquiry. So much obfuscation has arisen from squabbles over Coleridge's distinction between Imagination and Fancy that it is still worth following out the implications of his theory. And for the present purpose it is illuminating to compare his theory with Kant's. Coleridge's strenuous labours with the Kantian philosophy ended in respectful repudiation; whatever affinity there was between their minds was the affinity of direct opposites. Not only does Kant's theory of imagination reveal the technical mind and Coleridge's the contemplative, but Coleridge recognized the distinction and specifically drew attention to it within his own theory of imagination.

The *locus classicus* for Coleridge's theory is found at the very end

[1] Coleridge's influence upon theories of imagination dates from 1800. His ideas play a much more important role in Wordsworth's Preface to *Lyrical Ballads* (1800, 1802) and in the 'Essay Supplementary' (1815) than is generally recognized. It is also interesting to notice how persistently the Shakespeare passages quoted above ran through Coleridge's head during the *annus mirabilis* at Nether Stowey (1796–8), and how important a part they played in shaping his vocabulary of imagination.

[2] This summary view of Coleridge's position is set forth at length by D. G. James in *Scepticism and Poetry* (1937). The account that follows diverges, however, in several respects from Professor James's discussion.

of the tantalizingly evasive thirteenth chapter of *Biographia Literaria*: 'The Imagination then I consider either as primary, or secondary. The primary Imagination I hold to be the living power and prime agent of all human perception, and as a repetition in the finite mind of the eternal act of creation in the infinite I AM. The secondary Imagination I consider as an echo of the former, co-existing with the conscious will, yet still as identical with the primary in the *kind* of its agency, and differing only in *degree*, and in the *mode* of its operation. It dissolves, diffuses, dissipates, in order to recreate: or where this process is rendered impossible, yet still at all events it struggles to idealize and to unify. It is essentially vital [*i.e.* organic], even as all objects (*as* objects) are essentially fixed and dead.' The primary Imagination is the imagination operating at its most elementary level in the direct act of perception, organizing whatever is perceived instantly into a meaningful pattern without the intrusion of analysis or 'thinking'. In this Coleridge anticipates the *gestalt* psychology: in all his psychological inquiries he insists that every psychic event is integral. But nowhere else does he discuss the primary Imagination; and he seems never to have completed the 'theory of perception and its dependence on the memory and imagination' promised in *The Friend*.

The secondary Imagination engages a twofold activity which resolves itself in a synthesis, an integrated psychic unity. This activity is not a spontaneous mechanism but 'co-exists with the conscious will'. And this feature of the secondary Imagination—important for the distinction between Imagination and Fancy—is clarified by a celebrated passage in the fourteenth chapter of the *Biographia*:

'[The poet] diffuses a tone and spirit of unity, that blends and (as it were) *fuses*, each into each, by that synthetic and magical power, to which I would exclusively appropriate the name of Imagination. This power, first put into action by the will and understanding, and retained under their irremissive, though gentle and unnoticed control, *laxis effertur habenis*, reveals itself in the balance and reconcilement of opposite and discordant qualities: of sameness, with difference; of the general with the concrete; the idea with the image; the individual with the representative; the sense of novelty and freshness with old and familiar objects; a more than usual state of emotion with more than usual order; judgment ever awake and steady self-possession with enthusiasm and feeling profound or vehement; and while it blends and harmonizes the natural and the artificial, still subordinates art to nature; the manner to the matter; and our admiration of the poet to our sympathy with the poetry.'

The earlier phrase, 'co-exists with the conscious will', is now clear. He does not mean that the secondary Imagination is *co-extensive* with the conscious will, but that it cannot function without the infusion of the will and understanding. Again, primary and secondary Imagination are the same in *kind* of agency, but differ in the *mode* of operation by the presence or absence of will and understanding: they differ in *degree*, because we are conscious only of the synthesized *product* of primary Imagination, whereas we are intensely aware of the synthesizing *process* of the secondary Imagination. But 'the rules of Imagination are themselves the very powers of growth and production': Imagination is not simply an act of will, but a dynamic activity developing from within, self-creating, lightly controlled and in part sustained by the will and understanding.

The link between primary and secondary Imagination is more clearly described in *The Statesman's Manual* as 'that reconciling and mediatory power, which, incorporating the reason in images of the sense, and organizing (as it were) the flux of the senses by the permanence and self-circling energies of the reason, gives birth to a system of symbols, harmonious in themselves, and consubstantial with the truth of which they are conductors'. The elements which Imagination 'dissolves, diffuses, dissipates, in order to recreate' are, then, images—whether the objects corresponding with those images are physically present, or remembered, or both. When the synthesizing process is complete a new whole has been created; and somehow both it and its constituents have been raised to symbolic status, made permanent and significant, partaking of reality—they have become windows opening upon reality. This synthesis is both the condition and outcome of the poet's integration; for 'The poet, described in *ideal* perfection, brings the whole soul of man into activity, with the subordination of its faculties to each other according to their relative worth and dignity.' Coleridge would agree with Croce that in a sense *homo nascitur poeta*—certainly in the instant integrity of direct perception, and probably also in the general manifestations of the secondary Imagination; but when it is a matter actually of constructing a work of art, the poet engages in an activity peculiar to himself.

'The sense of musical delight, with the power of producing it, is a gift of imagination; and this together with the power of reducing multitude into unity of effect, and modifying series of thoughts by some one predominant thought or feeling, may be cultivated and improved, but can never be learned. It is in these that "*poeta nascitur non fit*".'

Kant's account of imagination in the *Critique of Pure Reason* is drawn up in strikingly similar terms; but it starts from and returns to a very different attitude of mind.[1] The imagination he considers to be 'a blind but indispensable function of the soul', 'the faculty of representing in intuition an object that is *not itself present*'.[2] (We notice at once that he singles out the feature of imagination which is central in the popular view.) The imagination, in Kant's view as in Coleridge's, operates in two orders or modes: these he calls 'reproductive' and 'productive'. The reproductive imagination fashions empirical intuition into 'images', its synthesis being 'entirely subject to empirical laws, the laws, namely, of association'.[3] In an important note Kant indicates at what a radical level he conceives imagination to function.

'Psychologists have hitherto failed to realize that imagination is a necessary ingredient of perception itself. This is due partly to the fact that that faculty has been limited to reproduction, partly to the belief that the senses not only supply impressions but also combine them so as to generate images of objects. For that purpose something more than the mere receptivity of impressions is undoubtedly required, namely, a function for the synthesis of them.'

---

[1] The passages quoted in the following account are taken from Norman Kemp Smith's translation of the *Critique of Pure Reason* (1929); the central passages—on imagination, synthesis, and schemata—are found in pp. 112, 165, 182 of that text. I have profited much from Kemp Smith's *Commentary to Kant's 'Critique of Pure Reason'* (1923), especially pp. 263–70, 334–42.

[2] Kant's term 'intuition' (*Anschauung*) is not much like the popular sense of that term, being almost the equivalent to 'perception' but not involving any particular psychological or ontological theory about the relation between the perceiver and the thing perceived. See the first part of 'Transcendental Aesthetic' in the *Critique of Pure Reason*: 'In whatever manner and by whatever means a mode of knowledge may relate to objects, *intuition* is that through which it is in immediate relation to them, and to which all thought as a means is directed. But intuition takes place only in so far as the object is given to us. . . . Objects are *given* to us by means of sensibility, and it alone yields us *intuitions*. . . . The effect of an object upon the faculty of representation, so far as we are affected by it, is *sensation*. That intuition which is in relation to the object through sensation, is entitled *empirical*.'

[3] Cf. *Critique*, p. 112: 'To bring this synthesis [of imagination] to *concepts* is a function which belongs to the understanding, and it is through this function of the understanding that we first obtain knowledge properly so called.' See also my p. 57 below.

Coleridge, then, has evidently taken a clue from Kant in distinguishing a phase of imagination at the level of perception, and has substituted the more convenient, less restrictive term 'primary' for Kant's 'reproductive'. But already their views diverge. Kant considers that the reproductive imagination commands discrete empirical intuitions into recognizable and relatable forms for cognition: Coleridge regards the primary imagination, not as a higher faculty which supervenes upon perception, but as an integrative process within perception itself. Perception for Coleridge is immediate, meaningful, and integral; he sees imagination operating in perception and assigns to it a function other than that of producing what is not actually present, because he recognizes that perception is (in his own word) *unific* and in that important detail exhibits the distinctive character of imagination.

The productive imagination (to continue with Kant's distinction) is a spontaneous and self-determining faculty which synthesizes intuitions into schemata; intuitions are the unformed objects of thinking. The reproductive imagination operates 'through and in accordance with' the productive imagination; but images and schemata are different in kind. (Kant does not give any account of the commerce between images and schemata.) Schemata provide the basis for empirical concepts; and pure *a priori* concepts (the categories) supply the relational forms for all knowledge. Images are 'never completely at one with the concept'; consequently empirical observation, even when commanded and clarified by the reproductive imagination, can play no primary role in what Kant calls 'the unitary consciousness'. The hierarchical character of his outline appears in the notion of a supreme 'intellectual synthesis' which secures 'combination through the understanding alone, without the aid of imagination' and commands the 'figurative synthesis' supplied by imagination.

At the level of *verbal* exposition, Kant's distinctions between productive and reproductive imagination, and between imagination and intuition, are clear enough. But when we recall Kant's insistence that form and content mutually condition each other, we wonder why Kant introduced these distinctions; for we are entitled to assume that he *meant* to show that imagination was a synthesis of functional relations and not a faculty mediating between intuition and understanding. It might be argued that he was hampered by an inherited Leibnizian terminology not suited to his central purpose, and so in the end does not define clearly enough the difference between categories (the formal structures of understanding) and schemata (pure conceptual forms isolated from the particular and referable to the *a priori* categories). It has been argued that his architectonic scheme deflected him from the account of imagination that he might otherwise have given; for he asserts that intuitions without concepts are blind and that concepts without intuitions are empty. Nevertheless it is a fact that he fails to show how there can be a single unbroken arc between empirical intuition and the unified life of understanding. The reason for this failure, though difficult to detect, lies at the roots of the difference between Kant and Coleridge.

On one point Kant is consistently clear: the *generation* of unified experience is primarily due to the productive imagination. The distinctive character which he assigns to imagination explains, however, why the imagination was an embarrassing notion for him to handle, and why he does not devote as much attention to it as Coleridge does. Kant's primary purpose is to discriminate *pure* reason, to show what conditions must be postulated if knowledge of the *a priori* is to be possible. For Kant, all knowledge involves awareness of self and of objects; it is an activity of the conscious mind. Yet by postulating imagination he has introduced an unconscious faculty, 'an *art* concealed in the depths of the human soul'; we can be conscious of the products of imagination but (in Kant's view) not of imagination itself. Of the schemata provided by the productive imagination Kant says that they are 'pure (without admixture of anything empirical), and yet are in one aspect intellectual and in another sensuous'. But we see that this recognition of the mixed intellectual and sensuous character of imagination is a bit perfunctory when he also writes that 'the transcendental unity of the synthesis of imagination is the pure form of all possible knowledge. Hence, through it all objects of possible experience must be represented *a priori*.' Images—the outcome of reproductive imagination—he takes to be always particular; schemata—the outcome of productive imagination—are always universal. By a confusion of the terms 'schema' and 'category', and by softening the outlines of his important term '*a priori*', Kant appears to have established some commerce between image and category by way of the schemata. His concentration upon the conscious mind and pure reason has led him to think of the schema as a third entity intermediate between the other two, and not as the functional relation which his doctrine required. Something in the whole set of his mind has led him to neglect that vital feature of imagination which

Coleridge—as practising artist and sensitive psychological observer —was so well equipped to illuminate: its incorrigibly physical and *im*pure character.

The radical difference between Kant and Coleridge may now be discerned; the difference is not unimportant for it bears upon more than the theory of imagination. Kant, seeking wholly to detach *pure* reason and the *a priori* from the empirical, thinks of the imagination as imposing *a priori* forms upon the actual or empirical; for he starts at the level of *a priori* synthetic judgments and works 'downward' towards intuition (perception), renouncing all interest in psychological inquiry. Coleridge, approaching the problem of knowledge (as it were) from the other end, knew from the nature of poetry that imagination discovers the *a priori* in the actual; and he would further maintain that the prime function of art is to bring into instant identity the particularity of the image and the universality of the (Kantian) schema: in art, he would say, the particular takes on sudden luminous universality, for in art the particular becomes a symbol. Between the two there is a difference of intension, a difference in the centre towards which each swings when confronted by a chasm in thinking or by the need for a delicate distinction. Kant tends to be driven back upon his concern for the relation between subject and predicate, even when dealing with issues not noticeably *logical* in character; for Kant is in love with metaphysics and seeks to make metaphysics a science through the rigorous application of a scientific logic. Coleridge falls back upon his concern for the *real* relation between subject and object—the relation being experiential or apprehensive—that interanimation of subject and object which lies at the centre of all artistic experience.[1] The shift in the meaning of 'subject' in this distinction indicates the radical nature of the difference. Coleridge was more than an amateur of metaphysics; he wished to extend the compass of metaphysics to embrace the poetical sphere; he also wished to break through the limitations of the Aristotelean logic. The opposite to poetry was, he saw, science; he wished to extend logic into the sphere of poetic. Coleridge's theory of

[1] Kant seems to have been aware of having to choose between these two basic positions. In his earliest attempt to encompass the generative activities of mind he appreciated that only the products, not the activities generative of consciousness, could be presented to consciousness. In the face of this requirement his distinction between the *real* understanding and the *logical* understanding collapsed (in the *Dissertation*); and it was at this point that he introduced imagination as a 'third thing' capable of transcendental as well as of empirical activity.

imagination is essentially an artist's view. Kant was once offered a professorship of poetry; yet his view if imagination is a scientist's view, the antithesis of the artist's.

Kant's notion of a supreme 'intellectual synthesis' finally establishes the dominance of understanding in his scheme. The intellectual synthesis secures 'combination through the understanding alone, without the aid of imagination', and commands the 'figurative synthesis' which imagination supplies. Kant's 'productive imagination', then, differs from Coleridge's 'secondary imagination' in the same important respect that the 'reproductive' differs from the 'primary'. For Coleridge's secondary imagination is not commanded by the understanding: it is under the irremissive but nonetheless gentle and unnoticed control of the will and understanding. And if it is argued that Kant's intellectual synthesis, being separated from imagination, is therefore outside the scope of Coleridge's secondary imagination, we must remember that for Coleridge there *is* no faculty or activity higher than that of the fully developed imagination. On the one hand, the imagination 'brings the whole soul of man into activity, with the subordination of its faculties to each other according to their relative worth and dignity'; on the other hand, imagination 'incorporat[es] the reason in images of the sense'. In Kant's scheme there is a chasm between imagination and understanding, between the images of perception and the concepts proper to the highest mental activity—understanding. Although he insists that both syntheses are 'transcendental', he has no means of bridging the chasm; his view of knowledge, starting from the reality of *a priori* synthetic judgments, will not allow him to find any genuine basis for knowledge in the radical and direct act of perception (intuition). In the Coleridgean theory there is no such chasm: each level of imagination is whole and unifying; the one flows out of the other; the higher development (secondary imagination) is instantaneously interfused at the upper end of the scale with 'Reason' (= Kant's 'understanding' in the translation), and at the lower end with the senses.

The crucial problem for a theory of art is to give a satisfactory account of the commerce between percepts and concepts. An adequate psychological theory of art requires that whatever is given in perception can mingle with abstract concepts and be submitted to conscious selection and criticism without losing its peculiar perceptual character—that is, without losing the charges of feeling it acquires in the act of perception. Kant's distinction between 'images' and 'schemata' is a valuable one; but the distinction, as he has drawn it, cannot lead into an adequate account of artistic process. (One must remark in passing that Kant had no intention of describing or establishing artistic process here.) Images, regarded as perceptual and charged with feeling-tone, are the irreducible units for imagination; and these alone are capable of achieving synthesis—a dynamic, self-constructed unity. 'Schemata', on Kant's own definition, are conceptual and devoid of feeling-tone; inasmuch as they are intellectual they are abstracted from the experiential reality from which art springs. Schemata are constructed by that intellectual vision which, being abstractive, is not contemplative: they are diagrams of 'ideas', the irreducible units for analytical or theoretical thinking.

I am not concerned to elevate Coleridge's theory at the expense of Immanuel Kant, but simply to distinguish certain operations of mind. When two theories are as similar as these, and yet so different, it is pertinent to ask whether they are two conflicting accounts of the same experience, or accounts of two different kinds of experience. Each one describes what he is convinced is the highest activity of the soul. The 'intellectual synthesis' was the most vivid and important experience that Kant—the philosopher, the impeccable connoisseur —had known.[1] Coleridge the poet is working from the basis of his most vivid and important experience—those times when the 'shaping spirit of Imagination' struck with its o'ertaking wing, and he found himself resolving, clarifying, objectifying events of reality into a poem.

Kant offers the classical account of ideation:[2] Coleridge offers the classical account of imagination. After patient and repeated study of Kant, Coleridge could find no resting-place for his mind in that philosophy: gradually, by imperceptible stages, he came to recognize the difference between his way of mind and Kant's. He had indicated in an early trenchant observation that the antithesis of poetry was not prose but science—and Kant was trying to establish a purely scientific metaphysics, a project with which at least some part of Coleridge's

[1] It is interesting to notice how reluctantly Coleridge recognized this 'set' to Kant's mind. 'In spite . . . of his own declarations, I could never believe, that it was possible for him to have meant no more by his *Noumenon*, or THING IN ITSELF, than his mere words express; or that in his own conception he confined the whole plastic power to the forms of the intellect, leaving for the external cause, for the *materiale* of our sensations, a matter without form, which is doubtless inconceivable. I entertained doubts, likewise, whether in his own mind he even laid *all* the stress, which he appears to do, on the moral postulates.'

[2] The *N.E.D.* definition is 'the formation of ideas of things not present to the senses'.

mind was in sympathy. Kant had held the word 'imagination' firmly
to the sense of an image-making faculty, taking as its most prominent
characteristic its ability to confront the mind with images of things
not actually present to the senses. Coleridge was less concerned with
this particular question, probably because he had studied it in close
detail in dream, fantasy, association, and eidetic imagery. But as soon
as he does discuss image-making, he is led to the distinction between
Imagination and Fancy—a distinction which Kant conceals by his
equivocal use of the term 'synthesis', and which several subtle
thinkers since Coleridge have seen fit to neglect or repudiate.[1]

'Repeated meditations [upon Wordsworth's poems]', Coleridge
tells us in the fourth chapter of the *Biographia Literaria*, 'led me first to
suspect (and a more intimate analysis of the human faculties . . .
matured my conjectures into full conviction) that fancy and imagination were two distinct and widely different faculties, instead of being,
according to the general belief, either two names with one meaning,
or, at furthest, the lower and higher degree of one and the same
power.' [2]   The account of Fancy is reserved for the 'sharp point' of
the famous thirteenth chapter, following immediately upon the
description of Imagination (p. 51 above). 'Fancy . . . has no other
counters to play with, but fixities and definites. The fancy is indeed
no other than a mode of memory emancipated from the order of time

---

[1] See, for example, T. S. Eliot, *The Use of Poetry and the Use of Criticism* (1933),
pp. 76–81; J. L. Lowes, *The Road to Xanadu* (1928), pp. 103, 488. Basil Willey's
Warton Lecture of 1946, 'Coleridge on Imagination and Fancy' (now reprinted in his
Nineteenth Century Studies (1949)), gives an admirably clear and persuasive account of
the distinction. More extended discussions are to be found in D. G. James's *Scepticism
and Poetry* (1937) and I. A. Richards's *Coleridge on Imagination* (1934, revised 1951).

[2] In Italian the word for 'fancy' is *imaginazzione*; the word for 'imagination' is *fantasia*.
In eighteenth-century criticism the two words were virtually synonymous; and Coleridge observes characteristically (still in the fourth chapter of the *Biographia*): 'It is not,
I own, easy to conceive a more opposite translation of the Greek φαντασία than the
Latin *imaginatio*; but it is equally true that in all societies there exists an instinct of
growth, a certain collective, unconscious good sense working progressively to desynony-
mize those words originally of the same meaning, which the conflux of dialects
supplied to the more homogeneous languages, as the Greek and German: and which
the same cause, joined with accidents of translation from original works of different
countries, occasion in mixed languages like our own.' (Coleridge, however, was guilty
of disseminating an inversion of the scholastic terms 'understanding' and 'reason' by
exalting 'Reason' as the more noble term.) Miss Wilma L. Kennedy's *The English
Heritage of Coleridge of Bristol 1798* (1947) accumulates some useful material to support
Coleridge's claim to originality in this distinction: the text of the book, however, is
not much more elegant than the title.

and space; while it is blended with, and modified by that empirical phenomenon of the will, which we express by the word Choice. But equally with the ordinary memory the Fancy must receive all its materials ready made from the law of association.' This is very Kantian language indeed; but in his *Lectures on Shakespeare* (1811–12), where he had already suggested the distinction as it applied to Shakespeare, he writes entirely in his own terms. 'As soon as [the mind] is fixed on one image, it becomes understanding [? Kant's 'intellectual synthesis'], but while it is unfixed and wavering between [images], attaching itself permanently to none, it is imagination. . . . The grandest effects of poetry are where the imagination is called forth, not to produce a distinct form, but a strong working of the mind, still offering what is still repelled, and again creating what is again rejected; the result being what the poet wishes to express, namely, the substitution of a sublime feeling for the unimaginable for a mere image.' This not only clarifies his direct account of Fancy, but anticipates Yeats's doctrine of the *Hodos Chameleontos* (the Chameleon's Way), and looks towards Keats's sketch of that gift 'which Shakespeare possessed so enormously—I mean *Negative Capability*, that is, when a man is capable of being in uncertainties, mysteries, doubts, without any irritable reaching after fact and reason——'

It is clear that the Coleridgean Fancy is identical with the faculty Kant had postulated to produce the 'figurative synthesis'. But Coleridge's imaginative synthesis does not coincide with Kant's 'intellectual synthesis'; for the one is a synthesis of images, the other a synthesis of concepts. Coleridge then has not only singled out a 'faculty' which Kant does not recognize, but he has characterized it in three senses: in terms of faculties, of the data the faculties work upon, and of the relations that hold between those data. Fancy is 'the faculty of bringing together images dissimilar in the main by some one point or more of likeness'; the images of Fancy are constructed by the exercise of will and logic—the logic often inverted and fantastic; and being toneless they are grouped by collocation into diagrams. Imagination—'the greatest faculty of the human mind'— is 'the power by which one image or feeling is made to modify many others, and by a sort of fusion to force many into one'; the images of Imagination are constructed by an unwilled constellating process of memory, are richly toned with feeling, form and true syntheses by fusing themselves dynamically into each other and into their context. Finally, Imagination by 'combining many circumstances into one moment of consciousness, tends to produce that ultimate end of allhuman thought and human feeling, unity'.

The associative link for Fancy is always an idea, a *fixed* connection between counters 'fixed and definite'; the images of Fancy are static, toneless, decorative, stable because they have been raised out of their experiential context and have lost the indeterminacy of outline and richness of meaning that intense feeling would give them. The images of Imagination are single, immediate, and singular; by sudden collisions and fusions they wield the whiplash of hitherto unrecognized relations. Are the abstract and conceptual images of Fancy to be associated with the technical mind, and the individual, palpitating and cohesive images of Imagination to be associated with the contemplative mind? Can we say that the feeling-tone which typifies Imagination is the sign, not only that the whole man is engaged, but also that here is an activity arising from an event of reality? If so, we have the keystone of the aesthetic arch; it should be possible to trace an unbroken creative arc from the primal events of perception to the completed work of art. The central term for such an account will be *feeling*; and it will be necessary to show how in art feeling and memory combine in a process where analytical thinking plays only the marginal (though not insignificant) role of critic and casual stimulant.

Before proceeding with such an account, however, an important observation remains to be made. Coleridge has conducted his description of Imagination at two levels. Sometimes he regards it as a special mode of image-making, a function of memory; sometimes he regards it as a transcendent activity which terminates in a poem whose constituent images are produced by the special mode of image-making. No matter how closely related the two processes may be—and indeed one must flow seamlessly out of the other—two processes can and should be discerned. Aware that two processes were being confused, Coleridge strove to separate them by reserving the word Imagination for the image-making faculty and coining a new word for the other. In the thirteenth chapter of the *Biographia* (as Basil Willey wittily observes), when he was 'face to face at last with his central problem, and alarmed by his own chapter heading . . . [he] slips lizard-like into a thicket of learned excerpts, and vanishes from sight, leaving in our hands his tail only—a letter from himself to himself about his forthcoming masterpiece'.[1] The chapter heading reads: 'On the Imagination, or Esemplastic Power.' The word 'or' was unfortunate; for more than a century it has concealed the sharp outlines of an analysis which, far from being superseded, has scarcely been rediscovered.

Some years before writing that chapter heading Coleridge had been searching for a word to identify the sovereign activity in art—we can watch him in a notebook entry: 'How excellently the German *Einbildungskraft* [Kant's word] expresses this prime and loftiest faculty, the power of coadunation, the faculty that forms the many into one—in-eins-bildung! Eisenplasy, or esenoplastic power, as contradistinguished from fantasy, or the mirrorment, either catoptric or metoptric—repeating simply, or by transposition—and again, involuntary as in dreams, or by an act of the will.' Mr J. Isaacs has observed that in the passage on the imagination as a reconciliation of opposites (quoted on p. 51 above) Coleridge 'calls only on distilled phrasing and sensitive balance, and throws overboard his whole armoury of *esemplasy*, *multeity*, and *coadunation*'. This is so; and yet it is a serious misrepresentation. Coleridge did not need his whole armoury to *describe* the imagination: but he did need a suitable label to indicate a special kind of experience which was not very much like what his contemporaries called Imagination, and only one feature of which was the image-making faculty he had distinguished from Fancy. The German word *Einbildungskraft* indicates very clearly the kind of activity it stands for. The word Imagination bears in its body no such meaning; and by the end of the eighteenth century it was difficult to hold the word to any precise meaning at all. Kant had used an admirable term, but had applied it only to man's response to 'Nature': artistic experience was beyond the range of his knowledge and so beyond the range of his inquiry. What Coleridge required was not a word to translate Kant's *Einbildungskraft*, but a word to stand for the 'synthetic and magical power' in whose miracles of integration he himself was inexhaustibly interested—the power that could fuse discordant elements and achieve organic unity in the paradoxical poise between spontaneity and conscious selection. If the problem could have been solved simply by substituting 'esemplasy' or 'coadunation' for Imagination, Coleridge was the last person

---

[1] It occurs to me that, with slight modification, Professor Willey's sentence admirably describes the critic's responsibility—to 'slip lizard-like into a thicket of learned excerpts, and vanish from sight, leaving in our hands the poem only'.

in the world to hesitate to do so. To avoid being forced into the mechanical associationist explanations popular in his own day, he had thought in terms of faculties and powers. But he needed to go a short step farther. He could only have solved his terminological problem by rejecting his translation of the Kantian word, and by rethinking his psychology in terms of process.

Since it is no longer very difficult to think in terms of process, we may venture to give a name to each of Coleridge's two senses of the word Imagination, and then discuss them separately. I shall confine the term *imagination* to the primary process of image-making. For the more comprehensive process which enfolds the first and terminates in a poem, I suggest that the term *symbolic extrication* might be used; for we require some such self-evident term to indicate a process in which the poet, through an unwilled and self-generating feat of integration, extricates himself from immersion in reality by incarnating in a symbolic entity the feeling of that reality.

V

Imagination: Image-making

Visionary Power
Attends upon the motions of the winds
Embodied in the mystery of words.
There darkness makes abode, and all the host
Of shadowy things do work their changes there,
As in a mansion like their proper home;
Even forms and substances are circumfused
By that transparent veil with light divine;
And through the turnings intricate of Verse,
Present themselves as objects recognis'd,
In flashes, and with a glory scarce their own.

WILLIAM WORDSWORTH

JOHN LIVINGSTON LOWES in *The Road to Xanadu* triumph-antly fulfilled his claim to have disclosed for the psychology of poetry 'a group of facts which have never before been reckoned with'. He shows (in part at least) how fragmentary images and even single words, accumulated without conscious design from widely scattered sources and from personal experience, were fused into *The Ancient Mariner* and *Kubla Khan*. Recognizing that some plastic and energetic function of memory was an indispensable condition of poetry, Lowes found his centre of emphasis in memory and associa-tion. His figurative name for memory is the Well. Into this 'Deep Well' all items of experience sink—everything seen, heard, felt, touched, known; and there, by some alchemical process of associa-tion, selection, accretion, the individual particles of experience are

64

submerged, related, separated, changed, enriched. But the Well is not responsible for the whole of poetic activity

'There enter into imaginative creation three factors which reciprocally interplay: the Well, and the Vision, and the Will. Without the Vision, the chaos of elements remains a chaos, and the Form sleeps forever in the vast chambers of unborn designs. Yet in *that* chaos only could creative Vision ever see this *Form*. Nor without the cooperant Will, obedient to the Vision, may the pattern perceived in the huddle attain objective reality. Yet manifold though the ways of the creative faculty may be, the upshot is one: from the empire of chaos a new tract of cosmos has been retrieved; a nebula has been compacted—it may be!—into a star' (*The Road to Xanadu*, p. 432).

Lowes frankly admits that, as far as a psychological theory of poetry is concerned, he can offer only a working hypothesis, 'the provisional conclusions of the layman'; his primary concern was for the facts. Several unjust strictures have been brought against Lowes on the fallacious assumption that because he uses little of the jargon of the new psychology he is not writing psychology at all.[1] But Miss Maud Bodkin (*Archetypal Patterns in Poetry* (1934), p. 40) has noticed that 'in his general theory Lowes seems to take no account of emotional forces as determining either the selection or the fashioning of the material of the poem'; and this charge cannot easily be dismissed. Is Lowes correct in regarding memory as chaotic? Are the 'elements' images or something else? And what is the virtue of retrieving a new tract of cosmos from a random and chaotic memory? For surely it is not the glory of the poet (as Lowes suggests here) that his Vision is directed upon and gives an ordered 'objective reality' to the huddle and chaos of memory. Lowes shows a profound respect for his materials; but respect may impede inquiry by introducing gratuitous mysteries.

The Road to Xanadu has given a powerful impetus to those who would collect facts of memory and association. To the introspective

[1] Lowes himself deals with this charge implicitly in his crushing attack upon Robert Graves's psycho-analytical interpretation of *Kubla Khan* (*The Road to Xanadu*, pp. 593–6). Writing in the 'twenties, Lowes added stature to his work by not becoming uncritically intoxicated by the Freudian interpretations of literature then fashionable. And there is some hard sense in Basil Willey's passing comment in 'Coleridge on Imagination and Fancy': 'To-day we talk familiarly about the subconscious, and think we are speaking more scientifically than our predecessors who discoursed about "the soul".'

evidence of artists and thinkers there has now been added great store of psychologists' clinical reports and speculations. How are these to be brought into relation to provide a reliable account of this most fully documented aspect of poetic process? I have suggested that the term 'feeling' may offer a satisfactory centre of reference; Miss Bodkin would seem to prefer the more usual and troublesome term 'emotion'. Let us examine Wordsworth's celebrated introspective report of poetic activity, offered in his Preface to *Lyrical Ballads*.

Early in the Preface Wordsworth asserts without qualification that 'all good poetry is the spontaneous overflow of powerful feelings'. The phrase evidently needs to be expanded and explained, and presently, abandoning the oracular and dogmatic tone, Wordsworth returns to the attack. 'Poetry is the spontaneous overflow of powerful feelings: it takes its origin from emotion recollected in tranquillity; the emotion is contemplated till, by a species of re-action the tranquillity disappears, and an emotion, kindred to that which was before the subject of contemplation, is gradually produced and does itself actually exist in the mind. In this mood successful composition generally begins, and in a mood similar to this it is carried on.' This passage calls forth three observations. First of all, the terms 'feeling' and 'emotion' are confused and treated as though they were interchangeable; this confusion appears not only in Wordsworth but (as far as I know) in every writer on poetic experience and the nature of poetry. Second, the central term in this account is feeling (or emotion) and not the poetic image. And finally, one is constrained to ask how an emotion can be 'the subject of contemplation'. If these three issues are dealt with in turn, the ground can be cleared for a discussion of imagination as a process of image-making.

Feeling and emotion, though in some respects closely related, are not to be regarded as synonymous; indeed one of the most important tasks for a philosophical critic at the present time is to distinguish clearly between them. Since I have chosen the term 'feeling' to represent the irreducible energetic principle for all psychic organization, a brief sketch for such a distinction may be offered. In the light of this distinction I should further urge that the word 'aesthetics' be taken to mean (in accordance with its Greek derivation) the inquiry into states and processes of feeling.

The difference between feeling and emotion seems to me to turn upon the difference between person and personality. Emotion necessarily involves personality, feeling does not. By personality I mean the jealous sense of the self as primary. Personality is that model or projected self constructed out of the secret recognition of our capacities and incapacities, of our strength and weakness; that dignified, impressive, flippant, aggressive armour—compounded of 'character', assumed gaiety, and an amiable self-indulgence—behind which the naked vulnerable self marches into the world.[1] Emotion is a complex of feeling which nourishes and protects this personality, this *persona*, this mask. Emotion is centripetal; it turns the attention inward exclusively upon the self; it tends to isolate the person from the outside world and inhibits his response to it; it is a limitation in awareness. Emotion is rightly distrusted and decried; characterized by strength, aggressive defensiveness, and vagueness, it is a form of psychic irresponsibility, implying a self-indulgent infidelity of response which may lead to every form of egotism, rigidity, stultification, and harmful fantasy.

Feeling is personal only in the sense that it is generated in a person. As an energetic principle in psychic organization it cannot be separated from concern and value; in this important respect it differs from those forms of energy postulated for physical organizations and mechanisms. Feeling is energy in the Greek sense—$\dot{\epsilon}\nu\dot{\epsilon}\varrho\gamma\epsilon\iota\alpha$, the inner working, the actuality, the existence in action. 'Feeling' is then not so much a component of 'intension' (see p. xxvii *n* above) as a specific aspect of intension. Feeling is the orientation of the person in a dynamic and directional sense. Feeling may manifest itself in part as physical energy—as electrical charges, currents, potentials, or chemical changes. Physical energy is so conceived in science that it shall be quantitatively measured, that it be dispersed throughout the universe, and that its character shall remain unchanged whether or not it is engaged in an actual physical event: feeling, however, can only be regarded in a qualitative sense, for it is generated in persons as an indispensable feature of actual psychic events and exhibits a great variety of force, pattern, and physical manifestation. 'Nature or reality as known to poets and tramps', Yeats has said, 'has no moment, no impression, no perception like another; everything is unique and nothing unique is measurable.'

When considered as a basic principle in artistic experience, feeling

---

[1] The power to charm or compel devotion and obedience in others, when exerted without conscious design, is a genuine manifestation of the true or essential self; in my use of terms this would be called style and not personality. But style is as impossible to describe or enjoin in behaviour as it is in art.

always has a double character; and that double character does not correspond to the positive and negative polarity postulated for physical energy. Feeling as exhibited in art is always both a feeling *of* something, and a feeling *for* something; an entering into something, and a concern for something. Feeling and concern are inseparable; and feeling in this sense is one aspect of value arising in events of reality. Feeling, properly speaking, is not a 'feeling *about* things', nor is it an 'emotional response' to things; feeling dislodges the self from his detached personal vantage-point, and engages him in a widespread sympathetic response which somehow constructs the thing perceived. In another of its aspects, emerging in vital action, feeling is the passion so frequently regarded as an essential quality in works of art; and passion in its ironic duplicity—as suffering and as an overmastering delight—prefigures ecstasy, the final moment of peace, the fulfilment and resolution of powerful feeling. It is in this sense that Yeats can assert that 'Passions, because most living, are most holy . . . and man shall enter eternity borne upon their wings.' Wordsworth had asserted that 'The Reader cannot be too often reminded that Poetry is passion: it is the history or science of feeling.' For passion is feeling when it is most clearly personalized.

Feeling is centrifugal, vectorial, outward-moving, pointing insistently outside the self in which it is generated; like charity it 'doth not seek its own' but energetically releases the self into fullness of response and into freedom of action. The fulcrum for feeling is the self, the central point of departure and return. Evanescent yet indestructible, energetic but not assertive, this self-being is revealed in nothing so clearly as in the pure activity of feeling. Paul Valéry has well described this secret, most personal centre.

'And as the ear catches and loses and catches again, and loses again through all the varying movement of a symphony some grave and persistent *motif* which ceases to be heard from moment to moment, but which never ceases to be there—so the pure *ego*, the unique and continuous element in each being in the world, rediscovering itself and then losing itself again, inhabits our intelligence eternally; this deep *note* of existence itself dominates the whole complication of circumstance and change in existence from the moment that it is heard.'

A state of pure feeling can seldom be achieved, and when achieved cannot for long be sustained; but it is the goal towards which all who are genuinely artistic or religious strive—a state of powerful and wholly disinterested being which will realize itself in whatever action (or restraint from action) an individual event demands. That is why artists as artists have no personality; that is why Keats's Shakespearean doctrine of Negative Capability holds for the psychology of art the same central position that Shakespeare holds for the history of poetry. And that is why artists strive constantly to transcend emotion and personality, and to purify their experience into states of liberated and passionate awareness.[1]

*　　　*　　　*

Two important assumptions may be recalled. First, that reality is a matter of relations. In the second place, a work of art is not a 'thing' to be examined by the methods normally exerted upon physical entities; a work of art is the physical embodiment of an event of reality with particular emphasis upon the event as valuable. Our starting-point must therefore be the event—if we can discover it —and not the physical work of art; we wish to know the event of reality embodied in the poem and not the poet's history of personality. What we want to know is somehow 'inside' the poem; we have to discover how to get at it. Many recent accounts of poetry have

[1] T. S. Eliot makes this point with characteristic pungency in 'Tradition and the Individual Talent': 'The poet has, not a "personality" to express, but a particular medium, which is only a medium and not a personality, in which impressions and experiences combine in peculiar and unexpected ways. . . . Poetry is not a turning loose of emotion, but an escape from emotion; it is not the expression of personality, but an escape from personality. But, of course, only those who have personality and emotions know what it means to want to escape from these things.'

Mr Eliot, however, does not distinguish between emotion and feeling, and more often than not uses the word 'emotion' uncritically where I suggest that 'feelings' are in question. Herbert Read, in *Form in Modern Poetry* and in *Annals of Innocence and Experience*, takes issue with Mr Eliot in drawing a contrast between 'character' and 'personality'; these terms correspond with what I have called 'personality' and 'style'.

Paul Valéry writes in his *Leonardo Da Vinci*: 'Each person being a sport of nature, a *jeu de l'amour et du hasard*, the most beautiful purpose and even the most learned thought of this re-created creature inevitably recall his origin. His activities are always relative, his masterpieces are fortuitous. He thinks mortally, individually, by fits and starts; and he finds the best of his ideas in casual and secret circumstances which he refrains from making public. Besides, he is not sure of being positively *some one*, he disguises and denies, more easily than he affirms, himself. Drawing from his own inconsistency some strength and much vanity, he puts his most cherished moments into fictions. He lives by romance, sees himself in a thousand roles. His hero is never himself.'

found their central term in the poetic image; but in doing so they seek the security of ready-made instances in poems while they neglect, assume, or gloss over, the connections between poetic images and perceptual experience. Wordsworth does not offer an alternative to a theory based upon the poetic image: he starts from and sustains his inquiry at a more radical level. And at that level it is possible (even though Wordsworth did not do so) to show the connection between perception and expression, between feeling and image.

Wordsworth maintained that the poet is a person 'possessed of more than usual organic sensibility'; he also ascribes to him a 'more than usual capacity for deep thinking'. Wordsworth's *theory* of perception (if he had one at all) was naïve; but his condensed statement points unambiguously to the special gift with which the poet, at the elementary level of sense-perception, must be endowed. The poet has an exceptionally acute awareness, an especially refined delicacy of response; not only can he 'see' things with more than usual clarity, but he is unusually successful in organizing, in all their primal richness, the feelings that such power of vision involves. It is in perceptual experience, experience most notable for its directness and immediacy and for its demands upon fidelity of response, that feeling is most powerfully generated. The senses, one might say, offer means of contact with the outside world; and through them the energy implied in a real universe flows. But if that external energy is to be regenerated into powerful feeling, the window of access must be wide open; there is required active awareness, responsive co-operation as well as passive sensitiveness. This regeneration of feeling is not simply a mechanical response to external stimuli; yet one cannot fail to notice that practically all theories of perception—even those which take into careful account the physiological concomitants of perception—regard perception as a detached and passive response. For an artist, perception is nothing of the sort; it is energetic, exuberant, at times overwhelming, always passionate, acute, incisive; it is the spring and source of his poetic energy.

The artist's perception then has to be regarded in two aspects; in terms of feeling as well as in the usual sense of clarity or distinctness.[1] But clarity and feeling are intimately connected in any perceptual event, even when the feeling is too slight for conscious recognition. The feeling (which is also concern) arises in events of reality at their

---

[1] A sketch for a theory of perception based upon this twofold discrimination is offered in the note appended to this chapter (pp. 95–103 below).

very inception. The feeling which is associated with vivid perception does not follow upon or result from a clearly differentiated grasp of particular 'things'. Actually, feeling is in one sense an impulse towards further clarification. No distinguishable thing can ever be completely separated from its context without losing its identity; it is the matrix of relationships which intrinsicates the event itself, gives it depth, and leads far beyond the particular happening. The clarifying impulse is satisfied in two senses: as a progressive refinement and clarification of the feeling itself, and by a progressively acute sharpening of the sensory data. And this second mode of clarity is intimately related with the first; for the more clearly the artist sees or hears, the more distinctly and powerfully he feels.

When Wordsworth speaks of contemplating a past emotion he is not using his words in a precise philosophical manner. What he means to convey is the notion of recalling, reconstituting, sustaining, the feeling of a past event. Observe that he says nothing about recalling the scene or the sounds or the setting of the event, but the feeling. He knew—if Coleridge had not told him—that if the feeling is accurately recalled the sensory elements will follow. Coleridge had observed in dreams and in certain pathological states that 'imagination, . . . the true inward creatrix, instantly out of the chaos of elements or shattered fragments of memory, puts together some form to fit' a feeling. In a waking state, however, or in a mood of concentrated awareness, the content of memory may be expected to assume forms more appropriate to the feeling than those arresting dream-images whose humble function is to keep us asleep; and Wordsworth himself noticed that 'each man is a memory to himself'. Yet the feeling it is that the poet will convey in his poem, and all the imagery of poetry subserves that purpose. In the act of recall and in the subsequent agitation of memory, perceptual details in a fully clarified visual or auditory form are less important to the poet than the feelings they are associated with. For a poet's states of feeling are intricate as well as powerful; and although feelings are primarily perceptual in the sense that they are firmly linked with perceptual experience, there are many 'pieces of feeling' which cannot be classified under any one of the five senses.

For the poet has an exceptional gift of sympathy, a flair for 'getting the feel' of things and persons, for 'experiencing' things—even inanimate things—by repeated acts of self-projection and identification. Vico noticed this long ago in the *Scienza Nuova*: 'The most sublime labour of poetry is to give sense and passion to insensate things; and it is characteristic of children to take inanimate things in their hands and talk to them in play as if they were living persons. This . . proves to us that in the world's childhood men were by nature sublime poets.' Poetic sympathy is a more subtle and intricate business than Ruskin seems to have thought when he coined his baleful phrase—the Pathetic Fallacy. That some minor poets—and even major poets in their off-moments—are guilty of reprehensible self-projection there can be no denying. But 'things-in-themselves' simply are not accessible to knowledge in a way that allows us to determine the kind or degree of self-projection in any particular instance. Poets are incorrigible—they will never become good little positivists. And since it is the poet's world we are trying to discover, it is well to use the poet's eyes.

'I have at all times endeavoured to look steadily at my subject'—that is Wordsworth's claim to the poet's birthright. But what was the subject for him? Wordsworth's greatest poetry is not the descriptive verse of an enthusiastic nature-lover or naturalist: it is his rendering of those

> *sounds that are*
> *The ghostly language of the ancient earth.*

'The power of a peculiar eye', he observes, 'could find no surface where its power might sleep'; 'the language of the sense' was

> *The anchor of my purest thoughts, the nurse,*
> *The guide, the guardian of my heart, and soul*
> *Of all my moral being——*

and he recognized that it was also the well-spring of all poetry. The poet is not simply an acute observer; he is endowed with a capacity for sympathy, for withness, which gives him special insight

---

[1] Wordsworth opens the 1815 Preface with a statement of 'The powers requisite for the production of poetry', the first being: 'Observation and Description,—*i.e.* the ability to observe with accuracy things as they are in themselves, and with fidelity to describe them, unmodified by any passion or feeling existing in the mind of the describer; whether the things depicted be actually present to the senses, or have a place only in the memory.' But a little later on he modifies this apparently blunt statement: 'These processes of imagination are carried on either by conferring additional properties upon an object, or abstracting from it some of those which it actually possesses, and thus enabling it to re-act upon the mind which hath performed the process, like a new existence.'

into what Gerard Manley Hopkins called 'the inscapes of things'—the essence, life, or form of things, the inner nature which when vividly apprehended becomes 'the very soul of art'. The iridescent ambiguity of the word 'inscape' is in some sort an image of the poet's sympathy—of the 'perpetual reaching out of this sympathy towards objects otherwise unattainable', a reaching out for the abundance of life in things, an outward movement which is the true antithesis of *escape* for it is a plunging into reality, losing and discovering the real self in a real world.[1]

The capacity for sympathetic identification permeates all poetry and accounts for the force of its non-scientific rendering of natural phenomena. This intense feeling has sometimes been vividly recorded. Keats for example writes to Benjamin Bailey: 'You perhaps at one time thought there was such a thing as Worldly Happiness to be arrived at, at certain periods of time marked out— . . . I scarcely remember counting upon any Happiness—I look not for it if it be not in the present hour—nothing startles me beyond the Moment. The setting Sun will always set me to rights—or if a Sparrow come before my Window I take part in its existence and pick about the Gravel.' And Coleridge gives a similar report: 'From my very childhood, I have been accustomed to abstract, and as it were, unrealize whatever of more than common interest my eyes dwelt on, and then by a sort of transfusion and transmission of my consciousness to identify myself with the object.' The sharp agony of this feeling for the life of things is perhaps most vividly conveyed by an entry in one of Hopkins's journals. 'The ashtree growing in the corner of the garden was felled. It was lopped first: I heard the sound and looking out and seeing it maimed there came at that moment a great pang and I wished to die and not to see the inscapes of the world destroyed any more.' The more clearly and intensely an artist perceives, the less is he like a camera. For his intense perception engages the whole

---

[1] W. A. M. Peters (*Gerard Manley Hopkins* (1948), p. 1) defines the word *inscape* as 'the unified complex of those sensible objects of perception that strike us as inseparably belonging to and most typical of it, so that through the knowledge of this unified complex of sense-data we may gain an insight into the individual essence of the object'. The word *inscape* carries just that sense of vitality, of dynamic interpenetration, which the English word *pattern* lacks and which the German word *gestalt* to some extent sustains. Hopkins's conceptions of *inscape* and *instress* deserve attentive examination, and could (with sensitive and accurate application) enrich both philosophy and criticism. But since they express notions widely separated from common-sense views they are in danger of rapid erosion unless used with fastidious clarity.

person in a flow of outward-turning response to his world, the world being grasped as a delicately poised and intricate texture of feeling. And a human being in a state of wholeness is a great deal more complex and energetic than any photographic emulsion.

All of us in various ways are capable of sympathy, of suffering with somebody else, and even occasionally of entering into the existence of something else. But few of us can achieve the complete identification I have been describing, probably because it is alarming suddenly so to lose one's identity. Yet artists consistently court such experiences, and they are able to do so because they do not completely lose either identity or self-consciousness. Hopkins in one of his meditations gives a memorable account of this persistent 'otherness', this sense of self-distinctness.

'I find myself both as man and as myself something most determined and distinctive, at pitch, more instinctive and higher pitched than anything else I see; I find myself with my pleasures and pains, my powers and my experiences, my deserts and guilt, my shame and sense of beauty, my dangers, hopes, fears, and all my fate, more important to myself than anything I see. And when I ask where does all this throng and stack of being, so rich, so distinctive, so important, come from—nothing I see can answer me. And this whether I speak of human nature or of my own individuality, my self-being. . . . And this is much more true when we consider the mind; when I consider my self-being, my consciousness and feeling of myself, that taste of myself, of *I* and *me* above and in all things, which is more distinctive than the taste of ale or alum, more distinctive than the smell of walnutleaf or camphor, and is incommunicable by any means to another man. . . . Nothing else in nature comes near this unspeakable stress of pitch, distinctiveness, and selving, this self-being of my own. Nothing explains it or resembles it, except so far as this, that other men to themselves have the same feeling.' [1]

[1] Coleridge in a notebook entry records some misgivings about this sense of distinctness: 'Has every finite being (or only some) the temptation to become intensely and wholly conscious of its distinctness and, as a result, to be betrayed into the wretchedness of *division*? Grosser natures, wholly swallowed up in selfishness which does not rise to self-love, never even acquire that sense of distinctness, while, to others, love is the first step to re-union. It is a by-word that religious enthusiasm borders on and tends to sensuality—possibly because all our powers work together, and as a consequence of striding too vastly up the ladder of existence, a great *round* of the ladder is omitted, namely, love to some . . . of our own kind. . . .' (*Anima Poetae*, p. 184).
Cf. also Gabriel Marcel's note in *Being and Having* (1949): 'I am more and more

In the act of poetic perception, overwhelming though it may be, the 'self-being' is not destroyed; indeed it is intensified. For this reason we should rescue from misuse an excellent term introduced by Lipps—the word 'empathy', *Einfühlung*. For the word (if I understand Lipps correctly) was intended to indicate precisely this simultaneous self-identification and self-scrutiny that I have been trying to describe. In empathy the person is able to discern, sometimes attentively and with a sort of fascinated detachment, his own sympathetic response, without at the same time interrupting the full development of that response. The artist is best capable of sustained empathy because his tendency to refer all experience to his medium (of language, music, and the like) makes him able to distance his experience while it is happening. This I suppose is what Coleridge had in mind when he noted that 'The eye hath a two-fold power. It is, verily, a window through which you not only look *out* of the house, but can look into it too.'

When in one person a peculiar virginity of consciousness and the gift of empathy come together you have a great artist or a great critic. The artist's memory is richly charged not only by his direct sensory contact with the world—'that infinite cluster of images'—but also by his grasp of those hard and wiry shapes, those stern intractable knots of thought and feeling which other artists have distilled into their work. Books, music, paintings—the sort of equipment that Shelley catalogued in *Epipsychidion* for his sojourn on an island of love and contemplation—these give the artist vivid access to a multitude of real worlds of the spirit. The artist's feeling for these is not less powerful nor less immediate than his feeling for whatever his actual world may bring to him: indeed in many cases it is more acute; for he brings the same discriminating and delicate awareness to what is already selected, significantly arranged, and passionately transmuted into an appropriate medium of feeling. The good reader's experience, or the listener's or beholder's, is essentially perceptual and terminates in intricate states of feeling: the only difference from ordinary perceptual experience is that the physical objects are removed, the work struck by the difference between the two modes of detachment: the one is that of the spectator, the other of the saint. The detachment of the saint springs, as one might say, from the very core of reality; it completely excludes curiosity about the universe. This detachment is the highest form of participation. The detachment of the spectator is just the opposite, it is desertion, not only in thought but in act. Herein, I think, lies the kind of fatality which seems to weigh on all ancient philosophy—it is essentially the philosophy of the spectator.'

of art becomes a direct channel for feeling. To be able to observe and render into language this regeneration of ordered feeling is to be a true critic; and that explains why great artists are usually the best critics.

Wordsworth, when he spoke of contemplating a recollected emotion, may have been elliptical but he was not wrong. It is the energetic charge of feeling upon the contents of memory, the feelings stamped upon 'images' in direct perceptual experience, which distinguish the poet's images from the images of the 'ordinary man'. Whether one should think of sensory images charged with feeling, or of feelings with certain sensory characteristics, is by no means clear. Yeats, at all events, has said that 'it is not possible to separate an emotion or a spiritual state from the image that calls it up and gives it expression'. Once sensory feelings have been transmuted into words to become poetic images they may seem to have a predominantly sensory character; but many important poetic images have little or no distinct sensory character. The charge of feeling cannot be separated from perceptual vividness; nor can it be detached from the conviction in vivid perception that what is seen is known beyond argument. Ezra Pound defines a poetic image as 'that which presents an intellectual and emotional complex in an instant of time'.[1] I am inclined to believe that feeling is not something added on to sensory images, but that the feeling *is* the image; that it is the feeling that abides in memory, secretly combining with and modifying other feelings. When these feelings emerge into the light and seek a body they take on the aspect of images in poetry or painting or sculpture—but not so obviously in music; and in a comprehensive theory of art that would be a serious consideration.

★   ★   ★

This worthless present was designed you, long before it was a play, when it was only a confuse'd mass of Thoughts, tumbling over one another in the dark; when the Fancy was yet in its first work, moving the sleeping images of things towards the light, there to be distinguished, and then either chosen or rejected by the Judgement.—JOHN DRYDEN.

Memory is the central factor in the process of image-making: without memory there can be no poetic creation.

[1] *Make it New* (1934), p. 336. He continues: 'It is the presentation of such a "complex" instantaneously which gives that sense of sudden liberation; that sense of freedom from time limits and space limits; that sense of sudden growth, which we experience in the presence of the greatest works of art.'

Not what it leaves behind it in the light
But what it carries with it to the dark
Exalts the soul.

And unless a man be endowed with 'more than usual organic sensibility' to supply memory with a constant shower of intense experience, his memory cannot be stirred to the richness of its secret fashioning; a paradeigmatic event cannot occur. Ruskin, speaking in *Modern Painters* of Turner's imaginative processes, gives a striking picture of the artist's memory.

'Imagine all that any of these men [Dante, Scott, Turner, Tintoretto] had seen or heard in the whole course of their lives, laid up accurately in their memories as in vast storehouses, extending, with the poets, even to the slightest intonations of syllables heard in the beginning of their lives, and, with the painters, down to minute folds of drapery, and shapes of leaves and stones; and over all this unindexed and immeasurable mass of treasure, the imagination brooding and wandering, but dream-gifted, so as to summon at any moment exactly such groups of ideas as shall justly fit each other: this I conceive to be the real nature of the imaginative mind.'

Here, as in Lowes' general theory of imagination, Ruskin regards the imagination as a selective faculty—'brooding and wandering, but dream-gifted' to be sure—working upon the materials stored up in memory; like Lowes' huddle and chaos of memory, Ruskin's memory is an 'unindexed and immeasurable mass of treasure'.[1]

[1] Roger Fry, in his *Reflections on British Painting* (1934), probably with this same Ruskin passage in mind, draws from Turner's work a different judgment. 'He [Turner] drew and studied incessantly, and he had filled his mind with a vast repertory of precise images. He knew more than anyone. He knew how a wave curled. How the spring of a branch of an elm differed from that of an ash, how a tree roots itself in the ground, what all kinds of cloud and rock form are like. But he had looked at all this, had collected it all, in a practical spirit. These images were his stock-in-trade and his tools. He knew that any fact about the look of things might come in useful in his business at any time. They were essential to the business of making pictures, and that was his passion, to make pictures, and to make them superlatively well, and, incidentally, to beat others at the job . . . In Turner the contemplative impulse was, I think, almost in abeyance. He never saw things with a really disinterested passion.'
Shakespeare, through Holofernes' lips, gives a more playful account of this same aspect of imagination. 'This is a gift that I have, simple, simple; a foolish extravagant spirit, full of forms, figures, shapes, objects, ideas, apprehensions, motions, revolutions: these are begot in the ventricle of memory, nourished in the womb of *pia mater*; and delivered upon the mellowing of occasion: But the gift is good in those in whom it is acute. . . .'

About the memory and its workings we know embarrassingly little; it is probably better to retain the term, ascribing to it certain spatial and temporal characteristics in a frankly figurative manner, than to dismiss it as an anthropomorphic fiction. But I cannot see any reason for separating imagination from memory, any more than I can see any reason for separating value and feeling from the elementary stages of perception. For the poet and the 'ordinary man', the Well of memory and its processes are *potentially* the same: actually, however, the processes are very different in force and extent because of the greater quantity, vividness, and distinctness of the experience, images, and feelings the poet discharges into his Well.

Ruskin's description however—like Lowes' or Wordsworth's—goes farther than is needed to understand the place of memory in imagination. Between an event of reality and the embodiment of that event in a poem there lies an act of distancing, a period of gestation sometimes short, sometimes long. The 'emotion', Wordsworth said, must be recollected in tranquillity. Rilke, in his *Letters to a Young Poet*, asserts this theme more powerfully. '*Everything* is gestation and then bringing forth. To let each impression and each germ of feeling come to completion quite in itself, in the dark, in the inexpressible, the unconscious, beyond the reach of one's own understanding, and await with deep humility and patience the birth-hour of a new clarity: that alone is living the artist's life—in understanding as in work.' [1] Imagination as a process of image-making may profitably

[1] In *Die Aufzeichnungen des Malte Laurids Brigge* Rilke restates this view. 'And still it is not yet enough to have memories. One must be able to forget them when they are many and one must have the immense patience to wait until they come again. For it is the memories themselves that matter. Only when they have turned to blood within us, to glance and gesture, nameless and no longer to be distinguished from ourselves —only then can it happen that in a most rare hour the first word of a poem arises in their midst and goes forth from them.' And Gide notes in one of his *Journals*: 'Wait for the work to become silent in you before writing it.'

Camille Pissarro makes two interesting observations to his son Lucien, in 1883 and 1892. 'Degas says that there is one way of escaping Legros' influence, the method is simply this: it is to reproduce, in your own place, from memory, the drawing you make in class. . . . You will have your difficulties, but a moment will come when you will be astonished by the ease with which you retain forms, and curiously enough, the observations you make from memory will have more power and be much more original than those you owe to direct contact with nature. The drawing will have art—it will be your own—this is a good way of escaping slavish imitation.' And again: 'I am more than ever for the impression through memory, it renders less of the object —vulgarity disappears, leaving only the undulations of the truth that was glimpsed, felt.'

be described in two modes: first, in its direct relation with perceptual experience, as an unconscious and unwilled process of fusion working upon the sleeping images in the deep Well of memory; and then as selecting and fashioning the images of memory into the luminous arresting patterns called poems.

Memory retains and associates images in the mode of feeling; and it exhibits the salient characteristics of imagination because it is self-integrating. Memory, to use Coleridge's phrase, is 'tenacious and systematizing'; but its system, like the system of any self-integrating process, is unpredictable though always 'unific'. Lowes' figure is an excellent one: memory is a Well of dissolving, crystallizing, fructifying water. Memory, like Orsino's love, is

> all as hungry as the sea,
> And can digest as much.

And we recognize, from ordinary experience as well as from poetry, that memory not only stores images but also—in a process usually called association—constellates them, fuses them, works sea-changes upon them to form novel and even unique patterns.[1]

There is reason to suppose that everything that impinges upon awareness is somehow retained in memory. But memory obtrudes, or offers for conscious recall, only 'significant' images; or perhaps we regard as significant those images which memory retains and obtrudes: in either case memory seems only to reintroduce into consciousness those things which we somehow endowed with significance in the act of perceiving them. 'In life,' Delacroix observes, 'we preserve the memory of those feelings only that move us; all the rest becomes less than what has actually occurred, because nothing any longer lends it colour in our imagination.' Mr Eliot treats the question more cautiously, but there is no doubt in his mind about the fact of the matter.

'Why, for all of us, out of all that we have heard, seen, felt, in a

---

[1] Nobody, and least of all a poet, can deny the *fact* of association. But the word association has become so entangled with the various corpuscular and mechanistic theories of *associationism* (especially in the eighteenth and nineteenth centuries) that it has fallen under suspicion. T. S. Eliot, for example, writes in *The Use of Poetry* (p. 147): 'I will not say . . . "associations", for I do not want to revert to Hartley.' What he failed to notice was that Coleridge (whom he is discussing in this passage) was not reverting to Hartley either, having renounced him and all his ways by 1800. Yet Eliot himself in the next page gives a memorable account of association which I quote on this and the following page.

lifetime, do certain images recur, charged with emotion, rather than others? The song of one bird, the leap of one fish, at a particular place and time, the scent of one flower, an old woman on a German mountain path, six ruffians seen through an open window playing cards at night at a small French railway junction where there was a water-mill: such memories may have symbolic value, but of what we cannot tell, for they come to represent the depths of feeling into which we cannot peer. We might just as well ask why, when we try to recall visually some period in the past, we find in our memory just the few meagre arbitrarily chosen set of snapshots that we do find there, the faded poor souvenirs of passionate moments.' [1]

Memory may in fact retain all our impressions whatsoever; but the memories which are stamped with an unknown significance, the memories that 'represent the *depths of feeling* into which we cannot peer', these ones are most tenaciously preserved and obtrude themselves without—and often indeed in spite of—the will or desire to recall them. The images that memory does not obtrude are those which received no charge of feeling in the act of grasping them; they remain inert, if retained, and are inaccessible to that process of recall at which Wordsworth hinted and which Coleridge—acutely aware of the curious 'hooks and eyes of memory'—describes. 'What is forgetfulness? Renew the state of affection or bodily feeling—same or similar, sometimes dimly similar, and, instantly the trains of forgotten thoughts rise from their living catacombs.'

Returning to Coleridge—for there is some advantage in keeping to the theory of imagination from which we started—we find that he too noticed how deep feelings are associated with vivid images but with indistinct ideas, and that they are difficult to recall at will. He observes in *The Friend* that 'deep feeling has a Tendency to combine with obscure ideas in preference to distinct and clear notions'; and again, that 'by a wise ordinance of nature our feelings have no abiding-place in our memory, nay the more vivid they are in the

---

[1] *The Use of Poetry*, p. 148. An interesting parallel is offered by a passage in Thomas Mann's *Lotte in Weimar* (trans. H. T. Lowe-Porter): 'The strange thing was that these pictures and memories had their extreme vividity and brilliance, their fullness of detail, not, as it were, at first hand. It was as though memory had not originally been so concerned to preserve them in all their detail, but had had to yield them up afterwards, bit by bit, word by word, out of its very depths. They had been searched out, refashioned, reproduced with all their attendant circumstances—given, so to say, a fresh coat of paint and hung in a strong light, for the sake of the significance which they had unanticipatedly taken on.'

moment of their existence the more dim and difficult to be remembered do they make the *thoughts* [? ideas] which accompanied them'. And an early notebook entry links this observation with Hopkins's note on the vividness of self-being: 'By deep feeling we make our *ideas* dim, and this is what we mean by our life, ourselves. I think of the wall— it is before me a distinct image. Here I necessarily think of the *idea* and the thinking *I* as two distinct and opposite things. Now let me think of *myself*, of the thinking being. The idea becomes dim, whatever it be—so dim that I know not what it is; but the feeling is deep and steady, and this I call *I*—identifying the percipient and the perceived.' Yet in the 'streaming continuum of passive association' the 'images of memory flow in upon the impulses of immediate perception' to form 'nuclei in the reservoir of the soul'.[1] And those nuclei, nebulae, constellations are retained in memory as feelings, combine as feelings, emerge as feelings; for their elements were charged with feeling in the primal instant of perception, and were at that first stage in the process of gestation endowed with, and known as, feelings.

To suggest (as newspaper articles do from time to time) that anybody's 'subconscious' may contain a great poem, painting, or symphony is journalistic nonsense—even though Edward Young in his *Conjectures on Original Composition* (1759) and Croce in his *Estetica* (by a split hair of misplaced emphasis) fell into this trap. Few people possess the acute awareness, the refined capacity for feeling, that is required to store memory with the impressions and feelings that may become a poem. Rilke, in *Malte Laurids Brigge,* has reported upon the poet's need for vivid experience; the passage has often been quoted but is still worth repeating.

'One ought to wait and gather sense and sweetness a whole life long, and a long life if possible, and then, quite at the end, one might perhaps be able to write ten good lines. . . . In order to write a single verse, one must see many cities, and men and things; one must get to know animals and the flight of birds, and the gestures that the little flowers make when they open out to the morning. One must

---

[1] Cf. Yeats's reference to Byzantine decoration as

> Those images that yet
> Fresh images beget.

Elsewhere he speaks of 'forms that represent no creature eye has ever seen, yet are begotten one upon the other as if they were themselves living creatures'.

be able to return in thought to roads in unknown regions, to un-expected encounters, and to partings that had been long foreseen; to days of childhood that are still indistinct, and to parents whom one had to hurt when they sought to give one some pleasure which one did not understand . . . ; to childhood's illnesses that so strangely begin with such a number of profound and grave transformations, to days spent in rooms withdrawn and quiet, and to mornings by the sea, to the sea itself, to oceans, to nights of travel that rushed along loftily and flew with all the stars—and still it is not enough to be able to think of all this. There must be memories of many nights of love, each one unlike the others, of the screams of women in labour, and of women in childbed, light and blanched and sleeping, shutting themselves in. But one must also have been beside the dying, must have sat beside the dead in a room with open windows and with fitful noises. And still it is not yet enough to have memories.'

Exposed to such a chain of experiences only a person endowed with peculiar awareness and capacity for feeling could produce a poem. Most people literally cannot see clearly enough to feel deeply: the connection between perceiving and feeling is as direct and intim-ate as that.[1] The poet, the artist, must have eyes for the vision of reality—

> . . . *these eyes*
> *By water, herb and solitary prayer*
> *Made aquiline, are open to that light.*

To write a poem is much more than a technical achievement; it is not some sort of conditioned reflex, some mechanical response neces-sarily set in motion by exposure to certain kinds of experience. Every phase of the poet's consciousness is structuring and integral: his per-

---

[1] Roger Fry in *Vision and Design* notices the limitations of the ordinary man's percep-tion: 'With an admirable economy we learn to see only so much as is needful for our purpose: but this is in fact very little, just enough to recognise and identify each object and person; that done, they go on to an entry in our mental catalogue and are no more really seen. In actual life the normal person only reads the labels, as it were, on the objects around him, and troubles no further.' Paul Valéry makes a similar observation 'The majority of people see with the intellect much more frequently than with the eyes. . . . They see through a dictionary rather than through the retinae, they come so ill to an object, so vaguely to knowledge of the pleasures and pains of sight, that they have had to invent *beautiful views*. Of everything else they are unaware. But at the beautiful view they regale themselves on a concept swarming with verbal associations. . . . And since they reject as nothing that which has not a name, the number of their impressions is limited in advance.'

ception, his memory, his feeling. His initial grasp of a particular event of experience is itself integral: not only is it an act of penetration and vision, not only is it in some way an instance of primal knowing in which the whole person is engaged and suspended, but it is also an act of imagination. As each image of passionate perception enters the well of memory 'the images of memory flow in upon the impulses of [that] immediate perception'; the whole content of memory regroups, constellates into fresh patterns; the fresh image does not have to find for itself a place in that bright company for (in the words of Coleridge's Moon-gloss) it enters 'unannounced, as lords that are certainly expected and yet there is a silent joy at their arrival'.

The 'object seen' or the 'sound heard' may for the poet be anything whatsoever: what matters is not the nature of the 'thing-in-itself', but the nature and fidelity of responsive feeling in the presence of the thing. It may be convenient to use the word Beauty to indicate the moment of arrest, the perfect instant of knowing and self-realization which is the end both of art and of contemplation; but Beauty is not a quality to be conferred upon objects or situations to which artists seem most inclined to respond. 'The essential advantage for a poet', Eliot has said, 'is not, to have a beautiful world with which to deal: it is to be able to see beneath both beauty and ugliness; to see the boredom, and the horror, and the glory.' The artist can satisfy his restless search and hunger, not in certain things called beautiful, but in reality. Where there is no vivid perceiving there is no reality; when there is no vision the people perish. So it is that the artist is withdrawn, secret, of no personality, his self-being disclosed only in his work, arrogant and brutal even to defend his capacity for feeling and to preserve the integrity of memory. 'Our fire', Yeats says, 'must burn slowly, and we must constantly turn away to think, constantly to analyse what we have done, be content even to have little life outside our work, to show, perhaps, to other men, as little as the watch-mender shows, his magnifying glass caught in his screwed-up eye. Only then do we learn to conserve our vitality, to keep our mind flexible for expression of the emotions of life as they arise.'

When a poet breaks down as a poet and ceases to write, it is (I believe) because the images cease to constellate and to well up from memory; imagination has failed at its primitive and secret source.[1]

[1] Gerard Manley Hopkins notices that 'insight is more sensitive, in fact is more perfect, earlier in life than later and especially towards elementary impressions' (*Correspondence with Dixon* (1935), p. 38). Vico in the *Scienza Nuova* made this fact an

The poet's patience, his suffering, his need for tranquillity is not merely his waiting for the poem to come; it is also the means of preserving a vigorous imagination; only in this way can he ensure that a poem *can* come at all. And here, perhaps more than in any other phase of the poet's experience, is the balance extremely delicate and vulnerable. It is a balance of concentration and passivity, a fearless courting of dangerous—even destructive—experience so that imaginative vitality shall not decay or the integrity of imagination be shattered. It is a poise between the mounting tension of the need for utterance, and the patient waiting for the thing that is to be uttered to come forth into the light. The poet carries in his head no prefigured model of his completed poem: he must discover his poem in making it. Nor does he *cause* the poem to be made: he allows and encourages it to make itself. Without the poet's collusion, the poem cannot make itself; but the poet must wait until what was known and forgotten makes itself known afresh in a new and singular light, constellated in secret, enucleated out of the black fire of memory.

*　　　　*　　　　*

It's certain there are trout somewhere
And maybe I shall take a trout
If but I do not seem to care.

W. B. YEATS

'In the hollow of humility,' Jacques Maritain writes in *Art and Poetry* (1943), 'a painter meditates and gazes, he sees the vines that God has made, the olives, the nettle trees, the bulls, the unicorns—the moors and skies of Brittany—and the labours and movements, captured in slow-motion, of men whom God also made; what he receives through his eyes falls into the silence of a fervent lake of contemplation and vegetates slowly until its resurgence in a work capable of acting as a talisman that would bring peace to the heart.' How does this resurgence occur, and under what conditions?

Strictly speaking the single abstract term 'image' cannot mean very much in the phrase 'image of memory'. The function of the latent but energetic imagination is to constellate perceptual images as well

argument for the quality of primitive poetry: 'In childhood memory is most vigorous, and imagination is therefore excessively vivid, for imagination is nothing but extended or compounded memory. This axiom is the explanation of the vividness of the poetic images the world had to form in its first childhood.'

84

as to retain them; when they emerge into the light to take their place in a work of art they are already complex, carrying with them a context of feeling and thought which is not the original perceptual context. Every image which strives towards poetic embodiment implicates other images, other feelings. The history of a single image can never be traced; for the image is not fully known until it has found its body in a poem, and the image embedded in the poem—the intersection of many currents of feeling and thought—is not identical with any single image as it was when it first dropped into the well of memory. But it is a convenient verbal device—perhaps an indispensable one—to use the term 'image' as though we could, by thinking, detach a single image from its matrix of feeling.

Energetic though the state of latent imagination may be, it strives (like any other energetic system) to maintain equilibrium. In the case of the artist this equilibrium is fragile, susceptible to minute intrusions; and it is to these intrusions, these poetic germs, that we must trace the genesis of the poem as a verbal and rhythmic entity. The germ may present itself in perceptual experience, or it may for no detectable reason emerge into consciousness; it may be a distinct visual image, a sound, a cluster of words, a rhythm, a feeling; it may simply 'turn up', or be noticed for no particular reason, or arise in a process of willed recollection. Generally it makes a random appearance; when it appears it is recognized as valuable even though one could not have known beforehand what to look for. The poetic germ has this single and singular power; it conturbates the images of memory, stimulates the latent imagination to such unusual activity that a paradeigmatic event is generated, demanding expression, clamouring for a body. This, in different terms, is what Wordsworth meant when he said that 'the emotion is contemplated till, by a species of re-action, the tranquillity disappears, and an emotion, *kindred* to that which was before the subject of contemplation, is gradually produced.'

The poetic germ is not the subject or theme of the poem; its function is to crystallize, to 'seed' the images of memory into a pattern which is felt to be significant even though the significance cannot be known until the poem has been fully extricated. By insemination the germ generates an event of reality which is compact of numerous instants of reality, remembered and forgotten, and with none of which it can be identified. One mark of poetic genius, I suspect, is the knack of recognizing the germ and fostering the mounting process of parturition, by a dainty poise between passivity and concentration, between astonished acceptance and critical severity, between stimulation and selection.[1] Nowhere has the poetic germ been more vividly described than by Henry James in his Preface to *The Spoils of Poynton.*

'A lady beside me made in the course of talk one of those allusions that I have always found myself recognizing on the spot as "germs". The germ, wherever gathered, has ever been for me the germ of a "story", and most of the stories straining to shape under my hand have sprung from a single small seed, a seed as minute and wind-blown as that casual hint for *The Spoils of Poynton* dropped un-wittingly by a neighbour, a mere floating particle in the stream of talk. What above all comes back to me with this reminiscence is the sense of the inveterate minuteness, on such happy occasions, of the precious particle—reduced, that is, to its mere fruitful essence. Such is the interesting truth about the stray suggestion, the wandering word, the vague echo, at touch of which the novelist's imagination winces as at the prick of some sharp point: its virtue is all in its needle-like quality, the power to penetrate as finely as possible. This fineness it is that communicates the virus of suggestion, anything more than the minimum of which spoils the operation. If one is given a hint at all designedly one is sure to be given too much; one's subject is in the merest grain, the speck of truth, of beauty, of reality, scarce visible to the common eye—since, I firmly hold, a good eye for a subject is anything but usual. . . . Life being all inclusion and confusion, and art being all discrimination and selection, the latter, in search of the hard latent *value* with which alone it is concerned, sniffs round the mass as instinctively and unerringly as a dog suspicious of some buried bone. The difference here, however, is that, while the dog desires his bone but to destroy it, the artist finds in *his* tiny nugget, washed free of awkward accretions and hammered into a sacred hardness, the very stuff for a clear affirmation, the happiest chance for the indestructible.'

How imagination makes its interfusing connections; how a single word or the fragment of a tune may call to itself the whole substance

---

[1] Compare Paul Valéry's statement: 'The essential principle of the poetic mechanism —by which I mean the production of poetic sensibility by the use of words—lies, or so it seems to me, in the harmonious interchange between expression and impression. Our poetic pendulum begins in sensation, moves towards an idea or a sentiment, and returns again to a memory of the initial sensation, or to an act which is capable of reproducing that sensation.'

of a poem; how (as Eliot records in *The Music of Poetry*) 'a poem, or a passage of a poem, may tend to realise itself first as a particular rhythm before it reaches expression in words, and . . . may bring to birth the idea and the image'; how the growing cluster of words or sounds or rhythms may evoke other images and words and sounds more essential than the first ones: these are unexplained mysteries, facts to be accepted because plentifully and responsibly recorded, but facts which can be illustrated and interrelated only in metaphors and analogies.[1] I wish now to introduce two analogies: one taken from chemistry to illustrate the activity which a poetic germ induces in the latent imagination; the other taken from wave mechanics to illustrate the poet's total response to a poetic germ.

In his essay 'Tradition and the Individual Talent' Mr Eliot introduced the now-familiar analogy of contact catalysis to show how the poet is a medium who brings tradition and the present into relationship and retransmits them in a novel and vital combination. He invites the reader to consider 'the action which takes place when a bit of finely filiated platinum is introduced into a chamber containing oxygen and sulphur dioxide. . . . When the two gases . . . are mixed in the presence of a filament of platinum, they form sulphurous acid. This combination takes place only if the platinum is present; nevertheless the newly formed acid contains no trace of platinum, and the platinum itself is apparently unaffected: has remained inert, neutral, and unchanged. The mind of the poet is the shred of platinum.' Eliot is here concentrating upon the neutrality, the impassivity of the artist. This analogy, with its terms altered, illustrates the action of the germ upon the images of memory; but first the analogy must be developed with more faithful regard to the chemist's conception of catalysis. Furthermore the air of mystery—

---

[1] As long ago as 1894 Valéry in his *Introduction to the Method of Leonardo Da Vinci* complained against 'a kind of reciprocal coquetry of silence on the part of artists as to the origins of their work—to the extent of too carefully hiding them even. We fear that they are humble, these origins, even that they are mere nature. And though very few artists have the courage to say how they produced their work, I believe that there are not many more who take the risk of understanding it themselves. . . . Such an understanding is necessary if we are not to believe that minds are as profoundly different as their products make them appear.' Scrupulous inquirer into the genesis of works of art, Valéry has recorded in *Variété V* (1944) a remarkable instance of his being gripped and possessed by a rhythmic and musical *donnée*—'far more complex than I could have made it by any purely rational use of my normal rhythmic faculties'—an experience which, being no musician, he could not transmute into artistic expression.

or mystification—should be removed. The catalyst does not *caus*
the reaction, as Eliot seems to suppose; it changes the rate of a proces
which is already occurring. In the case cited by Eliot the catalys
accelerates a reaction which would have completed itself eventuall
even if the platinum had not been present; and in other case
catalysts are used to slow down reactions which would be incon-
veniently or dangerously rapid.

This feature of catalysis is important if we are to illustrate imagination. The poetic germ does not *cause* a mental activity different ir
kind from whatever was occurring slowly and secretly before the
germ appeared: it accelerates or intensifies the fusing and constellating processes of latent imagination. When the catalytic and passionate
germ appears, the images of memory enter upon a condition of con-
turbation; for (as Coleridge observed) 'the property of passion is no
to create, but to set in increased activity'. This poetic catalysis is no
like an explosion; it is neither automatic nor predictable; the reactior
may complete itself instantly, or in extreme cases—as with Goethe'
Faust—spread out over the better part of a lifetime.

In another respect the analogy is very precise. The chemist canno
say how a catalyst accelerates a reaction or why a particular substance will catalyse a particular reaction and not another; he merely
knows by empirical observation that some substances will catalyse
some reactions. The poetic germ is minute, incisive, and highly selective. Not only does it accelerate imaginative activity and induce ar
exceptionally energetic state, but it directs that impulse in a certair
direction and indicates patterns of relevance which offer the poet a
basis for discrimination while he guides and criticises the developing
process. For the poet, the poetic germ is random; it is an accidenta
discovery; but while the germ works the poet introduces from his
own end (as it were) other catalysts to sustain and clarify the reaction
'Enthusiasm', Valéry observes, 'is not the writer's state of mind.
However powerful the passion may be it only becomes active and
useful when it is utilized upon a subject where art can direct it.
There must be well-placed checks to prevent it from being dissipated, and a delay must be adroitly imposed on the invincible movement back to equilibrium so that something may be abstracted before
the ardour diminishes.' Over against the swift and energetic intensity
of the mounting poetic state, we must set the poet's Negative Capability, his patient slowness, his tolerance of doubts, uncertainties,
mysteries. Thomas Mann, describing Goethe through the eyes of his

amanuensis Dr Riemer, speaks of the cumulated weight of darkness and silence behind the 'dramatic flow of words, poured out hour after hour without a pause save when it trips over itself for fullness'.

'His hands behind his back, his gaze lost in distant visions, he invokes the word, he invokes the form, with sovereign and as it were spontaneous power and reigns in an intellectual kingdom of bold and untrammelled freedom—. . . Yet it is useful to bear in mind that one is not dealing with an improvising mind; rather with one which hesitates, procrastinates, is very undecided and circumstantial. Above all, it is very easily tired, works fitfully, never sticks long at the same task, and often when most active is most digressive, so that it will take years to bring a particular work to completion. It is a nature given to slow and secret growth and unfolding; it must warm for years—perhaps since early youth—a work in its bosom before it can issue in reality. Its industry is quite essentially patience; by which I mean that even in all its need of variety it sticks stoutly and unremittingly, through long periods of time, to its task of spinning its web' (*Lotte in Weimar*, pp. 70–1).

The poet's state at the inception of a poem may be illustrated in a different way by using the analogy of the quantum theory.[1] Let us imagine an atom to be a very small model of the solar system. At the centre of the system lies the nucleus, around which planetary electrons move in elliptical orbits. When the atom is in its neutral state the orbits of the electrons lie as close to the nucleus as is consistent with the energy-structure of the system. When an atom absorbs additional energy radiated from other sources, the electrons move outward to another set of orbits, thereby neutralizing the atom with respect to any external magnetic field. The quantum theory states that in such changes, the electrons do not move out gradually, but assume a definite outer orbit as it were by a definite jump, as though the possible outer orbits were predetermined as a series of fixed tracks along which alone an electron could move. The matter can be restated in different terms: an atom will not absorb any quantity of energy whatsoever, but will accept only a quantity whose value is determined by its own structure. This value is called a quantum, and varies from one kind of atom to another. An atom will absorb only integral multiples of a quantum; a fraction of a quantum of energy will not be absorbed. (Within certain narrow limits an atom can absorb a value not exactly equivalent to a quantum by modulating

---

[1] I am here using the simple figurative account offered by Planck.

the wave-length of the received radiation and so modulating the value to a precise quantum.) 'The point of interest in this theory is that . . . some effects which *appear* essentially capable of gradual increase or gradual diminution are in reality to be increased or decreased only by certain definite jumps.' [1]

Let us now suppose that the poet's consciousness is the atom and that the quantum of absorbed energy represents the poetic germ. The germ must be a quantum-idea to be absorbed by the poet at all: it must be exactly the right thing, coming at exactly the right time, with the right force. The quantum-idea (and the word 'idea' is here used in the loosest possible sense) will be unique, because the individual poet is unique, and presents a constantly varying receptivity. [2] Once the quantum germ is absorbed, a widespread change occurs: the poet's whole person and organism alters and regroups itself to accommodate the quantum-idea. The outward movement of the electrons to their new orbits corresponds to the sudden generation of the paradeigmatic event: in poetic experience the event may be delayed or withheld but does not develop gradually. The inward movement of the electrons when the quantum of energy is again radiated corresponds to symbolic extrication, the activity which ends in the completed poem. At the end of the whole cycle, both atom and poet have returned to a neutral state—'invisible, refined out of existence, indifferent'. [3]

[1] A. N. Whitehead, *Science and the Modern World* (1933), Chapter VIII. His final comment upon the quantum theory is interesting: 'At any epoch the assumptions of a science are giving way, when they exhibit symptoms of the epicyclic state from which astronomy was rescued in the sixteenth century. Physical science is now exhibiting such symptoms.' This view, however, does not invalidate the analogy for our use; at least it represents—even if at a stage of scientific debility—a systematic expression of physical phenomena; and the process of step-change here invoked manifests itself in stages of learning, forgetting, and remembering as well as in some phases of poetic process. Psychology has suffered from applying analogies far simpler than the subject-matter to be illustrated. It is suggested that the most luminous psychological analogies may be found in those outermost fringes of scientific inquiry where new analogies have to be discovered to embrace anomalies which the old 'laws' cannot accommodate. It is worthy of notice that Jung—the only clinical psychologist to make any substantial contribution to the theory of art—unashamedly finds his analogies in ancient myths.

[2] Compare Jules Laforgue's remark in his essay on Impressionism: 'Chaque homme est selon son moment dans le temps, son milieu de race et de condition sociale, son moment d'évolution individuelle, un certain clavier sur lequel le monde extérieur joue d'une certaine façon. Mon clavier est perpétuellement changeant et il n'y en a pas un autre identique au mien. Tous les claviers sont légitimes.'

[3] I find that Paul Valéry has given an account of poetic experience in terms of a

Certain careful qualifications are required when we transfer this figure to the imagination. The quantum theory is expressed in terms of physical energy, and of reactions whose magnitude is a direct function of the amount of energy involved in the change. But feeling, or 'psychic energy', has a different character. There is no direct relation between the magnitude of the quantum-germ and the extent of the poet's imaginative reaction, in the same way that the amplitude of a reflex action is not a direct function of the amplitude of the stimulus that triggers the reflex; contact with the work of a very inferior poet or thinker has sometimes brought a great poet to his full powers (Coleridge and Bowles, Baudelaire and Poe, for example). The mind cannot be regarded simply as an energy system, even though some events in the nervous system may be described satisfactorily in terms of physical energy: memories, images, ideas, the value or intensity of a work of art, cannot be expressed in quantitative terms. But when these reservations have been made, the quantum analogy is most suggestive in emphasizing the fastidious selectivity of the poetic consciousness. Each atom has, we are told, its own quantum value which is a function of the atom's structure; the value of the quantum-germ constantly changes for each poet with the constant changes in his consciousness. The quantum-germ is not only unique, but must be absorbed *as germinal* to be a quantum idea at all.

The quantum analogy avoids the dangers of a crude mechanism by suggesting a self-determined and self-limiting responsive activity which yet bears a definite structural relation to an energizing intrusion. The analogy is intended to apply to the alterations of the poet's person when a poetic germ enters his consciousness. It leaves no room for the notion that poetry is, or should be, a stream of 'free association' which, once released, is 'significant' merely because it rises uncontrollably from the 'subconscious'. This kind of association, which the surrealists mistakenly supposed to have special artistic

much simpler electrical figure. He is describing 'certain states of mind which I am justified in calling *Poetic* because some of them find their ultimate fulfilment in poems.' 'They occur for no apparent reason and as the result of some purely accidental happening. They develop in obedience to the law of their own being, and, while they last, I am cut off from my normal mental discipline. As soon as they have done what they had to do, I slip back into the ordinary routine of exchange between life and thought. My circuit, so to speak, has been closed. But what has happened is that *a poem has taken form*. The closing of the circuit has left something behind. The completed circuit is the cyclical process of an act which has, in some way, provoked and externalized a potentiality of poetry.'

value, is probably called 'free' because it is the most mechanical operation the human mind is capable of. Free association bears impressive witness of obsessions and other forms of mental rigidity; in a court of law a witness who offers evidence as an uncontrolled stream of memory will probably be believed for his guileless suspension of selective intelligence.[1] But free association is not art; for art is selection and arrangement, concision and intension. 'All I would keep for myself,' Robert Frost declares, 'is the freedom of my material— the condition of body and mind now and then to summons aptly from the vast chaos of all I have lived through.' The singular character of the emergent poem is admirably delineated by Lowes (*The Road to Xanadu*, p. 304):

'The poem is not the confluence of unconsciously merging images . . . nor is the poet a somnambulist in a subliminal world. Neither the conscious impressions nor their unconscious interpretations constitute the poem. They are inseparable from it, but it is an entity which they do not create. On the contrary, every impression, every new creature rising from the potent waters of the Well, is what it now is through its participation in a *whole*, foreseen as a whole in each integral part—a whole which is the working out of a controlling imaginative design. The incommunicable, unique essence of the poem is its *form*.'

And the sudden sense of expansion and liberation, suggested by the instant outward movement of the electrons to their new orbits, is described in a sombre passage of Yeats's prose. In supporting the claim that the 'tragic ecstasy . . . is the best that art—perhaps that life—can give', he shows how that outward movement repeats itself in the beholder.

'Tragic art, passionate art, the drowner of dykes, the confounder of understanding, moves us by setting us to reveries, by alluring us almost to the intensity of trance. . . . We feel our minds expand convulsively or spread out slowly like some moon-brightened image-crowded sea.'

★   ★   ★

Under the inseminating impulse of the germ, the poetic process develops out of imagination into symbolic extrication; at this stage

[1] See for example the scene in which Mistress Quickly gives evidence against Falstaff (2 *Henry IV*, II, i).

a mediating activity is invoked. This dialectical [1] activity is well described by Samuel Alexander as 'not parthenogenesis but bisexual creation'; for in this the poet assumes a double role, bringing forth images and criticizing them as they come into the light. (Alexander does not discriminate very clearly however in applying the terms 'passive' and 'active' imagination; the first corresponds with association, the other embraces the rest of the poetic process.) Mr Day Lewis, adapting an image Dryden had used, speaks of 'the undisciplined behaviour of the faculty—whatever it is—that brings up images into the consciousness'.

'I may compare this faculty, perhaps, with an enthusiastic but woolly-witted dog; it goes bounding off again and again into the undergrowth, and returns to lay at one's feet so seldom the game one is after, so often a bird shot long ago by another poet or some object that has nothing to do with the chase at all.' [2]

The poet is at once his own woolly-witted dog and the wary but never wholly disinterested critic of the quarry he so hopefully seeks. Into imagination he sends thoughts, words, images, and selects from whatever they may bring forth. Croce speaks of putting ideas back into the crucible. 'When a man writes any work of genius,' Yeats said, 'or invents some creative action, is it not because some knowledge

---

[1] In this essay the word 'dialectical' is used in the Socratic sense of question-and-answer; no pseudo-mystical Marxist overtones are implied.

[2] Did Milton, for example, alter 'humming tide' in *Lycidas* to 'whelming tide' because he recognized a feather of Shakespeare's bird?

Lycidas 155–8:

> *Where e'er thy bones are hurl'd,*
> *Whether beyond the stormy Hebrides,*
> *Where thou perhaps under the humming tide*
> *Visit'st the bottom of the monstrous world.*

Pericles III, i:

> *nor have I time*
> *To give thee, scarcely coffin'd, in the ooze,*
> *Where, for a monument upon thy bones,*
> *And aye-remaining lamps, the belching whale*
> *And humming water must o'erwhelm thy corpse,*
> *Lying with simple shells.*

Mr Day Lewis in *The Poetic Image* develops at some length the figure of the patient fisherman to illustrate the poet's fastidious fostering of imagination. Is this also the fisher-king of *The Waste Land*? And compare Rémy de Gourmont's remark (*La Culture des Idées* (1916), p. 47): 'La mémoire est la piscine secrète où, à notre insu, le subcontient jette son filet; mais la conscience y pêche aussi volontiers.'

or power has come into his mind from beyond his mind? It is called up by an image, as I think . . . but our images must be given to us, we cannot choose them deliberately.' So this activity, as Coleridge insisted, is lightly controlled by 'the will and understanding'. A light touch is needed, the quarry must not be frightened away; for the making of a poem is an act of discovery—'the poet', Louis MacNeice tells us, 'is often not completely sure what he is trying to say until he has said it. He works up to his meaning by a dialectic of purification.' The meeting of pen and paper, of ear and rhythm and tone and meaning, the 'struggle to turn blood into ink' —these show the poet plunging his hands through the interface at that meeting-place of memory and dream and fantasy, of action, passivity, and suffering, which is reality. Each poem is a unique discovery; each poem is a new problem. A poet is a person whose feelings refer themselves to words and seek verbal incarnation. It is difficult to see how anything less than the clamorous power of an event of reality could ever bring a man successfully to fulfil that intricate feat of translation. On this point Yeats may well have the last word.

> We sat together at one summer's end,
> That beautiful mild woman, your close friend,
> And you and I, and talked of poetry.
> I said, 'A line will take us hours maybe;
> Yet if it does not seem a moment's thought,
> Our stitching and unstitching has been naught.
> Better go down upon your marrow-bones
> And scrub a kitchen pavement, or break stones
> Like an old pauper, in all kinds of weather;
> For to articulate sweet sounds together
> Is to work harder than all these, and yet
> Be thought an idler by the noisy set
> Of bankers, schoolmasters, and clergymen
> The martyrs call the world.'

A NOTE ON PERCEPTION

It is astonishing how little attention has been paid in aesthetics to what Coleridge called 'the original unific consciousness, the primary Perception'. The reason is perhaps—again in Coleridge's words—'its extreme difficulty'. Through failure to inquire closely into perception, aesthetics has failed to describe the single unbroken arch of poetic process. Either perception has been taken to be a spontaneous but mechanical neural response to external stimuli; in which case there is no means of accounting for the variety and value of art. Or else, in the attempt to show that art is a 'spiritual' activity—neither a neural mechanism nor an activity dominated by 'intellect'—the physical and perceptual character of art has been ignored or vaporized out of existence. All scientific theories of perception—and some philosophical ones—suffer from a misguided zeal for simplicity. Searching for a simple instance of a complex phenomenon, they carry analysis below the level of relevance and start with 'ordinary' perception. In this way an inert and confused middle term is mistaken for the prototype of perceptual experience.[1] The *gestalt* psychology avoids some of these abstractive excesses by insisting that every perceptual experience is integrated at its most rudimentary stage and is at once an act of discrimination and interpretation; but this school has not yet proceeded beyond highly artificial laboratory experiments which have little to offer to a theory of art.

I take it that if the facts of artistic perception are accepted as the starting-point for a theory of perception, the facts of 'ordinary' perception will readily accommodate themselves to that doctrine. Such an account, finding its centre of emphasis in artistic experience and

[1] The same difficulty arises when uncontrolled analysis is applied in an attempt to isolate 'life' or 'mind', or when a study proceeds from apparently simple organisms to more complex organisms. Either the vanishing (or emergent) point of life and mind cannot be determined, and life and mind crop up unaccountably in isolation at one end of a scale of phenomena: or else life and mind are limited to what can be explained by the analogies of cause and of energy-systems. In the second case life and mind have to be dismissed either as elaborate figments of the unscientific mind or as falling outside the range of inquiry. Physiologists carefully avoid the term 'life', and psychologists use the term 'mind' with caution. For the bearing of this general principle upon the problem of perception, see A. N. Whitehead, *Science and the Modern World* (1933), p. 139; Whitehead, *Symbolism* (1928), p. 6; Sir Charles Sherrington, *Man on his Nature* (1946), pp. 265–6.

not elsewhere, will recognize whatever conclusions scientific psychology and neurology may offer, but will be philosophical and to some extent speculative.

What features of artistic experience must be included in a theory of artistic perception? The artist's perception presents a double character, in the simultaneous sense of 'withness' and 'otherness'; in 'ordinary' perception only the sense of 'otherness' is recognized. We must show, not only how images of objects are taken up into the mind, but also how perceptual experience can claim the status of knowledge, how Value enters at the level of perception and not as an afterthought, how feeling enters as an inseparable feature of perception, and what part feeling plays in establishing knowledge and Value. I wish to summarize one possible account and to indicate its implications for a theory of art.

Artistic experience is energetic and intricate; yet the poet, unlike the 'ordinary' man, seeks to sustain and clarify his experience until, by embodying it in a physical artefact, he has discovered the experience to himself. This process of embodiment is arduous, usually painful, and often prolonged; and the vividness of artistic experience is more a matter of suffering than of delight or 'happiness'. There is no convincing way of explaining why an artist should submit to this discipline of self-abnegation, unless by saying that he recognizes some peculiar value in his experience and in the activity which flows from it. In my earlier chapters I have attempted to show that an event of value is refracted into simultaneous modes: it has the perceptual character of exceptional vividness, clarity, distinctness; and the psychological character of powerful and patterned feeling; and it is cognitive—something is genuinely and directly known. The nature of this 'prelogical knowing' which establishes itself without analytical thinking or logical verification, is difficult to describe. *What* is known is at once the value and the event and the event as valuable; for the event is known, not merely as an external occurrence or set of circumstances, but as self-constructed, self-determinate, self-contained, self-evident—an event in which the *person* plays an indispensable constructive role and is not simply an observer or a recording instrument. It seems to me that all these features must enter paradeigmatic experience at the instant of perception; it is impossible to find a point of entry for any of them at a later stage without misrepresenting the character of that experience as reported by artists and as manifested in works of art.

96

The sense of 'otherness', the sense of perceiving something separate from the self, of receiving a direct impact from 'things outside', is the most prominent feature of 'ordinary' perception; it has therefore usually been regarded as the irreducible feature of the perceptual situation. It is by concentrating upon this feature alone that we are led to postulate a figment called the 'sense datum', the 'image', the thing 'seen in the mind's eye', a mental construct which can be scrutinized and even recalled, bearing some structural relation (it is supposed) to the 'thing seen'. But this is an attempt to smuggle in a substantial criterion where substance is not in question and where no independent criterion is possible because all criteria are subject to the same distortion as the eyes whose aberrations are to be tested. Paradoxically, the artist's sense of 'otherness' is most vivid when associated with his sense of 'withness'; it is in the empathic state of self-identification that the sense of 'otherness' is specifically a sense of the *self's* otherness, and not merely a sense of the object's distinctness. In this state he enters into the thing, thereby discovering in an act of astonishing penetration what it feels like to be that thing; and he endows it with a life and character which is not merely the projected life and character of the artist.

The double character of artistic perception appears in another sense; in a double concern and excitement, not only for the thing or event perceived but also for the medium in which he works. This excitement—often a sense of loathing as well as one of delight or enthusiasm—helps to sustain the state of feeling throughout the activity of composition. Perception is not always, or even characteristically, an instantaneous flick of a shutter; and even in 'ordinary' perception the feeling for a physical medium helps both to sustain and to clarify the perceptual feeling. The most modest amateur painter or photographer knows how his feeling for the medium helps him to sustain and intensify the perceptual character of an event by holding the attention concentrated.

Alfred North Whitehead has offered, as a special instance of his doctrine of prehensions, a theory of perception which embraces the features of artistic perception. He distinguishes two simultaneous modes of perception (corresponding with the double character of artistic perception), and accounts for feeling and value as perceptual recognitions and not as conceptual constructs.[1] He analyses the

[1] Whitehead elaborates his theory of prehensions and of perception in Chapter III of *Process and Reality* (1929), and in various parts of *Science and the Modern World*. His

relations between things, and between things and persons, in terms of 'prehensions'—the 'feelings' that things have for each other. These prehensions may be positive or negative—that is, either energetic or neutral. Complex and vital organisms are capable of complex positive prehensions; inert objects (like stones) have weak or negative prehensions. Whitehead maintains that when subject and object come into relation, a dynamic mutual interpenetration occurs between them; a flow of 'feeling' or 'energy' passes between them; and this interchange, when combined with responsive activity, constitutes an event of experience. 'The subject-object relation of experience is fundamental, Whitehead holds, not in the specialized epistemological sense, but in the sense suggested by the Quaker word "concern". Each entity is an experiencing centre whose nature is constituted out of the selective responses it makes to other entities of the environment, and at the same time the multiplicity of other events is organized into a new unity, as the universe from that perspective . . . Whitehead does not think of a prehension as the reaction of one self-subsistent entity to another self-subsistent entity. Both entities are thought of as fluid processes, and a 'prehension' . . . is transmuted in the prehending subject into a new unity which Whitehead calls a "concrescence".' [1] In perceptual experience, the prehending subject is not simply an organism of a high and complex order but a *person*; the flow of feeling therefore has widespread consequences—consequences both 'unconscious' and 'conscious', neural and visceral as well as 'mental'. Furthermore, the percipient being a person and not merely an organism, the state of the person has important effects upon those responsive developments. We should have to take into account in any actual event the neural 'tone' of the percipient, his 'set' (the nature and direction of his habitual interests), the degree of attention or concentration; for all these can be altered at will, or artificially (by drugs, fatigue, derangement, absent-mindedness and the like).

Perceptual response is immediate, direct, and widespread; simple in its immediacy, and complex in its range and implications. Various

most minute account of perception is found in *Symbolism: its Meaning and Effect* (1928)
Miss Dorothy Emmet expounds the doctrine of prehensions in *Whitehead's Philosophy of Organism* (1932), and gives a short and admirably clear summary in an appendix to *The Nature of Metaphysical Thinking* (1945). The passages quoted in my note are taken from Whitehead's *Symbolism* (especially pp. 97–9), unless otherwise identified; but my summary owes a great deal to Miss Emmet's exposition.

[1] Dorothy Emmet, *The Nature of Metaphysical Thinking*, p. 228.

phases of response flow seamlessly from one into another; but even if these phases of response were spread out widely enough in time to permit us to distinguish certain patterns, we should not be entitled to think of those phases as distinct 'faculties'. For the flow of response is not linear but eccentric; as the process develops, the nexus of prehensions becomes more and more complex.

Whitehead distinguishes two modes (not 'faculties') of primary perception; that is, we see or hear simultaneously in two senses. In the mode of Causal Efficacy we perceive the causal relations between the entities within an event; in the mode of Presentational Immediacy we perceive the spatio-temporal relations. Contrary to all previous theories of perception, Whitehead holds that Causal Efficacy precedes and is more 'natural' than Presentational Immediacy, because Causal Efficacy is the more practical mode: it alone is needed for mere physical survival. Our notions of spatio-temporal relations are vague compared with our grasp of causal relations: we run away from the lion before we have fixed his position with more than general accuracy.[1]

There is no such thing as 'pure perception' in which neutral data are presented for interpretation: the datum for awareness is the product of a discriminatory and interpretative response. Perception occurs only in one or other or both of these primary modes, and neither mode is the product of analytical thinking. The evidence diffracted in these two modes intersects however in a third mode which Whitehead calls Symbolic Reference. This mode is not only the bridge between the two primary modes, but the mode in which conceptual activity may be engaged. Thinking can proceed only when the perceived entities have been abstracted and referred in Symbolic Reference to groups of symbols established in memory. But thinking proceeds so quickly and naturally out of perception that in many cases—particularly in practical situations—it is difficult, if not impossible, fully to separate thinking from perceiving. We no sooner see *what* something is and *where* it is, than we start thinking *about* it. But sometimes the thinking does not proceed at all; and at

[1] Samuel Alexander, *Beauty and Other Forms of Value*, suggests an example. If I am walking at night along a road and suddenly perceive a loud noise and bright light close behind me, I immediately jump into the ditch. The fact that I *did* jump into the ditch tells me *afterwards* that I knew I was in danger; I did not first decide that I was in danger and then jump. But if the noise and light were not very startling my response would probably follow a more sophisticated pattern and terminate in more sophisticated behaviour.

any time either mode of perception may be limited or eliminated at will or physiologically.

According to this doctrine we should not think of a person 'seeing something'; but rather, that we project our immediate prehensions of a simultaneous (not causally related) situation into the contemporary world. There are no 'bare sensations' which are *first* experienced and *then* projected: 'the projection is an integral part of the situation, quite as original as the sense-data'. Perception is a primary phase in the self-production of an occasion of actual existence. The mode of Causal Efficacy objectifies things under the guise of affective relations; the mode of Presentational Immediacy objectifies things by projecting sensations outward under the guise of immediate presentation.[1]

We may conveniently follow Miss Emmet by substituting the term 'adverbial mode' for Whitehead's mode of Causal Efficacy, and 'accusative mode' for Presentational Immediacy: in the adverbial mode we perceive *how* we are engaged, in the accusative (or 'pointing') mode we perceive *with what* we are engaged. The adverbial mode is productive of feeling and carries the sense of 'withness'; the accusative mode, barren of feeling, is a mode of discriminative clarity and projection, and carries the sense of 'otherness'. 'The result of Symbolic Reference', Whitehead says of the synthetic process which fuses the two modes into single perceptions, 'is a datum of experience productive of feelings, emotions, satisfactions, actions, and finally the datum for conscious recognition when the mind intervenes with its conceptual analysis.' (Whitehead here uses 'feelings' in the ordinary sense of 'emotions'; 'feeling' in Whitehead's special sense is always vectorial and efficacious, seeking to discharge in a certain direction and in a certain pattern.)

The 'energy' or 'feeling' generated in perception discharges into action along certain paths. (*a*) Pure instinctive action, Whitehead

---

[1] Cf. Sir Charles Sherrington, *Man on his Nature*, pp. 325–6: 'Projection is a term helpful in dealing descriptively with sensual space. Perceptual space might be written here instead of sensual space, except that it is wished here to stress its derivation from sense. The vexed question of the mode of origin or genesis of sensual space we have not to enter on. We accept the brute fact that our mind's perception through the senses immerses us in "space". To see a thing is to see it somewhere. And so with all the other senses. That may seem nothing to wonder at, but to reflection it is perennially astonishing. We can only observe it, leaving it a "final inexplicability". . . . Sensual space is always just "3-dimensional" space, Euclidean space; Euclidean space is 3-dimensional because just sensual.'

maintains, is the response to pure Causal Efficacy (the adverbial mode). (*b*) Reflex action depends wholly upon sense-presentation in both modes, but without analysis of Causal Efficacy in Symbolic Reference. (*c*) Symbolically conditioned action occurs by symbolic transference from the accusative to the adverbial mode: and symbolically conditioned action quickly decays into reflex action unless refreshed by conceptual activity.

(*d*) When Whitehead considers artistic activity he states that 'The whole question of the symbolic transfer of emotion lies at the base of any theory of the aesthetics of art.' 'A poet is a person for whom visual sights, and sounds, and emotional experiences refer symbolically to words. . . . By concentrating on a certain selection of sense-perceptions such as words . . . there is a chain of derivations of symbol from symbol whereby finally the local relations between the final symbols and the ultimate meaning, are entirely lost. Thus these derivative symbols, obtained as it were by arbitrary association, are really the results of a reflex action suppressing the intermediate portions of the chain. We use the word "association" when the intermediate links are so suppressed.' Whitehead regards Symbolic Reference as a perceptual mode; although conceptual activity may flow out of and into this mode, whatever remains in this mode preserves its perceptual character of feeling-tone. Once any datum for awareness has passed from the perceptual to the conceptual sphere it has lost its feeling-tone. So it is that any perceptual experience dominated by conceptual activity presents itself only in the accusative mode (Presentational Immediacy), which by definition is barren of feeling. Actually the adverbial mode is not in this case eliminated; but it appears to be, because the feeling generated in this type of perception is below the threshold value for recognition. (This is what Valéry had in mind when he complained that most people see through a dictionary and not through their retinae.)

It is possible with the help of this doctrine to show why artistic experience is properly regarded as primitive, and why the artist's perceptual experience is different from 'ordinary' perception. Whitehead holds that the adverbial mode is the more 'natural' mode because it is the more practical: this does not mean that the adverbial mode alone is primitive. In the primitive state, and in artistic perception, the two primary modes are fused. The differentiation into two modes, which Whitehead discovered in contemporary persons, is a specialization occurring in response to practical necessity. As man

learns, through the device of abstraction, to control his environment
with increasing success, the need for instinctive action diminishes.
As a condition of ordered society the feeling-tone of the adverbial
mode becomes diverted (by custom, law, ethical codes) from immediate instinctive action; instinctive action is suppressed for reasons
which in the new situation of society have become practical. In the
shelter of social organization the adverbial mode is suppressed, and
the accusative mode gains prominence, eventually becoming so refined that the adverbial mode no longer seems to operate in normal
experience. This applies particularly to the sense of sight. The adverbial mode still remains the energetic mode—otherwise there would
be no mainspring for action. But once the direct link of instinctive
action is broken, feeling-tone is sublimated through Symbolic
Reference into conceptual activity. Ordinary civilized perception is
thus characterized by its neutrality, by absence of feeling-tone; it
appears to operate exclusively in the accusative mode (Presentational
Immediacy). It is interesting to observe that in philosophy most of
the metaphorical words for conceptual activity are metaphors of
vision, as though seeing were only (in the common phrase) 'seeing
things'; for it is in the sense of sight particularly that this specialized
sublimation of the adverbial mode has occurred.[1] Intuition is
'vision' of concepts in the accusative mode; contemplation however
is gazing upon reality in both modes.

The artist's 'more than usual organic sensibility' is to be interpreted as a fusion of the two primary modes of perception. The
perceptual feeling-tone, instead of resolving (in the primitive manner)
into instinctive action or (in the sophisticated manner) into pure conceptual activity, sublimates into the accusative mode without predominant conceptual reference. The effect of this fusion of the
adverbial and accusative modes is an extensive range of sensitivity,
exceptional clarity and vividness of perception. This may be called
a 'cognitive ring' (on the analogy of a molecular ring), or a state of
resonance. It is this state of resonance that I have called 'paradeigmatic
experience'.

Whitehead's mode of Symbolic Reference, a function of memory
whose activity is 'association', is another name for what I have called
'imagination'. 'Imagination' and 'ideation' are two responsive processes into which a person may be orientated by perceptual feeling;
and since the degree and complexity of perceptual feeling is a func-

[1] This point is discussed again at pp. 155–6 below.

on of the person's habitual attitude and contemporary state, the
esponsive organization may be discerned by determining the char-
cter and force of feeling in a particular instance. This (in different
erms) is the basis of Coleridge's distinction between Imagination
nd Fancy.

VI

Symbolic Extrication

It is the duty of human understanding to understand that there are things which it cannot understand, and what those things are. . . . The paradox is not a concession but a category, an ontological definition which expresses the relation between an existing cognitive spirit and eternal truth.

KIERKEGAARD

Then as th'earths inward narrow crooked lanes
Do purge sea waters fretfull salt away,
I thought, if I could draw my paines,
Through Rimes vexation, I should them allay,
Griefe brought to numbers cannot be so fierce,
For, he tames it, that fetters it in verse.

JOHN DONNE

The friends that have it I do wrong
Whenever I remake a song
Should know what issue is at stake:
It is myself that I remake.

W. B. YEATS

TOWARDS the end of the last chapter we ran into a familiar landscape in the discussion of imagination. We must continue a little farther to inquire into inscrutables before moving with the relative freedom of the critic. I suggested that a poem springs from a paradeigmatic event, that a poem is in some sense the resolution of an event of reality. A germ, a catalyst, a quantum of 'poetic energy', intrudes into consciousness; the associative function of memory which we call imagination is stimulated and orients itself in a particular manner. The activity that proceeds etween the paradeigmatic event and the finished poem I have called *ymbolic extrication*. And by this term I mean to imply, not simply the ritical activity by which a poem is guided finally to completion, but lso the activity which makes a poem necessary at all. Symbolic xtrication is the activity by which the poet extricates himself from an ntolerable reality (the paradeigmatic event) by transferring his feeling or that reality to a system of symbols. The poem is not merely a y-product of that withdrawing movement but the necessary con-ition of it. If the transfer of feeling to symbols is not faithful and omplete, the rhythmic movement by which a man preserves his ontact with reality is interrupted, and the capacity for making poetry lisappears—perhaps temporarily, perhaps permanently. But before liscussing the nature of symbols and the way feeling is transmuted nto language we shall consider symbolic extrication in its meta-hysical and psychological aspects.

A paradeigmatic experience is, in one of its aspects, an event of nowing characterized by vivid perception, intense feeling, and a onviction of value. This differs from what is usually called 'know-ng' because it does not rely upon or grow out of verification. But erification, though essential to practical and technical knowing, may ot be essential—or even possible—in moral and aesthetic knowing:

> *Swift to the soul the piercing image flies. . . .*
> *Fancy precedes, and conquers all the mind;*
> *Deliberating judgment slowly comes behind;*
> *Comes to the field with blunderbus and gun,*
> *Like heavy Falstaff, when the work is done.*
> *Fights when the battle's o'er with wondrous pain,*
> *By Shrewbury's clock, and nobly slays the slain.*[1]

Paradeigmatic events are self-contained systems like closed electric

---

[1] Christopher Smart, Prologue to *A Trip to Cambridge*. Verification either tests the rounds of conviction by collecting additional sensory evidence, or it tests whether he conviction is consistent with other conclusions and beliefs. In either case an act f will or habit is required. Verification is an afterthought, a test of the truth or false-ess of propositions made about an experience; it is not and cannot be a test of the onviction or of the reality of the event in which the conviction arose. Cf. the Intro-luction to Russell and Whitehead, *Principia Mathematica* (1910): 'In mathematics, he greatest degree of self-evidence is usually not to be found quite at the beginning, ut at some later point; hence the early deductions, until they reach this point, give easons rather for believing the premises because true consequences follow from them, han for believing the consequences because they follow from the premises.'

circuits. They are sometimes so overwhelming that they are 'in-
credible': yet paradeigmatic experience is a state of profound belief,
a state of faith. For faith, as Kierkegaard has asserted, 'is not an
aesthetic emotion but something far higher, precisely because it has
resignation as its presupposition; it is not an immediate instinct of the
heart, but is the paradox of life and existence'. In an event of reality
we see the world suddenly in a fresh and astonishing light; and what
we know in that instant may be unassailably at variance with our
previous settled beliefs. The literature of religious conversion and
mystical vision shows that a single experience of this kind may
uproot and recast a whole lifetime of carefully ordered attitude or
firm habitual belief.

The only proposition that can be made *in* such an event is an
affirmative cry which is not truly propositional: 'This is real' or 'This
matters'. Abstraction is not a necessary preliminary to this kind of
knowing. What is known is not the abstract relations between
'things' or 'ideas', but the whole event; consequently the expression
of this knowledge is not a group of related propositions but a total
assertion, a work of art, a physical embodiment of the event of
reality *in its own terms*. Suddenly, and in a manner that cannot be
explained, everything chimes together, becomes resonant, assumes
a self-sustaining clarity; but this state is fragile and unstable—'the
mind in creation is like a fading coal'. And this resonance, this
sense of enfolding and of being enfolded, this sympathetic fusion
with the outside world, also carries with it the need to clarify and
resolve both the event and the self—to withdraw, to extricate oneself
from the event of reality and so to embrace it.

A state of heightened feeling is a state of disequilibrium; equilibrium is restored by discharging the energetic feeling. Paradeigmatic
experience manifests itself as a complex state of heightened feeling.
But, being an event of value and of reality, it demands that the discharge of feeling be appropriate to the value—even though the vision
be blinding, and the feeling insupportably powerful. The 'ordinary
man' discharges his states of heightened feeling without much delay
in overt action or in inarticulate cries: the feeling may be satisfactorily
discharged, but the action is seldom an appropriate vehicle for the
feeling. It is like lightning, random and uncreative: a charge accumulates until it can no longer be sustained, then it jumps where and
as it may.

The poet is not satisfied with a random escape from feeling; for he is a contemplative nature and feeling is his window opening upon reality. He is prepared closely to criticize the quality of action; he does not prize mere action for the sake of 'doing something'—as ordinary people tend to do out of self-deception or justification.

> *Action is transitory—a step, a blow*
> *The motion of a muscle—this way or that—*
> *'Tis done; and in the after-vacancy*
> *We wonder at ourselves like men betrayed:*
> *Suffering is permanent, obscure and dark,*
> *And has the nature of infinity.*[1]

The culture of a poet's reality is a dark and obscure suffering; he must sustain the suffering of reality until he can find a body for it—otherwise he will betray and lose himself. For a poet, feeling has the intensity of suffering. But the complexity and pattern—the 'contours' —of his feeling are as important to him as the intensity: he must find some means of arresting his states of feeling, of holding them contemplatively in their complex vitality until he has transmuted them faithfully into language. From this arises the poet's patience; and patience is also suffering. The poet's capacity for suffering is the 'wound' that Gide speaks of—'cette blessure qu'il ne faut pas laisser se cicatriser, mais qui doit demeurer toujours douleureuse et saignante, cette blessure au contact de l'affreux réalité.'

A poem is not first conceived and then expressed; a poem in the making discovers itself to the poet. A poem is 'expressed' in the most vivid sense of that word: it is pressed out of the poet, forced out of him. 'It is', Hopkins notes in a journal, 'as if the blissful agony or stress of selving in God has forced out drops of sweat or blood, which drops were the world, or as if the lights lit at the festival of that "peaceful Trinity" through some little cranny striking out lit up into being one "cleave" out of the world of possible creatures.' The poem (as we have seen) will be a patterned cry and not a discursive

---

[1] These lines, surprisingly, appear in Wordsworth's early and bad play, *The Borderers*; he later used them, with some expansion, as an epigraph to *The White Doe of Rylestone* (1837). Cf. a passage in T. S. Eliot's *The Dry Salvages*:

> *For our own past is covered by the currents of action,*
> *But the torment of others remains an experience*
> *Unqualified, unworn by subsequent attrition.*
> *People change, and smile: but the agony abides.*

statement;[1] it must be an embodiment of feeling, not a description of feeling.

Artistic expression is cathartic, but in a special way. The work of art is so made that it shall carry away in its body the intolerable feeling of being immersed in reality. Is that perhaps what the prophet meant when he said that 'the fear of God is the beginning of wisdom'? To possess is to destroy; reality is so much more powerful than any person that to possess reality is to be destroyed.[2] To escape from reality is not difficult; but the poet seeks to incarnate reality, by becoming a medium through which that reality may pass. And this perhaps is what is meant by saying that a poet is 'inspired'; for it is reality, and not merely his own 'experience' or states of mind, that he expresses. His action might be called *inscape*—the opposite of *escape*; for he resolves the paradeigmatic feeling by a closer and closer identification with the event; by holding the event to himself he clarifies the feeling of that event as minutely and accurately as he can. If the process is to be cathartic, the expression must assume form—a form growing from within itself and self-bounded, to correspond with the form of the feeling. In this activity the poet discovers to himself the reality in which he is immersed, and extricates himself from it. The 'images of memory', steeped in feeling, are the psychic raw materials which assume form; and the indelible and physical mark of reality is rhythm. By transmuting the paradeigmatic event into rhythmic language, the poet passes from a state of tension to a state of luminous contemplative arrest, and on to that cathartic repose in which the self is emptied, annihilated, remade. He transfers the 'feeling of reality' to a unified system of images; these bear as precisely as may be the same intensity and pattern as that single intricate feeling. In this way the poet disengages himself from reality.

*　　　*　　　*

[1] This is as true of a poem like *Paradise Lost* as it is of a lyric; for Milton's theme, his 'felt vision', is embodied in the whole poem and is not to be identified with the programme offered in the title or in the long opening sentence.

[2] A passage in Kierkegaard's *Journal* for May 1842 reads: ' . . . And it was the delight of his eyes and his heart's desire. And he stretched forth his hand and took hold of it, but he could not retain it; it was offered to him, but he could not possess it alas, for it was the delight of his eyes and his heart's desire. And his soul was near to despair; but he chose the greater suffering, of losing it and giving it up, to the lesser, which was to possess it without right; or to speak more truly . . . he chose the lesser suffering of being without it rather than to possess it at the cost of his peace of soul . . . and strange to relate, it came to pass that it was for his good.'

By concentrating upon the *perceptual* character of paradeigmatic experience I may have given the impression that such experience can only develop when material objects are actually present to vivid perception. But poetry is very rarely the spontaneous overflow of powerful feelings *in situ*; there is always a certain 'psychic distance' between any event and the poem which dramatically reconstructs it. It is an advantage that, as in Wordsworth's case, the 'emotion' be 'recollected in tranquillity'; the paradeigmatic event is then liberated, and given a distinctively energetic freedom, by being separated from the accidental sequence of any actual event.

> *Strange, but the man who made the song was blind;*
> *Yet, now I have considered it, I find*
> *That nothing strange; . . .*

This second instance of paradeigmatic experience is not in any important respect different from experience in response to things actually perceived; for even at the most rudimentary level in perception, the poet's feelings have started to refer themselves to language and remembered images. In both cases the perceptual and sensory centre stands firm; and from this a vitally important feature of poetry is to be understood. When the imagination comes into resonance with some commanding passion, the 'images of memory' orient themselves, like iron filings in a magnetic field; they form clusters and constellations, the appropriateness and significance of which the poet tests and discovers in the critical activity of composition. Similarly, a paradeigmatic event orients itself upon one or more focal entities—or not so much *upon*, as *through* these objects—whether actually present or only present 'to the mind's eye'. The central object itself may not be particularly significant in any other context; yet in the paradeigmatic event it assumes a strange luminousness, as though it were the lens through which the light of reality were being focused to a sharp point, or an electrode through which the energy of the prehended reality were flowing in. When an object assumes this central position it retains in memory a high charge of feeling. And it is these objects which become symbols; when separated from actual incidents, and enriched by repeated contemplation and thought, they become the foci of feeling and value in the poem.[1] Poetic images differ from

[1] Cf. Yeats, Preface to W. T. Horton, *A Book of Images* (1898): 'A person or a landscape that is a part of a story or a portrait evokes but so much emotion as the story or the portrait can permit without loosening the bonds that make it a story or a portrait;

other images—and particularly from 'ideas'—by being (in the sense just offered) more or less symbolic. If the poet is to extricate himself from reality, he does so by transmuting his feeling into symbolic language.

Since feeling includes a recognition of value, and since we attempt to distinguish most clearly what 'matters' most to us, the charge of feeling upon an image is the index by which we recognize images of value; it is also the impulse that urges us to clarify them. But since our conscious discrimination between feelings is rather coarse, we also differentiate images in terms of their sensory character and intensity: we cannot say definitely whether we see most clearly what most matters to us, or whether that matters most which we see most clearly. We need to discriminate our images according to their sensory quality, because the data for sustained response must be charges of feeling *on* something. A charge of feeling not firmly attached to an image and controlled by it becomes a 'free' charge; it will combine with other 'free' charges to swell the undirected stream of energy which I recognize as emotion.[1] If we distinguish between images and ideas, we can see why artists constantly strive to rid themselves of emotion; for emotion threatens to take charge whenever the content of consciousness is abstract and general, or when vaguely realized.

An image receives its charge of feeling-tone in actual perception, in events of value. In memory the image tends to hold this charge: the charge may decay, or remain latent for a long period, but an image can never acquire a charge other than in a perceptual event. A perceptual event, however, need not be a direct perceptual contact with the physical world—it may, in the case of a mature person,

but if you liberate a person or landscape from the bonds of motives and their actions, causes and their effects, and from all bonds but the bonds of our love, it will change under your eyes, and become a symbol of an infinite emotion, a perfected emotion, a part of the Divine Essence.'

[1] When we have had some practice in using language, we can discriminate accurately between a large number of *words*; and we can respond appropriately to whatever each word implies, even though we may not be able accurately to define the *meaning* of each word. But a word is an image, even though in many cases a neutral image. And our discrimination among feelings when they are not attached to words or other images is at best crude and tentative. This failure in discrimination is quite distinct from the lack of words to *refer to* or *describe* fine shades of meaning; yet the poverty of language in that respect may well reflect this failure in discrimination. It is one thing to talk *about* feelings; it is a completely different matter accurately to convey feelings in words.

be a perceptive contact with a book or poem, a picture or a piece of music.[1] Feeling-tone is the stamp of reality, however the contact with reality be made. Feeling is always perceptual and physical; that is, it refers to differentiated sensory images and arouses a widespread response, both physical and mental. The physical character of the charged image marks it off from neutral images, ideas, concepts; the response to these follows a linear pattern very different from the involute self-circling process of imagination which is unified within itself at all stages of its development.

*　　　*　　　*

The paradox of symbolic extrication is revealed in works of art in the way they can combine complexity with precision, vitality with subtlety, force with delicacy. Robert Frost notices this paradox in the prefatory essay to his *Collected Poems* (1943).

'Just as the first mystery was how a poem could have a tune in such a straightness as metre, so the second mystery is how a poem can have wildness and at the same time a subject that shall be fulfilled. . . . I tell how there may be a better wildness of logic than of inconsequence. But the logic is backward, in retrospect, after the act. It must be more felt than seen ahead like prophecy. It must be a revelation, or a series of revelations, as much for the poet as for the reader. For it to be that there must have been the greatest freedom of the material to move about in it and to establish relations in it regardless of time and space, previous relation, and everything but affinity.'

In poetry, sound can interweave with, diffuse, and fortify visual clarity; gentleness of feeling and ironic astringency are not incompatible; violent variations in pace, rhythm and texture, transitions from sight to sound and touch, and from sound to meaning, can be fused into single fluent utterance. Conflicting and inharmonious elements can combine by resonance simultaneously to engage several levels of awareness. And when this occurs there is a sense of inevitability, of 'rightness'—that here is manifested exceptional penetration,

---

[1] In such cases the charge of feeling is carried over from the writer to the reader through the mediation of the printed book, the spoken poem, the played music, etc.; but it is nonetheless perceptual in character. In any case the person whose images tend to be charged, whose memory is richly stored, and his attitude attuned in a creative and contemplative direction, must also be acutely susceptible to perceptual experience.

clarity, richness, a reality beyond the 'real life' normally accessible to us, and that it could not have been expressed otherwise. But rhythm is the great compulsive physical centre around which all this tense and random diversity takes form. And symbolic extrication, the final phase of incarnating an event of reality, is itself a rhythmic activity, a movement back and forth between the contemplative and the technical, between fashioning and criticizing, between synthesis and analysis.

Analysis and synthesis are not—as is commonly supposed—mirror-images of each other; they are two activities different in kind. Analysis (in the sense now commonly used) is a process for abstracting and comparing ideas, a process which destroys the intricate internal relations of an event of reality. The products of analysis can be pieced together into a *schema* (Kant's word), a diagram of abstractions, but not into a synthesis. Synthesis is rhythmic, self-formed, integrating; all its elements are sustained in vital connection. Analysis can enrich successive syntheses; but no amount of analysis can *produce* a synthesis. Analysis is of ideas; synthesis is a direct grasp of any event or aspect of reality in unified complexity. It is the pre-eminent function of the artist to achieve synthesis.

The full poetic rhythm, centred upon perceptual and contemplative experience, swinging from synthesis to analysis and back to synthesis, arises only out of paradeigmatic experience. Once the artist is immersed in reality—not from choice only but also by reason of his individual constitution—he must withdraw again into the everyday world; for reality is intolerable. To make a work of art is for the artist an urgent and clamorous need: it is his only means of withdrawing from reality, and the work of art faithfully—ruthlessly —made is the only condition of his returning into contact with reality again.

Rarely outside artistic activity or mystical experience is a full rhythm of analysis and synthesis achieved. The practical or the technical man, limited by the poverty of his perceptual experience, his mind oriented to a limited pattern of response, seldom if ever moves out of the analytical cycle: abstraction, classification, generalization, and the construction of abstract schemata.

> . . . *one watches, starves, freezes, and sweats,*
> *To know but Catechismes and Alphabets*
> *Of unconcerning things, matters of fact.*

When a mind does break out of the analytical cycle to engage in a more contemplative activity in science or philosophy and wrest from reality (let us say) a fresh analogy—then we have a Newton, a Darwin, an Einstein, a Bergson, a Whitehead, a Sherrington. On those rare excursions of discovery their vision is not merely intuitive but paradeigmatic; no matter what analysis may have contributed, the true discovery is always a synthesis.

The artist, to be sure, has the best of both worlds; but only at the cost of maintaining a delicate balance between conflicting claims upon his attention, continual threats upon the virginity of his responses. 'Isolated artists', Augustin Cochin observes, 'have survived, but like rocks battered by the sea of banality and ignorance, not like great trees in the forest.' The insistent clamour of practicality will importune his allegiance or his reaction, drawing him into one world or the other—into a world of make-believe, or into a world of technical fantasy. If it were not so, the artist would not have to assert his claim to integrity, always firmly, at times with brutal arrogance: for the casualties are heavy.

★ ★ ★

The technical problem for the artist then is to transmute a complex state of feeling into his chosen physical medium—in the case of the poet, into language. Artists seldom trouble their heads about the theory of this transmutation: they usually work until they feel that the result is 'right'; and on the whole works of art seem to be better made in this untheoretical way. Philosophers (until quite recently) have spoken as though the first step towards expression must be a translation of 'sense data' into ideas; and this error is inclined to persist because poetry seems to be more intelligible and accessible than it really is. But poetry does not make propositional or discursive arguments; it does not describe; neither is it an exposition. Poetry is a cry uttered out of the heart of reality, and although usually an intricately articulated cry its internal connections are other than the connections that can exist among ideas. I have attempted to show how the artist transmutes his feelings into expressive terms *before* ideas referring to those feelings have been constructed; and how in the process of composition he extricates and distils their particular 'significance' and 'relevance' from these words, rhythms, and clusters of images. Symbolic transmutation cannot be completed—the feelings cannot be finally embodied in word-images—without some intellectual and critical activity; but it cannot occur at all unless there has been some initial prelogical transmutation.

In the final stages of the poetic process, in the actual process of composition when the 'relevant' images are evoked, selected, and articulated, two unifying principles command the process—the single unifying passion which is the integrity of the event of reality, and 'style' which is the personal integrity of the poet. At this point in the discussion of symbolic extrication we pass from the sphere of psychology to the realm of criticism—from an attempt directly to describe psychic processes, to an attempt to infer activity from the physical manifestations of it in the poem. But there is another reason why criticism properly enters at this state. There are some psychic processes which are purely mechanical and spontaneous; but poetic process is different from all these because it always involves the person and not simply an organism. Accessible only to contemplation, value enters the process—if it is to enter at all—at the radical level of perception. And since this element of value must be sustained throughout the poetic process, the activity is inevitably centred upon the person. This is so even in the phase of imagination which seems most purely spontaneous and undirected. Throughout the period of gestation, sometimes in conscious flashes, but more often in the dark broodings of subconsciousness, the person has 'lain in the soil and criticized the worm'. At no level is the process innocent of selection and direct judgment. Any particular cycle of the process is what it is because it has occurred in this individual and unique person; not because he is an organism with certain peculiarities but because he is a *person* of unique nature, awareness, and concern. In the final stage of composition, however, the poet is seeking to discover a system of images to embody his grasp of reality—by quiet passivity, by dainty stimulation, by fastidious selection, and by the grace of that *curiosa felicitas* which Coventry Patmore called 'careful luck'.[1]

---

[1] Cf. two passages in Paul Valéry's *Note-Book B1910*. 'To benefit from the lucky accident. The true writer abandons his idea to the benefit of another that comes to him while seeking the words for the one desired, by those very words. He finds that he has become more potent, even more profound through this unexpected game of words—whose value, however, he sees at once. . . . And he passes for profound and creative—having been only a lightning-swift critic and huntsman.' 'The mind is luck. I mean that the very sense of the word, *mind*, contains, amongst other things, all the meanings of the word, *luck*. Its laws are acted out, mimicked by this lack [? of law]. But it is more profound, more stable, more intimate than any known, *conscious* law.

And this phase of which so many artists of all kinds have given moving witness—the final agony of turning blood into ink—may properly be regarded as criticism.

Any law I think out is unstable, restricted, constrained.' Gerard Manley Hopkins similarly observed in one of his journals: 'Chance then is the ἐνέργεια, the stress, of the intrinsic possibility which things have.'

A NOTE ON TOYNBEE'S DOCTRINE O WITHDRAWAL-AND-RETURN

It takes more courage to suffer than to act, more courage to forget than to remember.
KIERKEGAARD

Mr Arnold J. Toynbee's doctrine of Withdrawal-and-Return show interesting points of similarity with the scheme of Symbolic Extrica tion.[1] The process of Withdrawal-and-Return he considers to b revealed most distinctly in mystical experience, in the movement fror action to ecstasy and back to action: 'a disengagement and temporar withdrawal of the creative personality from his social milieu, an his subsequent return to the same milieu transfigures'. He quote Bergson's *Les Deux Sources de la Morale et de la Réligion*: 'In our eye the culmination of Mysticism is an entry into contact, and i consequence a partial coincidence, with the creative effort that manifested by Life. . . .' He concludes that 'This movement . . . something that is characteristic of Life in general', and cites the rhythr of fertility which is a central feature in primitive religions and whic St Paul in his account of the life after death uses for illustration i 1 Corinthians xv. Toynbee places the emphasis upon the half-phas of Return, upon the re-emergence into creative social activity: 'Th return is the essence of the whole movement, as well as its fina cause.' But clearly the process *as* process must be considered in complete rhythmic cycle: and in this aspect (although Toynbee doc not make the point as clearly as Bergson) the rhythmic character c the process is the stamp of life.

Withdrawal-and-Return, in Toynbee's view, is nothing if not *creative* activity; indeed it is *the* creative activity whereby civilizatior grow and mature. But his interest in the growth and decay of civiliza tions places the emphasis almost exclusively upon social action— action which is predominantly practical and technical. (A simila emphasis commands Plato's not-very-serious discussion of poetry i *The Republic*.) Consequently his inquiry does not penetrate below th broader biographical patterns of individual experience.[2]

[1] In *A Study of History*, III, 248–63, Mr Toynbee offers his general theory Withdrawal-and-Return, and in the same volume illustrates it in a number of sho biographies (pp. 263–332) and in certain social developments (pp. 332–77).

[2] Toynbee's neglect of artistic process leads him to discuss twentieth-century art i

The doctrine of symbolic extrication, on the other hand, regards poetic process as the fundamental psychic process in art, and in all knowing which is not technical; the emphasis is then upon the half-phase of transfiguration, or immersion in reality. For the artist this is the important half-phase, because his works of art must grow out of this part of his experience. But as man, as social man, the artist must return' from his vision, his ecstasy, his immersion in reality *as a condition of survival*; and the return is also the gage of his survival as an artist. The only way he can return is to transfer his experience of immersion to a physical artefact: and that is his half-phase of 'action', his return to the social world. But the social world (as I suggested earlier) is paradoxically an abstract world because of the logic of man's practical situation.

The artist's problem of transmuting his paradeigmatic experience into a physical medium is very much like the mystic's problem of translating his vision into intelligible mundane terms. The artist *as artist* is, however, 'detached': the practical application of his work is incidental and no concern of his; it works itself out only through the power that art may exert in integrating those who can experience it. Even Kipling mentions 'the detachment of the true artist who knows that he is but the vessel of an emotion whence others not he, must drink'.) Art can strengthen and purify, but not by the direct will of the artist: for the artist's 'action' within the poetic rhythm will be contaminated by any specific practical purpose. Disinterested action devoid of practical intention is the paradox of the artist's life: it explains why artistic processes and values cannot be accounted for in the logic of practicality; it also explains why the artist is a social anomaly when not a social necessity.[1]

very cursory manner. In describing the decay and barbarization of contemporary art V, 51–6) he seems not to recognize any distinction between proletarian commodity-art and sincere creative art; nor between the reasons for the mass popularity of vulgarized barbaric art and the reasons why serious creative artists of the last two generations have made a careful study of primitive artistic expression. This is strangely at variance with Toynbee's postulate of a creative minority and an apathetic mass.

[1] Jacques Maritain, in *Art and Poetry*, cites Dostoievski as evidence that 'it is possible to know that what you write will have an effect" without curbing on that account our art and thought'. Gide had observed that Dostoievski 'retains, in face of human reality, a humble, submissive attitude; he never forces, he never diverts the event toward himself'. 'Well and good,' Maritain remarks. 'This is to say that his art does not give way, while he uses it for his God.'
There is a striking passage in Valéry's *Da Vinci* on this matter of detachment. 'Since to write should be to be, to construct, as solidly and as precisely as one possibly can, the

In discussing the 'Process of Disintegration' (VI, 170–1) Toynbe
returns to the theme of Withdrawal-and-Return, by distinguishin
between Detachment and Transfiguration: 'While Detachment is
simple movement of sheer withdrawal, Transfiguration is a com
pound movement whose beat is likewise a withdrawal but who
second beat is a return.' Detachment, being arhythmic, cannot b
'creative'. But when Toynbee states that the 'difference between a
act of withdrawal and an act of withdrawal-and-return is not
difference between one road and another but merely a difference i
the number of stages traversed', he seems to have lost sight of th
rhythm. As I have attempted to show, the difference is absolute: it
the difference between life and death, between poetry and apath
Also, in a smaller sense, it is the difference between Fancy an
Imagination: the one linear and ideational; the other rhythmic an
integrative. It is not the difference between work produced 'by th
mind' and work produced 'by the imagination'. It is the differenc
between a single dissipating linear movement which, having no sel
determinate end, never turns back to complete itself; and a comple
rhythmic self-enclosing movement which completes itself at the en
of each rhythmic cycle. Linear progress offers a false interpretation
human history because it represents an arhythmic movement—
movement neither of life nor of morality.

machine of language in which the released activity of the spirit spends itself in conque
ing an opposed reality, a writer must become detached from himself. It is only ar
strictly when detachment is achieved that the whole man becomes *author*. Everythir
else is merely part of a part of him, escaped, it is not part of *himself*. Between the emoti
or the initial intention and those final forgetfulnesses, disorders, vaguenesses which a
inevitable results of thought, his business is to introduce the contrarinesses that he h
created, so that, interposed, they shall set some regenerating action and independe
existence against the transient nature of interior phenomena.'

VII

Science and Poetic

High on some mountain shelf
Huddle the pitiless abstractions bald about the necks.

W. B. YEATS

I N Chapter V a distinction was drawn between the contemplative and the theoretical ways of mind; and I said that the distinction would assume importance at a later stage. Each way of mind reveals itself in a particular use of language. And since the dominant way of mind at present is technical the discussion of poetic language will be greatly clarified if we can first establish our views upon the technical use of language.

Coleridge justly observed that the antithesis of poetry is science. By this I take him to mean that the scientific mind is the antithesis of the poetic mind. The antithesis to a poem, however, is not prose simply, but *technical* or scientific prose. The complete range of prose includes every conceivable shade of intension and feeling: at one extreme that 'other harmony' which (without being 'purple') legitimately claims the status of poetry; at the other extreme the prose of scientific exposition and description. But the technical pole exerts much the more powerful influence over the sphere of prose—an influence which Ezra Pound finds destructive. 'Most good prose arises, perhaps, from an instinct of negation; is the detailed, convincing analysis of something detestable; of something which one wants to eliminate. Poetry is the assertion of a positive, *i.e.* of desire, and endures for a longer period. Poetic satire is only an assertion of this positive, inversely, *i.e.* as of an opposite hatred.' At first sight this might seem to be the angry bias of an anti-rational poet. But if technical prose is indeed the antithesis of poetry, and if poetry is in some sense 'creative', science can be expected to show a desire for negation; it will not be content to describe and explain but will also seek to explain away. And if, as I have claimed, a difference of intention in the writer will leave an indelible mark upon his style, we can expect to find that technical language has a very distinct character. For the time being it is enough to remember that the function of poetic language is neither to describe nor to explain. Poetry may be called the expression of an unusual state of awareness. Poetry always implies awareness of something; but that something is never in the end merely a distinguishable object or notion. Herein rests the untranslatability of poetry.

Technical prose starts from a selected position or idea—a premiss, assumption, postulate, or established doctrine—and proceeds by a series of logically correct steps to a desired conclusion.[1] If the premiss be accepted, and the logic is flawless, the conclusion is inescapable. The problem for the technical writer is to prevent the reader's attention and judgment from wandering out of the logical path he has plotted for it. His solution is, to avoid ambiguity and emotional tone. This is the sort of thing that happens.

'The interaction of reflexes has been here so far spoken of chiefly in regard to the final common path, as if the arcs of reflexes met at the *final* common path only. But, as stated above, reflex-arcs, especially the longer ones and those commencing in receptors far apart, converge and meet to some extent before they reach their *final* common path. The receptive neurones, *i.e.* private paths of the receptors, usually—perhaps always—reach internuncial paths which in turn conduct and converge to final paths or to further internuncial paths. The internuncial paths are thus themselves in various degrees common to groups of receptive neurones impinging upon them. They are therefore themselves, to some extent, *common paths*.' (Sir Charles Sherrington, *The Integrative Action of the Nervous System* (1947), p. 147.)

Or consider a passage of expository description:

'The very peculiar spicules of the holothurian *Synapta*, where a

---

[1] The scope of this inquiry does not warrant a distinction between expository and ratiocinative prose.

tiny anchor is pivoted or hinged on a perforated plate, are a puzzle indeed; but we may at least solve part of the riddle. How the hinge is formed, I do not know; the anchor gets its shape, perhaps, in some such way as we have supposed the "amphidiscs" of *Hyalomena* to acquire their reflexed spokes, but the perforated plate is more comprehensible. Each plate starts in a little clump of cells in whose boundary-walls calcareous matter is deposited, doubtless by adsorption, the holes in the finished plate thus corresponding to the cells which formed it. Close-packing leads to an arrangement of six cells round a central one, and the normal pattern of the plate displays this hexagonal configuration. The calcareous plate begins as a little rod whose ends fork, and then fork again; in the same inevitable trinodal pattern which includes the "polar furrow" of the embryologists.' (D'Arcy Wentworth Thompson, *On Growth and Form* (1942), pp. 686-7.)

Both these passages admirably fulfil their purpose: they are perfectly clear, unambiguous, and free of emotional tone. There is no difficulty in understanding either passage; but most of us would need some sort of glossary of hard words, because few of the key-words in these passages are legal tender in lay circles. Technical words can be used in this single-track manner because they are designed to be words of a single meaning: as soon as their references begin to multiply they become unsuitable in technical prose unless they can be carefully defined and qualified for particular use. Here is another example of technical prose—this time taken from a philosophical work.

'Propositions, commonly statements asserting that something has or has not a certain characteristic, are often usefully taken as the "bricks" out of which any structure of reasoning or argument is to be built; the relation of Implication between propositions or groups of propositions is then a structural property whose assessment can contribute to our judgments of truth. It is of the final emerging proposition itself that "truth" or "falsity" might be predicated, but it is seldom possible to make such a decision unambiguously about many modern scientific propositions; the multifarious qualifications of truthfulness have given rise to the whole assemblage of difficulties in interpreting scientific explanations of Nature.' (Martin Johnson, *Science and the Meanings of Truth* (1946), 82.)

These passages exhibit the salient features of technical prose. Nouns predominate and carry most of the emphasis: consequently most of the verbs are passive, intransitive, or parts of the verb 'to be'. The intense effort to focus each single word into one unambiguous meaning suppresses the vigour of the verbs and produces double nouns (like 'reflex-arc') in preference to nouns modified by adjectives. This dominance of the static noun and passive verb removes all muscle and movement from the sentences. The sentences form patterns of abstracts; and if the sentence is unduly long we lose our way, forget some of the pieces, and have to turn back again. This, rather than the recondite vocabulary, makes the more obscure reaches of science and philosophy an arduous desert for the layman. Technical prose neither engages sympathy nor compels attention: you have to be 'interested in the subject' if you are to read much of it.

Ideas lack feeling-tone, either because they are conceptual in origin (arising in abstractive and generalizing modes of thought), or because they are images which have lost their charge of feeling by being introduced into a conceptual process. Ideas do not carry within themselves the charges of feeling that make images cohesive and energetic, mutually attractive and mutually selective; they cannot arouse imagination to that resonant state from which a work of art is brought to birth. Ideas and formulae, being either latent or overt propositions, are arhythmic and do not seek a form of their own: they can be illustrated, but they cannot be embodied.[1] On aesthetic grounds we distrust the logically impeccable system, the argument that 'leaves one cold', the 'dull' book or person, the 'mathematical' music, 'uninspired' speech, 'dry' painting, any work that is no more than a triumph of technique: these are the product of ideas, and do not convince us that they arise from an unusual state of feeling or

[1] The word *idea* has been used in so many different senses—even as a synonym for the imaginative *donnée* or germ—that it is difficult to hold it to such a specific meaning. Few philosophers, however, allow the word to be separated from some such meaning as 'a unit in conceptual thinking'. At many points in her book *The Nature of Metaphysical Thinking* Miss Dorothy Emmet approaches the view that all modes of knowledge may be referred to a primitive 'non-propositional knowing'; but whenever the word 'idea' turns up she withdraws from that position, presumably because in the back of her mind she conceives an 'idea' to be a unit for conceptual thinking and therefore cannot allow it to be a unit in a process of 'non-propositional knowing'. See for example pp. 19, 78, 95. But a passage on p. 207 shows that she is fully aware of the importance of this problem, and perhaps also of the need for some fresh terms. 'The possibilities of so entering into responsive awareness of other people and of things that we are conscious of their *being* in their own right is a question on which those who are thinking with discernment about the nature of "non-propositional knowing" may be able to throw light.'

awareness. A good novelist writing about a dull person or a dull life, however, does not write a dull book: the dullness he embodies will be a *felt* dullness taken up into the writer's imagination, experienced, and made real; the result might be oppressive, but not dull. On the other hand, wit and fancy, though characteristically conceptual, can endow work with a special quality of excitement—but only when they arise from an excited, amused, irreverent recognition of hitherto unrecognized connections in things. And this is perhaps the only case where ideas play a prominent role in art. We see it in some of the work of Donne, Pope, Swift, and Joyce, in the intricate texturing of Henry James's novels, and in some of George Eliot's work; it is a central feature of 'metaphysical' poetry; when combined with persistent intellectual power it becomes that quality of irony— 'safety in derision' is Yeats's phrase—which T. S. Eliot judged to be the gage of artistic permanence.[1] But even when the excitement is 'only verbal' or 'only intellectual', a poem requires that the excitement be embodied: and this embodiment ideas can never attain.

Scientific prose, however, is not *bad* writing—except in its debased forms.[2] It is a distinct species of writing determined by that posture of mind which I have called 'technical'. And this sort of writing is to be distinguished by the writer's intension and not simply by the kind of *words* he chooses. His intension is characterized by a conscious desire to convince his reader by unambiguous exposition, description, argument; he fulfils this purpose by concentrating upon meaning and by making his words refer 'objectively' only to meaning and not to feeling. Because of this conceptual emphasis, a sentence in scientific prose tends to become a diagram of semantic units joined together by prepositions and conjunctions to indicate their functional relations. The form of these diagrams is imposed deliberately by the writer and does not arise internally from the 'thought'. The reader does not grasp such a sentence as a whole, but moves along

[1] For the intellectual quality of irony, see Ezra Pound's statement (*Make it New* (1934), p. 171): 'The ironist is one who suggests that the reader should think, and this process being unnatural to the majority of mankind, the way of the ironical is beset with snares and with furze-bushes.'

[2] In the pseudo-sciences—some kinds of psychology, much literary and art criticism, most sociology, and practically all technical discussions of the theory of education—the typical features of technical prose can be seen in a grotesque debility. Technical and semi-technical terms (many of them of questionable parentage) proliferate like a jungle growth; and verbose formulae come to be used, not functionally, but as linguistic union-cards.

the sentence—like a fly crawling over a building 'with animalcular feet'—fitting together by inference from fragmentary evidence the design of the whole diagram.

Words, however, are not detached units of meaning; nor can single words be distributed into two classes—'untoned' (good) and 'emotive' (bad). All words are emotive, inasmuch as every single word can and must evoke some responsive feeling otherwise it could not even 'mean' in that very cold and specific way that science seems to demand. For perfectly legitimate methodological reasons, scientists strive to respond to their subject-matter in a purely conceptual and 'objective' way. The silent postulate for any piece of scientific description or analysis is: 'Let us suppose that a human being can so suppress his responsive feelings for things that he can become an impersonal recording instrument.' When a writer attempts to describe with complete scientific accuracy and detachment, his language—ideally speaking—will be a succession of utterly untoned abstractions to which a reader or listener can respond only in that subliminal state of feeling where he 'grasps the meaning', but is not aware of any transfer of feeling; for feeling is not, and should not be, transferred here—except possibly as the secondary excitement of 'interest' in the material.

But that 'interest in the subject' is for technical writing the thin end of the poetic wedge. The very finest scientific prose—whether of description, exposition, or argument—is toned in extremely subtle, almost indiscernible, ways by the author's passionate concentration upon his material. Sir Kenneth Clark discusses this point as it touches painting: and one would suppose that in painting the acme of precise scientific objectivity could be achieved. He is thinking of a Vermeer canvas in which 'the rendering of atmosphere reached a point of perfection that for sheer accuracy, has never been surpassed'.

'This unique work is certainly the nearest which painting has ever come to a coloured photograph. Not only has Vermeer an uncannily true sense of tone, but he has used it with an almost inhuman detachment. He has not allowed any one point in the scene to engage his interest, but has set down everything with a complete evenness of focus. Such, at least, is our first impression of the picture, and the basis of its popularity with those who do not normally care for painting. But the more we study the *View of Delft* the more artful it becomes, the more carefully calculated its design, the more consistent all its components. No doubt truth of tone adds to our delight, but this could not sustain us long without other qualities, and perhaps could not, by itself, have reached such a point of perfection, for the mood of heightened receptivity necessary to achieve it cannot be isolated from that tension of spirit which goes to the creation of any great work of art.' [1] It would be difficult to demonstrate in a single passage of prose exactly the degree of compelling veracity and secret passion that informs Vermeer's *Delft*: most probably it could best be detected in historical writing—in a passage such as the following from G. M. Trevelyan's *English Social History* (p. 440):

'The [Scottish] parish church, with its roof of turf or thatch, was a small and tumble-down building; it had no mediaeval splendours or amenities, and would in England have been deemed more fitted for a barn. In the country churches there were seldom pews, except for the elders and a few privileged families. Most men and women stood during the service, or else sat on "creepies", stools such as that with which Jennie Geddes had marked her disapproval of the Prayer Book service. Yet the hard, ill-furnished room was crowded every Sabbath for two services of three hours each by a congregation of whom many had come on foot long miles across the moor. So small was the space inside the church that an overflow of the pious was often crowded out into the churchyard, where the Bible was read to them by a lad put upon a tombstone.'

Such a shaping spirit of discreet accuracy and rapt detachment informs all the best technical prose. What is not generally recognized is that scientific language, in its attempt to arrive at the stability of mathematics, is the farthest limit to which language can responsibly be pressed and still communicate meaning. The primary function of language is to communicate between human beings. The problem of communication can never be solved because at its fullest it implies communion, some mutual identification of the persons. Only the deceptive search for 'scientific objectivity' could have suggested that

[1] *Landscape into Art* (1949), pp. 32–3. Cf. Adrian Stokes, *Art and Science: A study of Alberti, Piero della Francesca and Giorgione* (1949), pp. 16–17: 'A measuring of phenomena served the humanism of that age [the fifteenth century] to the end of supreme art, an art which therefore embraced, incorporated science. Behind Alberti's view of painting there lodged, of course, the Platonic idea of Absolute Beauty whose rules and regulations were to be appropriated. An aesthetic, drunk with outwardness, blind to any psychological consideration, which would seem, if applied to present-day circumstance, either jejune or sterile, mystic at best, was the impression and the means in the early Renaissance of a sublime exuberance, of man's most comprehensive attempt to rule the universe with the least withdrawal from the world of the senses. In art it has eternity.'

language has an existence and mechanism of its own, that it can be turned into a quasi-mathematical system of cyphers. The radical situation for language is intercourse between two persons, an 'I-Thou' relation. The scientific convention starts by ignoring this relation. And (as John Macmurray has pointed out in a recent article), 'If the quest for a pure objectivity in statement could succeed, it would achieve a pure meaninglessness. A purely objective statement would have to be made by nobody to nobody.' [1]

*   *   *

In recent years—and especially in the work of I. A. Richards—much has been made of the distinction between 'emotive' and 'unemotive' language; and the rumour has got about that the language of poetry is emotive and the language of science is rigorously unemotive. We have seen that good writers of technical prose are at great pains to avoid rhetoric and to preclude an emotional response to their writing. All that this tells us, however, is that emotion is subversive of the scientific spirit. But emotion is dangerous currency in any sphere of life, and it does not follow that, because science seeks to be unemotive, poetry must be an affair of the emotions.

The trouble is that the term 'emotive' has not been closely enough examined. I have already suggested that emotion consists of 'free charges' of feeling—charges of feeling which are neither attached to images nor controlled by them. We have also seen that when words and images are abstracted and taken up into a conceptual process they lose the charge of perceptual feeling which is the stamp of value and reality. Charges of feeling, when firmly attached to images in a pattern, induce a minutely ordered response; 'free' emotions discharge at random. When language is not controlled by a finely articulated pattern of feeling, a reader or listener is at liberty to respond in an entirely personal manner, according to the accidents of his own memory, interests, and associations: that is, an *emotional* response is invited, a response not controlled by the context.[2] The technical

---

[1] John Macmurray, 'Some Reflections on the Analysis of Language', *Philosophical Quarterly*, vol. I (1951), 319–37.

[2] Suppose, for example, that in the course of a violin concerto the solo instrument makes noises like the bagpipes. A listener who has enjoyed an unhappy love affair in Scotland may be roused by this sound to indulge a personal reverie over his amatory experience. Yet the music itself has nothing to do with Scotland (I have Glazounov's violin concerto in mind)—and probably not with bagpipes either.

writer cannot tolerate such 'trigger-responses' of emotion: they can too easily distract attention from what is in any case almost impossible to read. Neither can the poet tolerate an uncontrolled emotional response; but he can at least be sure that a 'good' reader's responses will be controlled by the poem. The scientist knows that his writing cannot control the reader's response; all he can do is to remove as far as possible every occasion of emotional trigger-response.

Technical language may well then be called 'ideo-emotive'; for it starts with ideas and ends—if in any responsive feeling—in an emotive response. Good technical prose is finely enough controlled to submerge the emotive response; but the ideo-emotive use of language is most clearly revealed in bad scientific prose and in sentimental verse. Excessive abstraction and generalization can leave the emotive door open; and so can a failure precisely to clarify or embody feelings. Ideo-emotive language lends itself admirably to all kinds of specious persuasion—at law, in politics, in advertising, and all other forms of propaganda. The emotional appeal of scientific and pseudo-scientific terms has not been overlooked in advertising; nor has the power of vaguely hinted social, sexual, and cultural 'ideals'. Ideologies and utopian fantasies rely upon a carefully concealed structure of abstractions and are nourished by exploiting the vulgar response to a deliberately uncritical use of language. One of the primary social functions of language is not so much revelation as defence, concealment, and deception. The 'language of the market-place', seeking to evoke powerful emotional response for practical purposes, fights with bare fists, without any nice regard for subtle shades of feeling. Abstraction is one of its most powerful weapons. Mass hatred and mass adulation are best generated when the object of hatred or adulation is absent or not clearly seen—when it is abstracted. The most dangerous, because the most imprecise and explosive, use of language always springs from ideas and generates emotion. And since ideas are the raw material upon which the technical mind works, every expression of the technical way of mind is prone to uncontrolled emotional response. For this reason good scientific prose strives to eliminate every possibility of emotive response. And since the technical mind requires abstractions as its springboard, it turns in its perfection to increasing orders of refined abstraction. In the hands of all but a few subtle masters of language, it becomes etiolated, dry, unexciting; and when we do not hold a key to the abstract terms, it becomes inelegant and meaningless. The emotive use of language does not combine or confuse the technical with the poetic use of language: it perverts the technical use and derives its power from the technical bias of the 'ordinary' use of language. For the technical use of language, with its strong practical intension, has conditioned syntax to such a degree that only an extraordinary use of language will serve a contemplative purpose.

*   *   *

Poetry, I have maintained, preserves the primitive functions of language; technical prose represents the latest and most sophisticated degree of abstraction. The distinction between the ideo-emotive and the poetic use of language can be demonstrated historically. Language appears to have developed in three phases which may be called the mimetic, the poetic, and the emotive. In the 'mimetic' phase words are magical and representative: they stand almost in the relation of totems to the things they refer to; they carry within themselves something of the stuff of what they refer to and are not completely separated from them. (Imitative and onomatopoeic words belong to a later phase of abstraction.) To *name* an object, and to repeat that name, gives a magical power over the object. In the 'poetic' phase the first stage of abstraction has been accomplished. Particular objects are indicated in a vivid and 'feeling' manner by combining in simile and metaphor the 'mimetic' names which through erosion have lost both their clarity and their magical potency. In this second phase language recovers some of its magical quality. In the final 'ideo-emotive' phase abstraction is complete. Particular objects can be indicated in generic terms, and abstract qualities and relations can be expressed directly without reference to particular objects. These three historical phases—the first of which is only possible in the most primitive state of man—coincide with the three basic psychic organizations of mind: the 'instinctive', the 'contemplative', and the 'technical'.[1] From this it appears that the poetic

[1] I am indebted to Rémy de Gourmont for the term *'idéo-émotif'*. In *Le Problème de Style* he suggests that all writers can be classified either as *visuel* (poetic) or *idéo-émotif* I had, before finding this passage, conceived on linguistic and anthropological grounds that there were three historical phases in the whole process of achieving abstraction. Miss Emmet notices that Cassirer in his *Philosophie der symbolischen Formen* distinguishes the same three stages in the development of thought: these he calls 'Representative' (or 'Mimetic'), 'Analogic', and 'Symbolic' (but using the word 'symbolic' in its mathe-

use of language which arises from the contemplative mind, is to be understood directly in actual poems, and not as a modification of the prose use—whether technical or emotive. 'Words', Gabriel Marcel has observed, 'are essentially magical; it is in the nature of the word, as such, to evoke a presence. But we have to use words for practical purposes; so little by little this magical, evocative power of words tends to disappear. The function of poetry is that of restoring this very power to language, but the conditions in which it can be restored, today tend to become more and more hermetic.'

Technical prose, in satisfying a particular and clearly distinguishable attitude of mind, is able to convey ideas by using words as though they were self-contained nuggets of abstract meaning. But all the words in a language cannot be classified into two groups—one technical and the other poetic. Only in a period of imaginative debility can one believe that certain words and forms alone are proper to poetry: it is when vitality flags—in the individual or in a society—that formulae are allowed to substitute for discovery. The use of formulae in art is death; for all formulae are of the nature of ideas. Mallarmé once remarked to Degas that poetry is not made with *ideas* but with *words*. Every word carries some charge of feeling, even though in some cases the charge be subliminal; and every word can—theoretically at least—be made to carry a precise and complicated charge of feeling, provided the time is ripe and the writer can invent and control an appropriate context. The outstanding feature of poetic usage is that it explores and exploits the capacity words have for carrying precise and complicated charges of feeling. Poetry assumes and affirms the intimate personal character of language. The meaning of a poem is not what the *words* mean, but what the *poet* means—what the *I* at the centre of the poem means, speaking passionately to a *Thou*, to another person intimately engaged. Poetry is in some sort a succession of cries uttered out of 'the desolation of reality'. In poetry, words and images become vehicles for feelings: the feelings, under fastidious control, evoke inaccessible ranges of meaning thereby discovering the 'significance' and 'meaning' for the dominant passion. Poetry communicates; but the poet cannot be much concerned with the way his work will in fact communicate.

matical sense). At the present time this threefold division is a structural feature of the mind. It would be difficult to decide whether historical development has imposed this structure, or whether in interpreting the anthropological evidence we project that existing structure upon the subject-matter.

But the feeling-tone of a single word can only be controlled and determined by a particular context; it does not mean very much to talk about single words in isolation, because the number and quality of associations any single word may have for a single person is an accidental and personal matter. We need to ask then: what kind of contexts control our responsive feelings to language? What attitude of mind induces these contexts, and what attitude of mind gives access to a comprehensive range of these contexts?

*   *   *

Art is contemplative, springing from and ever turning towards the vital immediacy of a reality directly grasped. Science is technical, a means to predictable action—even though, as in theoretical thinking, action is indefinitely suspended; science springs from and ever turns towards abstraction. Art is concerned with uniqueness, science with generality. Art, by concentrating upon the individual luminous event, points implicitly to the fundamental values in a human experience. Science, by concentrating upon classes of events and ignoring value by technical convention, constructs conceptual categories as classes of similar events; it points towards abstract universals or 'laws', seeking a single analogy by which all physical events may be correlated and predicted. Art achieves accuracy by an increasing particularity, distinctness, clarity, which is constantly referred to reality. Science achieves accuracy by stages of increasing abstraction and generality, by farther and farther separation from a reality directly grasped. (The supreme accuracy and translatability of mathematics arises from a second degree of abstraction, one degree removed from empirical generalization.) Science proposes to show what 'things' and 'events' *are*: Art—adopting a less cursory view of metaphysics— is content to show what events and things *feel* like. Artistic writing is to 'make something' in writing, to 'write something': scientific writing is to 'write *about* something'. The wide chasm between these two ways of mind is revealed in the way they use language.

The technical mind imparts to language a distinctive pattern which is called 'Logic'.[1] The term is frequently taken to mean the pattern of 'reasoning' or of accurate thinking. The word 'logic' however is an elided form of the Hellenistic term ἡ λογικὴ τεχνή—the

---

[1] The way the meaning of 'Logos' has developed from its original magical sense to an exclusively technical sense is discussed in Chapter IX (pp. 179–80).

raft or *technique* of reasoning. The elision conceals a fact of which Aristotle himself was acutely aware: that logic is a means of *testing* one's thinking, but is not a direct representation of the *act* of thinking; logic does not represent every mental and psychic activity. Properly speaking the word 'logic' does not mean 'a principle of coherence'; it is an adjective limiting the term 'method' or 'technique'.

It may be supposed that when the contemplative mind expresses itself in language it will require a different mode of coherence from that used by the technical mind. The terms 'poetic logic' and 'logic of poetry' have been used to indicate the artistic mode of coherence. The coinage, however, is unhappy: the word 'logic' should not appear at all in these phrases—not because poets are incapable of reasoning, but because 'logic' indicates a way of mind and a syntax which are not proper to poetry and the contemplative mind. I shall therefore use the term *Poetic* (on the analogy of Logic—and there is good Aristotelean authority for it) to indicate 'the method of making relations in art'.

Poetic differs from Logic most markedly in this: it has no rules of procedure and never can have. Rules belong to the technical and not to the contemplative way of mind; rules can be applied only 'from outside', but Poetic must grow 'from within' and determine itself. Poetic is the precise opposite of the abstract. It is not governed by the law of non-contradiction because it moves within the world of reality, and reveals a moral universe where everything is related with everything else, where exclusive isolations are unreal. Poetic fashions itself to the integral mind when the mind seeks to grasp reality as a whole. Poetic is the mode of synthesis in which entities and events are grasped and 'expressed' as total, unified, dynamic, real. In each instance an appropriate congruity of form must be discovered by the poet—and incidentally by the reader. In Poetic there are similiarities of effect but no identities; for in reality every event is unique, and every poem arising out of an event of reality is unique. Among these unique events and poems certain abiding principles may be disclosed; but it is not the function of poetry to explain these generalities even though poetry may be a powerful instrument for pointing to them. Working from within the event of reality, Poetic establishes complex relationships which reveal events as uniquely occurring in a *person* with a vivid history. In this intricate task it works by suspension, by seeking and not by exposition: it embraces paradox, seeking it not as pairs of alternatives for choice, but as a fundamental antinomy in the structure of reality. Poetic works by tensions and collisions, by paradox and controlled ambiguity, by conflict harmony, and resonance: it goes beyond meaning without abandoning meaning, it fuses the individual elements of a poem without destroying their individual clarity; by a compulsive but deliberate forward movement it arrives at a stasis which is the contemplative expression of that movement.

Whereas ideas are the starting-point for Logic and the proposition its smallest articulate element, feeling is the starting-point for Poetic and the image (or metaphor) is its irreducible unit in language. A rough table of parallels would run something like this:

Contemplative Way of Mind	*Technical Way of Mind*
Poetic—process of articulation	Logic—process of articulation
Word—as charged with feeling, textured, related with other such words; uncontrolled if not in a context.	Term—as uncontrolled unit of abstract meaning.
Image (or Metaphor) Poem—as synthesis, embodied event of reality, self-determinate and self-bounded form, self-sustaining.	Proposition (or idea) Abstract diagram of 'conclusions' (which were implied by premisses), relying for its validity upon relations with previous conclusions and with analytic observations.
The question of 'truth' does not arise directly within the sphere of poetry.	The question of 'reality' does not arise; the question is begged or suppressed, or the answer assumed.
Inasmuch as Poetic expresses itself in verbal language, it submits to some extent to the syntax of language, which is predominantly technical. Other arts do not suffer this limitation.	

*   *   *

Owing to the dominance of the technical mind in the last three centuries the notion that Truth is necessarily connected with Logic has been widely dispersed. Plato, for purposes of argument, maintained that poetry was 'untrue'; and many critics and aestheticians have found no satisfactory ways of avoiding the conclusion that because art is illogical it must be some kind of make-believe. The difficulty arises over the question of coherence and permanence: the

ogically impregnable general proposition seems to have a permanent
validity which the lyrical poem cannot claim. Dr Johnson—that
great master of Common Sense—seeks to establish the authority of
poetry by rejecting whatever will not survive the test of philosophical
impregnability. 'Nothing can please many, and please long, but just
representations of general nature.' More than half-deaf, and more
than half-blind, his response limited almost entirely to the conceptual
aspects of poetry, Johnson does not surprise us with such a statement. But his statement is wrong, if by 'general truths' he means
universally valid propositions.[1]

A work of art may evoke, but does not refer to or rely upon,
abstract universals. In science, and most philosophy, nothing is of
interest except as an instance of a general proposition or a universal
principle. In art this relation of *particular* to *universal* is replaced by an
indirect relation of *individual* to *universal*; for in art an event or entity
is an end in itself, and is treated emphatically as unique, individual,
self-contained. As long as an event is in some sense 'real', it *can* be
referred to universals, and the expression arising out of that event
may be referred to universals; but it is not the function of art to do so.
And even for thought itself, is thought the only criterion? or should
we inquire into the genesis of particular thoughts to determine their
validity? 'The first condition of right thought is right sensation— . . .
if you have seen and felt truly, then if God has given you the power
you may be able to think rightly.' Can it be that this conviction of
Eliot's is informed by something more serious than a poet's professional bias? 'To think?' Valéry cries: 'To think! it is to lose the
thread.'

Let us consider an actual passage of poetry—some lines from
Shakespeare's *King John*.

[1] This is a quintessentially Johsonian statement. Compare these statements, also
in the Preface to Shakespeare: 'The mind can only repose on the stability of truth. . . .
His [Shakespeare's] characters . . . are the genuine progeny of common humanity, such
as the world will always supply, and observation will always find. . . . In the writings
of other poets a character is too often an individual; in those of *Shakespeare* it is commonly a species.' And again in the *Life of Cowley*: 'Great thoughts are always general,
and consist in positions not limited by exceptions, and in descriptions not descending
to minuteness. . . . Truth indeed is always truth, and reason is always reason; they
have an intrinsick and unalterable value, and constitute that intellectual gold which
defies destruction. . . . The diction of poetry, being the vehicle of thoughts, first
presents itself to the intellectual eye: and if the first appearance offends, a further knowledge is not often sought.'

Grief fills the room up of my absent child,
Lies in his bed, walks up and down with me,
Puts on his pretty looks, repeats his words,
Remembers me of all his gracious parts,
Stuffs out his vacant garments with his form;
Then have I reason to be fond of grief.
Fare you well: had you such a loss as I,
I could give better comfort than you do.—
I will not keep this form upon my head,
When there is such disorder in my wit.
O Lord! my boy, my Arthur, my fair son!
My life, my joy, my food, my all the world!
My widow-comfort, and my sorrows' cure! [1]

If obliged to classify this speech one would have to admit that it is an instance of grief. Yet as written, and as an *expression* of grief, it is not simply an *example* of grief in the same way that a battle is an instance of warlike behaviour. The poet has embodied in words, and has conveyed to the reader, the feeling-of-this-person (imagined) in this event (imagined), grieving; he has charged this with his own feeling for the person and for the event; and the reader knows directly from those lines what it is to grieve—even though he may never actually have lost a child nor ever have grieved in exactly that way. The lines convey the quality of the grief, its significance in an individual event, its value in a self-contained occasion. The more minutely and particularly the unique event is rendered, the more luminously it implies the universality of the universal (in this case, grief) by drawing the reader into a recreated event of reality. Poetry by a minute singularity shows the abstract universal in its universal character; philosophy or science shows it only in its general character. The value of the statement arises, not because it represents a genuine example of grief, but because it has made universally valid a single occasion of grieving. Remarking upon his method in writing *The Countess Cathleen* Yeats makes an observation which is very much to the point here: 'At first, if it [a play] has psychological depth, there is a bundle of ideas, something that can be stated in philosophical terms . . . but gradually philosophy is eliminated until at last the only philosophy audible if there is even that, is the mere expression of one character or another.'

[1] I am grateful to Professor Louis Arnaud Reid for suggesting this passage for illustration.

The uniqueness of the artistic event does not depend upon the minuteness with which the event is rendered, but upon its being apprehended as an event of reality. But the perpetual uniqueness of reality does not require that every event be isolated from every other event. If we imagine reality as moving and changing in time, it would not be like a railway train passing through a succession of stations in the night, but something like a comet flying through space with a huge tail streaming away behind it and a luminous antenna in front. Many philosophical problems of immortality and love are bedevilled by the tendency the mind has to transmute intense feelings or a sense of supreme value into terms of time.[1] For this reason the philosophy of Value is of the utmost importance to aesthetics and criticism: for Value occurs only when a *person* is engaged in an actual event of reality, and the *duration* of the event has no bearing upon the Value. Once an event of reality has been embodied in a work of art it is potentially accessible to anybody at any time: only in this sense has it universal value. But it is accessible as a live event which can be relived; unlike the general instance of an abstract universal it arises from, and is capable of reproducing, an event of value. And in the ever unique and transitory present of art the individual and universal are indissolubly fused; this is what St Thomas called *claritas*, the incandescent instant of vision and being.

[1] Coleridge scribbled a note on the back endpaper of his copy of Fichte's *Versuch einer Kritik aller Offenbarung* (1793): 'Intensity & Extensity combinable only by blessed spirits—Hence it is that Lovers in their finite state incapable of fathoming the intensity of their feelings *help* the thought *out* by extension, *commute* as it were—& thus think the passion as wide in *time* as it is deep in essence—Hence—*auf ewig dein* [thine forever]!'

A NOTE ON IMAGES AND IDEAS

To speak of images and ideas as different in kind is a convenience of language; in fact when we think of an image or an idea we are postulating an entity in order to describe a process. In the sense I have been using the terms, an image is a perceptual entity which is most clearly to be understood in artistic activity; an idea is a conceptual entity which is most clearly to be understood in analytical thinking. If an idea is introduced into poetic activity, it takes on something of the character of an image; and an image in technical activity will become an idea. The only evidence for the difference is the introspective accounts offered by persons who recognize and can distinguish between the two processes.

Paul Valéry's contrast between poetry and abstract thought (in one of the essays collected in *Variété V*) is worth quoting at length. Of 'poetic emotion' he writes: 'I, personally, find the sure sign of its presence in this fact—that all the phenomena of normal life, whether subjective or objective, people, events, feelings, actions, while remaining *seemingly* unchanged so far as outward appearance goes, become suddenly adjusted to the general modes of my sensitivity in a way that, though impossible to define, is extraordinarily precise. What I mean is, that all these perfectly familiar things and people—or rather, the ideas which represent them—in some way change their value. They become linked in an associative relationship quite different from that which obtains in the ordinary contacts of daily life. They become (if you will forgive the expression) *musicalized*. It is as though they affect one another with a mutual resonance of which harmony is the prime feature.' Valéry speaks of ideas changing their value: this is what I meant by saying that ideas alter their character when they enter into a culture of feeling, or into the poetic sphere. 'I have noticed that, at other times [that is, when the "poetic emotion" is not active], some incident, in itself just as insignificant, has caused —or seemed to cause—a mental excursion of a totally different kind, the cutting off of the thinking processes from their daily routine, but in a way that, both in nature and in result, is totally unlike the poetic impulse which I have just been describing. For example, some sudden association of ideas, some analogy, will lay seige to my awareness. I can describe it best by saying that it is like the sound of a horn heard deep in a forest. We catch it. We prick our ears. Our muscles are, as it were, orientated in an entirely new direction. They become concentrated on some one point in space hidden within the leafy vastness. But this time, what is born is not a poem, but an impulse to analyse the resultant intellectual ferment, and what emerges, more or less easily, while I remain in this state of mind, is not a set of verses, but some proposition which is destined, thence-forward, to form part of my mental make-up, some formula which will become an instrument to be used in the work of intellectual exploration.'

Two points may be emphasized in this description of abstract thought. (a) The attention is concentrated upon a distant point, upon the sound of the horn; this, and the word 'exploration' recalls the scientist's activity, as described in the analogy of the interface. (b) The outcome of the conceptual experience is the *analysis* of an *intellectual* ferment ending in a *formula*.

I cannot claim to have expended much energy or resource in collecting evidence for the difference between conceptual and poetic thinking. From my own experience I am convinced that the difference is much as Valéry describes it. But the difference is much less marked in the beginning of these processes than in their resolution. The word *analysis* meant to Aristotle 'loosening a knot', gently disentangling a compact and ravelled skein; for the starting-point even in philosophical thinking is not logical in form—is not linear, propositional, or discursive. I have been told by some philosophers that the starting-point for any of their discoveries has been an inscrut-able cluster which (as it were) explodes on analysis; many lines of implication develop outwards simultaneously and may for a long time conceal the point of entry from which all the threads can be brought into a linear relationship. Some lines in Donne's *Satyre III* apply equally to philosopher and poet:

> On a huge hill,
> Cragged, and steep, Truth stands, and hee that will
> Reach her, about must, and about must goe;
> And what the hills suddennes resists, winne so.[1]

---

[1] Donne is here describing the mental process of discovery and not simply observing that truth is hard to come by: the lines immediately preceding show this.

> To adore, or scorne an image, or protest,
> May all be bad; doubt wisely; in strange way

One man, whose response to poetry is invariably a series of distinct coloured eidetic images, has told me that, when he studied philosophy, abstract notions and ideas also presented themselves to him as eidetic images and patterns. I am able to quote part of a letter written to him by the late W. G. de Burgh. 'It's curious what you say about having to translate all your thoughts into imagery. . . . I was talking with a great physiologist and doctor . . . of the difference between conceptual and image thinking. I scarcely ever visualize anything clearly, and find it always (or nearly always) an effort to translate poetry when I read it into images. He is just the reverse, though a man of Science. Now I'm sure you can conceive this very different type of mind, that thinks conceptually despite the contrast with your own.' [1] These instances are examples of an exclusive response: a poet and 'a man of Science' responding in a sensory manner to concepts, and a conceptual thinker failing to respond in a sensory manner to poetry. But Valéry experienced both kinds of thinking, and his sensitive discrimination between them affords impressive evidence that the distinction between image and idea is valid as well as useful.

To stand inquiring right, is not to stray;
To sleepe, or runne wrong is.

Compare Matthew Arnold's statement (*Essays in Criticism: Second Series*): 'But excellence is not common and abundant; on the contrary, as the Greek poet [which one?] long ago said, excellence dwells among rocks hardly accessible, and a man must almost wear his heart out before he can reach her.'

[1] From a letter of 23 December 1938; printed by kind permission of Mrs W. G. de Burgh and the addressee.

VIII

Metaphor

Pour le vrai poète, la langue n'est jamais assez particulière; il est obligé d'employer les mots en les répétant pour les délivrer de leur sens usuel, usé, trop général et pour leur conférer cette signification unique, évocatrice d'une seule réalité spirituelle très concrète, à quoi il veut atteindre.

ALBERT BÉGUIN

THE poet's task, in composing a poem, is to discover and fashion in words an equivalent for the complex state of feeling and awareness which accompanies paradeigmatic experience. He must give a precise body to those feelings; he is not concerned to *describe* either the feelings or the physical objects with which those feelings may have been historically associated. In making his poem, however, the poet cannot translate the components of feeling one by one into a sort of point-for-point replica of his state of consciousness. The technical use of language shows that—within certain limits—it is possible to transliterate components of 'meaning'; but then the pattern is imposed in such a way that the 'I–Thou' relation, essential to the transfer of feeling, is destroyed. The translation from visual to verbal in poetry, from the paradeigmatic event to 'the cold dropped pebbles of painless verse', involves a total change from one system of relations to another. Furthermore the congruity of a poem depends upon its finding a self-determinate form; although poetry moves within the ambit of normal syntax, its emergent form can dominate syntax and distort it to its own image.

The poem, in one of its characters, is what Eliot has called the 'objective correlative' of a state of feeling: 'A set of objects, a situation, a chain of events which shall be a formula of that *particular* emotion; such that when the external facts, which must terminate in sensory experience, are given, the emotion is immediately evoked.' [1] Let us suppose that within the unity of a poem we may distinguish smaller units which are objective correlatives of 'pieces of feeling'. When these units are suitably articulated, the poet has exhausted a particular state of feeling and has constructed a poem.

Strong feeling is dangerous currency in ordinary life because it is usually emotional: emotion is difficult to control, difficult to organize, and difficult to discharge in a socially appropriate manner. When it passes by way of the normal practical attitude into 'action' or 'ordinary language' the strength of the feeling is discharged, the tension is released, but the feeling has lost both distinctness and complexity. The poet who is by nature contemplative—'not a man of action' as Yeats puts it—feels that it is a self-betrayal to discharge strong feeling in an indiscriminate action or utterance. By transferring portions of his feelings to the words and images with which they have associated in his memory and imagination, the poet prevents the feelings from attenuating and eroding; he sustains the state of feeling until it is fully developed and has discovered itself fully to him. Furthermore he can organize and develop the state of feeling fully only by embodying it precisely; indeed the critical activity in composition is an essential phase in realizing the feeling. [2]

---

[1] T. S. Eliot, 'Hamlet', in *Selected Essays*. F. O. Matthiessen, in Chapter III of *The Achievement of T. S. Eliot* (1947), discusses Eliot's doctrine of the objective correlative at some length. Eliot here uses the word 'emotion' in the ambiguous sense which I have tried to avoid. Ezra Pound has stated that 'Poetry is a sort of inspired mathematics, which gives . . . equations for the human emotions' (*The Spirit of Romance*, p. 5). In such a statement the word *inspired* plays the same ambiguous role as the word 'glorified' in Stoll's remark that *The Ancient Mariner* is 'the ballad of tradition, though glorified'.

[2] The transmutation is probably never complete; there is always an untranslatable residue. This no doubt explains how poems and even novels tend to be written in families, as a series of approximations to a recurrent complex of feeling. Marlowe for example writes in *Tamburlaine*:

> If these had made one poem's period,
> And all combin'd in beauty's worthiness,
> Yet should there hover in their restless heads
> One thought, one grace, one wonder, at the least,
> Which into words no virtue can digest.

Cf. also Thomas Mann, *Lotte in Weimar*: 'All together, the world even of so mighty

Images, being vehicles of feeling, are energetic and in combination form rhythmic patterns. One could say in jargon that an image is a *feeling-vector*: not only is it the vehicle for a 'charge' of feeling, but it also has directional character—it seeks to move in a certain direction. These vectorial characteristics, which are attained in reality, in the act of cognitive perception, combine (figuratively speaking) to produce a resultant which *is* the rhythm.[1] The flow of related and conflicting images in a poem makes it possible for the poet to convey very accurately and vividly the interwoven patterns of paradeigmatic feeling. The complexity of the feeling, and the need for a succession of articulated images to convey that complexity, prevents the poem from crystallizing into a single word. The separate 'particles of feeling' can be sustained in patterned distinctness as long as they retain their sensory character as images; otherwise the feelings flow together into an energetic but imprecise resultant of emotion to produce sentimentality. The way word-images can become sensitive vehicles of feeling without collapsing into conceptual abstraction is indicated by Whitehead (*Symbolism* (1928)).

'Mankind also uses a more artificial symbolism, obtained chiefly by concentrating on a certain selection of sense-perceptions such as words for example. In this case, there is a chain of derivations of symbol from symbol whereby finally the local relations, between the final symbols and the ultimate meanings, are entirely lost. Thus these derivative symbols, obtained as it were by arbitrary association, are really the results of reflex action suppressing the intermediate portions of the chain. . . . Mankind by means of its elaborate system of symbolic transference can achieve miracles of sensitiveness to a distant environment, and to a problematic future.'

I shall now maintain that metaphor is the means by which feelings can be fused without losing their individual clarity; that metaphor is the fundamental mode for transmuting feelings into words; that

---

a spirit as Goethe, however spacious it is, is a closed world, existing within limits. It is a unit, where the motifs repeat themselves and the same presentation recurs at large intervals of time.' And Yeats remarks: 'I have spent my life saying the same things in many different ways.'

[1] Compare A. N. Whitehead's observation: 'Life is complex in its expression, involving more than percipience, namely desire, emotion, will, and feeling. It exhibits variations of grade, higher and lower, such that the higher grade presupposes the lower for its very existence. This suggests a closer identification of rhythm as the casual counterpart of life; namely, that wherever there is some rhythm there is some life, only perceptible to us when the analogies are sufficiently close.'

metaphor is the process by which the internal relationships peculiar to poetry are established.

★   ★   ★

Aristotle asserted that, for the poet, 'the greatest thing by far is to have a command of metaphor. This alone cannot be imparted by another; it is the mark of genius—for to make good metaphors implies an eye for resemblances.' Why should metaphor be singled out for such special attention? Is it not merely one of many kinds of 'figures of speech'?

In the last thirty years or so metaphor has been very narrowly examined and has served as excuse for many a subtle theory of ambiguity, paradox, and irony. But the standard dictionaries still follow Aristotle in describing it as 'the figure of speech in which a name or descriptive term is transferred to some object to which it is not properly applicable'.[1] 'Not properly applicable' in what terms? In logic? But logic belongs to the technical way of mind, not to the contemplative; and perhaps we may find in metaphor a clue to the principles of Poetic. For, as Coleridge learned, poetry has 'a logic of its own, as severe as that of science; and more difficult, because more subtle, more complex, and dependent on more and more fugitive causes'. But can we conceivably take for the fundamental principle in Poetic a figure of speech which makes improper attributions? Perhaps the dictionaries have not well defined the term.

Rémy de Gourmont, in *Le Problème du Style* (1902), expressed the view that primitive language was originally denotative and unmetaphorical; and that when primitive denotative words became eroded by use, metaphor emerged to restore the pristine clarity of language.[2] In these matters he was mistaken, for lack of anthropo-

---

[1] Aristotle's definition in the *Poetics* reads: 'Metaphor is the application of an alien name by transference either from genus to species, or from species to genus, or from species to species, or by analogy, that is, proportion.' Aristotle's high regard for metaphor is tempered by the specificity of this definition, and also by a passage in his next chapter: ' . . . if we take a strange (or rare) word, a metaphor, or any similar mode of expression, and replace it by the current or proper term, the truth of our observation will be manifest' (Trans. S. H. Butcher).

[2] He traces the emergence of metaphor from its absence in Homer and the Romance Cycles of Europe to its use by Flaubert. Since de Gourmont's time anthropological and other evidence has established (a) that the mark of primitive expression is not simplicity but complication; and (b) that the Homeric poems and Romance Cycles

logical and linguistic evidence. Primitive experience and expression are not simple but complicated. And metaphor—like many other features of the poetic mentality—is primal and primitive. Metaphor is complex because it renders the complexity of reality; primitive man grasps reality comprehensively because he does not know any more limited or protective way of apprehending the world around him. Primitive man is 'immersed in reality': he evolves the trick of abstraction in self-defence. But reality is still the source of life, no matter what attitude we may adopt towards it; and every determined attempt to grasp reality is a return—or advance—to the prelogical mentality, which is primitive but not barbaric.[1] Jacques Maritain states this point vividly in *Art and Scholasticism* (1933).

'In the youth of language, words were pregnant with such a terrible, magical and magnificent power. The powerfully metaphysical instinct of primitive man might go astray in particular applications; it still bore witness to the symbolic nature and to that astounding mystery bestowed upon the human race, of being able *to give* things *names*. But words are not pure symbols ("formal symbols"), they are imperfect symbols which become quickly loaded with subjectivity, each dragging after it the whole psychological stuff of a race. In particular a prolonged social use tends of itself to make them lose their spirituality, their symbolic nature, to change them into *things* of value in themselves, letting off mental reactions without the intervention of any meaning; the less intervention of fact, the more reaction.'

In the present state of Western civilization, most single words point to ideas rather than to images. A word is abstracted and referred to a class, a type, a category, or a group of remembered abstractions; a word seldom evokes a distinct feeling or an eidetic image (the image,

---

belong to an advanced stage of civilization. Otto Jespersen, for example, writes in *Language: Its Nature, Development and Origin* (1933): 'Primitive language had no great store of ideas, and if we consider it as an instrument for expressing thoughts, it was clumsy, unwieldy and ineffectual; but what did that matter? Thoughts were not the first things to press forward and crave for expression; emotions and instincts were more primitive and far more powerful. . . . The genesis of language is not to be sought in the prosaic, but in the poetic side of life; the source of speech is not gloomy seriousness, but merry play and youthful hilarity. . . . Language was born in the courting days of mankind.'

[1] This view of the origin of metaphor is discussed with approval in a review of G. Révész, *Ursprung und Vorgeschichte der Sprache* (1948), in the *Times Literary Supplement* (3 July 1948).

actually before the eyes, of an object not physically present). Few adults can achieve eidetic imagery, though most children seem to enjoy it; and in any case eidetic responses are not what a poet strives to induce. Poetry seeks to convey the force, simplicity, and immediacy of direct perception; for only in this way can feelings be conveyed precisely and in a complex form.

Since few single words now make an immediate and particular impact, metaphor arises—in ordinary speech as well as in poetry—as a concentrated means of making words clear or startling. This however is only the decorative or *pointing* use of metaphor: metaphor as a figure of speech, a grace of clarity proper to description: without loss of meaning we might conceivably (as Aristotle suggests) 'replace it by a current or proper form'. A wilted word can be refreshed by the cold water of an illogical connection; but there is logic in illogicality. The pointing metaphor is at best an inert instance of metaphor; it lacks the power of self-evident revelation for which the primitive metaphor is peculiar.[1] Given an extensive vocabulary and a lively wit anybody can evolve decorative and descriptive metaphors; but metaphor at its most fully developed—that is, in its truly poetical and primitive kind, as a dynamic verbal relation of *four* terms—this cannot be contrived by formula or applied by rote. Every poet, and every generation of poets, has to rediscover afresh the peculiar nature of metaphor; for it is the life-blood of poetry.

T. E. Hulme, then, misstated the case for poetry when he asserted that 'the great aim is accurate, precise and definite description'. And Middleton Murry has followed him into this error. 'Metaphor', he says in The Problem of Style (1930), 'is the result of the search for a precise epithet.' His position is not quite as vulnerable as Hulme's,

---

[1] Poets are well described as the 'antennae of civilization'. Any general social tendency towards persistent abstraction erodes the clarity of language. The consequent demand for clearer expression will stimulate decorative metaphor and fortify the primitive metaphorical use proper to the contemplative mind. Chaucer was able to use language almost wholly unadorned and unmetaphorical. The Elizabethan conceit is a reaction to humanist rationalism: the 'Romantic' poetry of the early nineteenth century is a reaction from Augustan rationalism in poetry and the social rationalism of the *Aufklärung*. The Victorians failed to react away from contemporary abstractions into rediscovering the metaphysical nature of poetry; this is the mark of their debility. But Hopkins achieved it and is therefore the most characteristic (though most individual) figure of his time. In this century the force of arrogant rationalism in a fragmented society has encouraged a conceited and allusive verse; and at the same time an unparalleled erosion of language has occurred through vulgarized education, propaganda and calculated imprecision.

but when he attempts to extend his account he describes, not the primitive metaphor, but the descriptive or 'pointing' metaphor. 'Try to be precise, and you are bound to be metaphorical: you simply cannot help establishing affinities between all the provinces of the animate and inanimate world: for the volatile essence you are trying to fix is quality, and in that effort you will inevitably find yourself ransacking heaven and earth for a similitude.'

But what is to be described? and what is the object of this precise epithet? Description is a matter for science, not for art. And science assumes as one of the rules of its games that an object *can* be described in isolation, separated from its human relations and from most of its physical relations too. Description in that style cannot serve the poet —even though a good many self-styled poets have indulged a taste for it. The poet's concern is to embody the feeling of reality. Reality is immersion or relationship; for a person, relationship is feeling; and complex feeling can only be embodied—and clarified and revealed —through the hitherto unrealized connections in things. Metaphor comes into the poet's hand ready-made from his grasp of reality. Baudelaire remarked how 'In certain states of the soul, the profound significance of life is revealed completely in the spectacle, however commonplace, that is before one's eyes: it becomes the symbol of this significance.' The poet does not describe merely 'the spectacle . . . that is before his eyes': he must describe it as the significant-symbolical spectacle before his eyes; he must convey, gather up into words, body forth the *feel* of the thing, as of value to him at this particular moment, and as somehow eternally valuable. And that cannot be achieved by 'accurate, precise and definite description' nor even by finding precise epithets.

Herbert Read, in *English Prose Style* (1942), admirably describes metaphor as 'the swift illumination of an equivalence'. 'Two images, or an idea and an image, stand equal and opposite; clash together and respond significantly, surprising the reader with a sudden light.' [1] His terms are not used in precisely the same sense as my own; but this passage emphasizes some valuable features of the process of metaphor—the notions of tension, collision, resonance, shock,

---

[1] It should be noticed, however, that the fully developed metaphor (the prototype) is a figure, *not* of two terms, but of *four* terms welded by a vigorous verb. Aristotle (*Poetics* XXI) is quite clear about this. 'The sun sows the light' = 'The sun scatters light the way a sower scatters seed.' This definition of metaphor prevents us from thinking that a metaphor is merely a simile with the word 'like' or 'as' omitted.

illumination. Metaphor establishes a relation between things not normally (logically) connected; thereby it illuminates a fresh relation between the metaphorical image and the poet, and in turn between the image and the reader. But the influence of metaphor is not confined to illuminating only the terms it brings into collision. It can strike out a fresh image which cannot be produced in any more elementary way—an image which is not the sum of its elements nor their identity but one which grows to its individual form by a process of mutual enrichment, the elements of the metaphor cross-fertilizing each other.[1]

*　　　*　　　*

Sensory clarity is a part of what Legouis has called 'the vibration of our consciousness in our relations with things'; and metaphor—at the lowest range of its capacity—renders visual clarity by drawing unexpected sensory relations.

> . . . *bright chanticleer explodes the night*
> *With flutt'ring wings*
>
> (CHRISTOPHER SMART)

> *Mark where the pressing wind shoots javelin-like,*
> *Its skeleton shadow on the broad-back'd wave!*
>
> (GEORGE MEREDITH)

---

[1] Dylan Thomas has described how this process of collision operates in his own practice.

'I make one image—though "make" is not the word; I let, perhaps, an image be "made" emotionally in me and then apply to it what intellectual and critical forces I possess; let it breed another, let that image contradict the first; make of the third image, bred out of the other two together, a fourth contradictory image, and let them all, within my imposed formal limits, conflict. Each image holds within it the seed of its own destruction, and my dialectical method, as I understand it, is a constant building up and breaking down of the images that come out of the central seed, which is itself destructive and constructive at the same time . . . The life in any poem of mine cannot move concentrically round a central image, the life must come out of the centre; an image must be born and die in another; and any sequence of my images must be a sequence of creations, recreations, destructions, contradictions . . . Out of the inevitable conflict of images . . . I try to make that momentary peace which is a poem.'

One hesitates to generalize from a single account, especially when written by a controversial contemporary poet: but it offers a suggestive illustration. For an analysis of this image-dialectic in Thomas's *After the Funeral* and in Hopkins's *Harry Ploughman*, see Day Lewis, *The Poetic Image*, pp. 123–8. But for a derogatory view of the method, see Geoffrey Grigson, 'How much me now your acrobatics amaze', in *The Harp of Aeolus* (1947 for 1948).

. . . the proud nostril-curve of a prow's line

(ROBERT BRIDGES)

According to Eliot's formula the internal images of a poem 'must terminate in sensory experience'. In these examples of 'pointing' metaphor the images clearly start from and terminate in sensory experience. And even when one of the elements of the metaphor is personified, the pointing metaphor still generates a predominantly sensory colour.

> *. . . the morn in russet mantle clad*
> *Walks o'er the dew of yon high eastward hill*

> *. . . the worshipp'd sun*
> *Peer'd forth the golden window of the east*
(SHAKESPEARE)

> *. . . the hazles form a rank,*
> *And court'sy to the courting breeze*
(SMART)

In the pointing metaphor the effect is (as it were) condensed upon a single object—the bird of dawning, the wind-driven shadows, the sheer of a clipper bow, the morning, the sun, the hazel trees. There is a concentrated clarity but the influence does not spread outward. And this is the legitimate ground for Johnson's complaint against Cowley: it was not so much that his images were far-fetched and logically incongruous but that each image was condensed upon itself; its influence did not embrace or engulf the whole poem (as Donne's imagery for example does). Not recognizing clearly enough the reason for his dissatisfaction, Johnson generalized upon the Metaphysical poets at large; they 'wrote rather as *beholders* than partakers of human nature'; their wish was 'only to say what they hoped had been never said before'; they 'lay on the watch for novelty'; 'their attempts were always *analytick*; they *broke every image into fragments*'. Much poetry of this century suffers from this same defect—an isolated brilliance of single images which fails to illuminate the whole passage or poem.[1] Even though the reality given in experience may

---

[1] Some of C. Day Lewis's poetry is remarkable in this way, despite the brilliance of such a conceit as:

> *Admiral earth breaks out his colours*
> *Bright at the forepeak of the day.*

147

be fragmentary and evanescent, art can reveal that reality only by
arriving at the integrity which is the primal aspect of reality. In
Jubilate Agno Christopher Smart proclaimed: 'My talent is to give
an impression upon words by punching, that when the reader casts
his eye upon 'em, he takes up the image from the mould which I
have made.' The 'punched' and 'moulded' word express well the
acuity of direct images of sense beyond which Smart with his
'infinite capacity for astonishment' seldom advanced; but it cannot
account for the brooding evocativeness which in poetry secures that
integrity.

The pointing metaphor makes for intense clarity, but a clarity
somehow visual, static, and sterile. The full process of metaphor—
the 'ringing' metaphor as I shall call it—makes for resonance, a
pervasive *tone* which spreads outward in rings of sound and light to
bring into sympathetic vibration other or all features of the poem.¹
Poetry is incorrigibly sensory, yet the end of poetry is not merely
sensory experience. One of Gerard Manley Hopkins's biographers
has stated this neatly by saying that the 'divination of the spiritual in
the things of sense, which also will express themselves in the things
of sense, is what we properly call poetry'. 'Ringing' metaphors have
a noticeable trans-sensory character, and even when removed from
their setting evoke something beyond sensory response.

> My soul . . .
> There like a bird it sits, and sings
> Then whets and claps its silver wings
>
> > (MARVELL)
>
> The holy time is quiet as a nun
> Breathless with adoration
>
> > (WORDSWORTH)
>
> . . . the nunnery
> Of thy chaste breast and quiet mind
>
> > (LOVELACE)
>
> I shall ebbe out with them, who home-ward goe
>
> > (DONNE)

¹ Throughout this discussion I have simultaneously in mind two meanings of
resonance: (*a*) Sympathetic vibration: *e.g.*, when you shout into the undamped strings
of a piano the sound continues to reverberate in the strings; (*b*) When two oscillating
objects or currents come into phase with each other the amplitude (height) of the
oscillations is reinforced and in favourable conditions will increase steadily. This

n the Marvell passage—which curiously anticipates Yeats's manner
—and in the Wordsworth lines, the identity of the metaphorical
erms is 'dissolved, diffused, and dissipated': the soul becomes a bird,
he time becomes breathless; the resonant tone spreads forward into
he word 'holy', and echoes in the words 'whets' and 'silver'. In some
nstances the tone is compelling enough to bring into resonance a
equence of 'broken images'.

> To-morrow, and to-morrow, and to-morrow,
> Creeps in this petty pace from day to day,
> To the last syllable of recorded time;
> And all our yesterdays have lighted fools
> The way to dusty death. Out, out, brief candle!
> Life's but a walking shadow; a poor player,
> That struts and frets his hour upon the stage,
> And then is heard no more: it is a tale
> Told by an idiot, full of sound and fury,
> Signifying nothing.
>
> (SHAKESPEARE)

> Soaring through wider zones that prick'd his scars
> With memory of the old revolt from Awe,
> He reach'd a middle height, and at the start,
> Which are the brain of heaven, he look'd, and sank.
> Around the ancient track march'd, rank on rank,
> The army of unalterable law.
>
> (MEREDITH)

There is no limit to the scope of poetic resonance. 'We should
avoid making two inconsistent metaphors meet on one object'; this is
Lindley Murray's common-sense eighteenth-century advice. Yet most
metaphors are logically *in*consistent; and in Poetic the most out-
rageous inconsistencies can be the most characteristic, and often
secure the most powerful effects. In Poetic there is only one test: it
must 'work', it must 'fit'; every element must drop inevitably and
finally into place to fulfil a purpose which is not fully known until
it is fulfilled.

A successful 'mixed metaphor' seems not so much to clarify
('point') the single image as to establish a certain 'tone'. The bemused

---

sense of resonance plays an important part in the theory of tides and has also been
invoked to explain the origin of the solar system.

astonishment of the drunken reapers in *The Tempest*, hearing the sound of Ariel's tabor, is rendered by an obvious disorientation of the senses:

> *. . . like unback'd colts, they prick'd their ears,*
> *Advanced their eyelids, lifted up their noses*
> *As they smelt music.*

Hamlet's violent desperation is conveyed by a wrenched incongruity

> *Whether 'tis nobler in the mind to suffer*
> *The slings and arrows of outrageous fortune,*
> *Or to take arms against a sea of troubles,*
> *And by opposing end them?—*

When Thomas Sturge Moore tells how Don Juan in middle age is carried home dead from his courting at a nunnery window, the shock of the metaphor springs from the grotesque evocation of Don Quixote's perplexity.

> *Dull brown a cloak enwraps, Don Juan,*
> *Both thy lean shanks, one arm,*
> *That old bird-cage thy breast, where like magpie*
> *Thy heart hopped on alarm.*

*   *   *

When I drew the distinction between the contemplative and technical ways of mind, I made much of the fact that the data for Poetic were perceptual and charged with feeling, and that the data for Logic were conceptual, abstract, and uncharged. Poetic, however, is not restricted to perceptual words and obliged to avoid abstract words. Poetic can make any word or group of words sensory; it can give them charges of feeling by controlling their aural and tactile qualities. Generally speaking, an exclusive use of sensory words belongs to description and produces an opaque and unresonant effect. Consider these lines from Shakespeare.

> *I know a bank where the wild thyme blows,*
> *Where oxlips and the nodding violet grows;*
> *Quite over-canopied with lush woodbine,*
> *With sweet musk-roses, and with eglantine:*
> *There sleeps Titania sometime of the night,*

Lull'd in these flowers with dances and delight;
And there the snake throws her enamell'd skin,
Weed wide enough to wrap a fairy in:
And with the juice of this I'll streak her eyes,
And make her full of hateful fantasies.

There is more of Poetic in the last four words than in the nine lines that precede them. And when Shakespeare speaks most memorably of Cleopatra he makes his appeal only obliquely to the senses, and ends with an impudent whiplash of irony.

But most startling perhaps of all is the genuinely metaphorical character of some passages in which the words say exactly what they mean, refer quite explicitly to what they say, and are in no evident way figurative or allusive. Consider a passage of Donne that Ben Jonson singled out for especial admiration:

No use of lanthornes; and in one place lay
Feathers and dust, to day and yesterday.

Or a section from Donne's *The second Anniversarie:*

Heaven is as neare, and present to her face,
As colours are, and objects, in a roome
Where darknesse was before, when Tapers come.

Or these anonymous lines:

Christ, that my love were in my arms,
And I in my bed again.

Or Donne's astonishing phrase—

A bracelet of bright haire about the bone.

A whole passage otherwise conventional may spring into sudden incandescence by the collision of two words not in themselves remarkable.

The glories of our blood and state
Are shadows, not substantial things;
There is no armour against fate;
Death lays his icy hand on kings:
Sceptre and Crown
Must tumble down,

And in the dust be equal made
With the poor crooked scythe and spade.

(SHIRLEY)

My Love is of a birth as rare
As 'tis for object strange and high:
It was begotten by despair
Upon Impossibility.

(MARVELL)

In Poetic, even the personal centre may suddenly shift, without any warning.

So I would have had him leave,
So I would have had her stand and grieve,
So he would have left
As the soul leaves the body torn and bruised,
As the mind deserts the body it has used.
I should find
Some way incomparably light and deft. . . .

(ELIOT)

In Poetic too, words may be endowed with texture—roughness, smoothness, jagged or intricate outlines. This is controlled by the clusters of consonants, and sometimes even (I believe) by the optical effect of the shapes and arrangement of letters. Words and phrases can make gestures of motion and sound. But it is by the sensitive control of vowel sounds that the quality of passionate or brooding song enters: this is often the dominant factor in establishing and modulating the tone of a poem.[1] All or several of these forces operate in Shakespeare's phrases: 'the dark backward and abysm of

---

[1] 'Tone' is not simply a detached musical or technical feature of poetry: it also projects the person of the poet in two senses, showing at once his 'style' or 'fineness' and his attitude towards life. Valéry remarks upon the sonic aspect of this double self-revelation. 'The "tone" of an author is the leading thing. We see at once by the tone whom he is addressing: whether he pictures an unthinking audience, a crowd, a superficial boy who must be dazzled, stunned, stirred—or a defiant individual hard to get into—or one of those light-profound people that let everything be said, that welcome, seize, shoot ahead, but quickly annul all that was written. Some, one might say, never dream of the silent response of their reader. They write for creatures that gape. . . . The man, the poet that gives in the most to the unconscious, that finds therein his vigour and his "truth", always counts more and more on the stupidity of his reader' (*Note-Book B1910*).

ime', 'the fierce vexation of a dream', 'Hard-handed men . . . have
oiled their unbreathed memories'; and in the lines

> Most true it is that I have lookt on truth
> Askance and strangely.

And in various ways these forces can give sensory character to
bstract words, or impart an exact shade of solemn gaiety.

> When as in silks my Julia goes
> Then, then (methinks) how sweetly flows
> That liquefaction of her clothes.
>> (HERRICK)

> I love thee to the level of each day's
> Most quiet need, by sun and candle-light.
>> (ELIZABETH BROWNING)

> Her feet beneath her petticoat,
> Like little mice, stole in and out,
> As if they feared the light.
>> (SUCKLING)

> Age cannot wither her, nor custom stale
> Her infinite variety: other women cloy
> The appetites they feed; but she makes hungry
> Where most she satisfies: for vilest things
> Become themselves in her; that the holy priests
> Bless her when she is riggish.

And some of the most profound effects in poetry have been achieved
with words which are, in the prose sense, entirely 'abstract'.

> And I have felt
> A presence that disturbs me with the joy
> Of elevated thoughts; a sense sublime
> Of something far more deeply interfused,
> Whose dwelling is the light of setting sun,
> And the round ocean and the living air,
> And the blue sky, and in the mind of man:
> A motion and a spirit, that impels
> All thinking things, all objects of all thought,
> And rolls through all things.

n such cases thought can be rendered (as George Eliot has said in

Middlemarch) 'with that distinctness which is no longer reflection bu
feeling—an idea wrought back to the directness of sense, like th
solidity of objects'. 'Abstract' words endowed with sensory qualitie
—of sound, of texture, of feeling—make a 'thought' which is no
Logic but Poetic. But within these thought-images the interplay o
sensory and 'abstract' can establish exquisite interfaces which, lik
the lips, transmit tingling shocks of acute sensation.

> *What is he whose grief*
> *Bears such an emphasis; whose phrase of sorrow*
> *Conjures the wandering stars, and makes them stand?*
>
> (SHAKESPEARE)

> *The Host with someone indistinct*
> *Converses at the door apart,*
> *The nightingales are singing near*
> *The Convent of the Sacred Heart,*
>
> *And sang within the bloody wood*
> *When Agamemnon cried aloud,*
> *And let their liquid siftings fall*
> *To stain the stiff dishonoured shroud.*
>
> (ELIOT)

★   ★   ★

My purpose so far in this chapter has been to show the integrativ
or 'resonant' action of metaphor and to indicate that this is the proto
type of Poetic. Since the process is in all its aspects a process o
synthesis, and its mode of articulation an embracing rather than a
discriminating one, our purpose is not well served by attempting to
classify varieties of metaphor. Indeed any classification of metapho
must be arbitrary, because metaphor is a fusing process which arrive
at total assertion by obliterating all the distinctions upon which a
system of classification might rest. The distinction between 'pointing
and 'ringing' metaphor is not properly a classification at all. It is an
attempt to separate out the metaphorical process which will revea
most clearly the basic articulation of Poetic. The 'pointing' meta
phor is a middle term between Poetic and Logic, in the same way
that Fancy (in Coleridge's use of the term) stands midway between
Imagination and Common Sense. Once it is possible to concentrat

upon metaphor as a process—upon 'ringing' metaphor—some important features of Poetic begin to emerge.

The end of metaphor is not acute *visual* clarity, nor even is it intense sensory clarity: it is a process in which words and images are made incandescent and resonant. When Rimbaud said, 'Il s'agit d'arriver à l'inconnu par le dérèglement de tous les sens', he uttered more than the technical manifesto of a school of poetry: this is the essence of Poetic. Although the terms of Poetic must have sensory character, metaphor disorients the individual senses so that they excite and fertilize each other. In this way Poetic establishes a novel interpenetration of thought and feeling, and—through the interinanimation of sound, rhythm, meaning, and sensory qualities—evokes complex meanings and paradoxical implications. In Poetic, sight can be converted into sound and texture and even scent; single words can assume physical shape, contour, fibre; groups of words may take on meanings not implied by their grammatical relations; savour, aroma, cachet may be conveyed in texture and rhythm. All this occurs in the transmuting crucible of feeling; the mouth of that crucible is the ear.[1]

This is what one would expect. The eye is the organ of abstraction,

[1] Paul Valéry states a different view in his *Introduction to the Method of Leonardo Da Vinci* (1894). 'The sense of sight', he remarks in a note on the limited perceptions of the 'ordinary man', 'seems to me more spiritual than the others. Visual images predominate in the mind. It is in relation to them that the faculty of analogy is most frequently exercised. . . . The form and colour of an object are so obviously primary that they enter into the conception of it formed by one of the other senses. If one speaks of the hardness of iron, it is nearly always the visual image, rarely an auditory one, that is produced.'

This, it seems to me, is an unsupported generalization: I for one first hear and feel —not see—the hardness of iron. And when he says that form and colour are 'so obviously primary' he is thinking of the abstracted and differentiated 'thing', which by being abstracted is already shifted into the mode of seeing. Analogy again, which is essentially an abstractive operation in Logic and not in Poetic, the forming of a spatial diagram out of abstracted elements, is also in the mode of sight and proves nothing about the 'spirituality' of the sense of sight. *Visual* images predominate in the mind because they are visual *images*; but in my view the mind and memory are more numerously and energetically charged with sensory elements—and verbal elements— which have no visual quality whatsoever until we attempt to isolate or analyse them and so shift them into the mode of visuality.

It is interesting to find Valéry writing in his *Note-Book B1910*: 'Odours, more than anything, give me the sensation of the unusual. It is through them that I find myself in a foreign city. Nothing new in odourless streets: and, if my olfactory sensitivity happens to increase, I shall walk about Paris like a foreigner.'

of logic, of the technical mind; and two of the words very prominent in the discussion of technical process—*idea* and *intuition*—are
metaphors of seeing. That 'image'—a visual word—should have to
be a central term in a description of Poetic shows how far the
technical mind has dominated our language in establishing a vocabulary of sight. Poetry actually suppresses or dissipates visual clarity;
the urgent forward movement of poetry prevents us from constructing
clear static pictures. Even when images of colour predominate, the
reader receives little visual response—unless he is the sort of person
who visualizes everything. A passage from *The Ancient Mariner* will
serve as illustration.

> But where the ship's huge shadow lay,
> The charmèd water burnt alway
> A still and awful red.
>
> Beyond the shadow of the ship,
> I watched the water-snakes:
> They moved in tracks of shining white,
> And when they reared, the elfish light
> Fell off in hoary flakes.
>
> Within the shadow of the ship
> I watched their rich attire:
> Blue, glossy green, and velvet black,
> They coiled and swam; and every track
> Was a flash of golden fire.

The ear is *par excellence* the organ of Poetic. It is more primitive than
the eye. Our response to sounds is more physical, and is intimately
related with the instinctive reactions required for self-preservation;
consequently what we hear transmutes less readily into conceptual
ideas. The ear is as finely discriminating as the eye, if not more so,
and since it cannot be focused with so much selectivity it is far
more comprehensive than the eye. Again, the ear shares with the
sense of touch the power of apprehending rhythms, shaped movements in time; and this the eye lacks to a marked degree. It is through
the ear that the most profound and characteristic features of Poetic
are grasped. Once the ear is engaged the other senses are roused to a
tenebrous activity which precludes both the static character of what
is merely *seen*, and the unmuscularity of what is merely *thought*.

A poem can scarcely be said to exist except when it is excellently

read by ear.[1] Attentive listening suspends that 'irritable reaching
after fact and reason' which Keats rightly deplored in the poet; it
sustains a state of 'uncertainties, mysteries, doubts', a posture of total
awareness and delicate response; it secures a personal integrity which
is yet outward-turning, and that virginity of consciousness which is
as priceless a gift to the reader as to the poet. And the poet, no less
than the reader, must be gifted with what Eliot has called 'the
auditory imagination', 'the feeling for syllable and rhythm, penetrating far below the conscious levels of thought and feeling, invigorating
every word; sinking to the most primitive and forgotten, returning
to the origin and bringing something back, seeking the beginning
and the end. It works through meanings, certainly, or not without
meaning in the ordinary sense, and fuses the old and obliterated and
the trite, the current, and the new and surprising, the most ancient
and the most civilized mentality.' Metaphor is the mode in which
Poetic integrates all its resources through sound and rhythm; it
works through the disorientation of the senses, and transmutes feelings into words—even abstract words—by making language sensory.

$$\star \qquad \star \qquad \star$$

The reason for Aristotle's praise of metaphor is now clear. But
many of the passages I have quoted in illustration, although resonant
within themselves, do not bring into resonance the whole poems in
which they are embedded. It is sombre to recollect how seldom even
Shakespeare can sustain to the extent of a sonnet the promise of such
passages as these:

> *When to the sessions of sweet silent thought*
> *I summon up remembrance of things past—*

[1] After writing this passage, I find that Wyndham Lewis had already said the same
sort of thing in his *François Villon*. 'Such is the ecstasy of his [Villon's] creative force,
the life he has breathed into his work, that it is seen and felt to be poetry absolute,
stirring the soul and the imagination like a fanfare of silver trumpets, fulfilling the
mind, vibrating, awakening that instant response which is the mark of high poetry.
This [reading aloud] is a test no lesser verse can pass. Villon possessed *le Verbe*, the
Word, and the magic formula (Rabelais has it, too) by which words are changed
into something beyond themselves and their arrangement transmuted into the language
of another world; a language in which the very shape and size and texture of words,
their resonance, their position and significance, becomes as it were faëry, charged with
tremendous, or mysterious, or ravishing music.'

> *'Gainst death and all-oblivious enmity*
> *Shall you pace forth; your praise shall still find room*
> *Even in the eyes of all posterity*
> *That wears this world out to the ending doom.*
>
> *Love's not Time's fool, though rosy lips and cheeks*
> *Within his bending sickle's compass come:*
>
> *The expense of spirit in a waste of shame*
> *Is lust in action.*

Coleridge observed that 'Images, however beautiful, do not of themselves characterize the poet. They become proofs of original genius only as far as they are modified by a predominant passion; or by associated thoughts or images *awakened by that passion*.' The *total* poem, the poem which is also a single image, is most often a lyric—a single agonized cry of joy, delight, sorrow, longing, renunciation, love— 'begotten by despair upon impossibility'.

> *O rose, thou art sick:*
> *The invisible worm*
> *That flies in the night*
> *In the howling storm,*
>
> *Has found out thy bed*
> *Of crimson joy,*
> *And his dark secret love*
> *Does thy life destroy.*

This poem of William Blake's is perhaps misleading; the visual imagery is unusually sharp and it may be supposed that the poem is unified by the two 'consecrated images' of the rose and the worm. But visual imagery has not that fusing power.

> *Our gaze is submarine, our eyes look upward*
> *And see the light that fractures through unquiet water.*
> *We see the light but see not whence it comes.*

The wholeness of a poem depends, not upon the persistence of a single image or of a conceit with many facets, but upon the compulsion of a single tone, a dominant passion. This quality is triumphantly exhibited in the central section of Andrew Marvell's poem *To His Coy Mistress*.

> *But at my back I always hear*
> *Time's winged chariot hurrying near:*
> *And yonder all before us lie*
> *Deserts of vast eternity.*
> *Thy beauty shall no more be found;*
> *Nor, in thy marble vault, shall sound*
> *My echoing song: then worms shall try*
> *That long-preserved virginity,*
> *And your quaint honour turn to dust,*
> *And into ashes all my lust.*
> *The grave's a fine and private place,*
> *But none, I think, do there embrace.*

An early reading of this poem suggests that the intensity must now relax, and that the later images are arbitrary and confused. In the closing section, however, fresh fierce images are introduced, and the tone steadily heightens from insolent cruelty to savage gaiety.[1] On the other hand, George Herbert's poem *The Flower* sullenly resists the redemption of these two perfect stanzas:

> *Who would have thought my shrivell'd heart*
> *Could have recover'd greenness? It was gone*
> *Quite under ground; as flowers depart*
> *To see their Mother-root, when they have blown;*
> *Where they together*
> *All the hard weather,*
> *Dead to the world, keep house unknown. . . .*
>
> *And now in age I bud again,*
> *After so many deaths I live and write:*
> *I once more smell the dew and rain,*
> *And relish versing: O my only light,*
> *It cannot be*
> *That I am he,*
> *On whom the tempests fell at night.*

Metaphor is the process by which unity of tone may be achieved in poetry; but metaphor—no matter how brilliant—cannot automatically secure wholeness of impression. Metaphor can establish a tune, an undertone both sonic and rhythmic; but it is the poet who

[1] Cf. T. R. Henn, *The Apple and the Spectroscope* (1951), pp. 25–33.

must keep the tune running in his head; the poet must in the end make his poem one song, one utterance, a single cry. Poetic wholeness is *form*: and form strives—if the poet will allow it—to grow from within and to realize itself as 'full, sphere-like, single'. And that singleness in the poet is 'a predominant passion'. Once the poet is 'on fire' with the poetic passion, he must then (as J. B. Yeats wrote to his son) *'work with cold logic and resolute purpose,* till he has created his work of art——' The paradox is that, when the work of art is completed, 'all the fire will be *in it* for ever'.[1] It is the passion of revelation that appears in the poem as *style*—'the self-conquest of the writer'. Then the words have fallen into resonance, ordained to a just precision, toughness, pace, *timbre*, duration. Metaphor, by an enveloping compulsion, defies the theoretical borders between one sense and another, between sense and feeling, thought and meaning, and moves towards a self-determinate form. Poetry has a double root—in reality and in the person. The intersection of these two is Value. From this twofold stem (which is yet single) grows the self-realizing discovery which is at once the poem and the transfigured person. But before the incarnation is complete there is needed a special kind of metaphor which I shall call *symbol,* and a special articulation of symbols which I shall call *myth.*

---

[1] J. B. Yeats, *Letters to his Son and Others 1869–1922,* ed. Joseph Hone (1944), p. 152 (October 1912). In the same letter he writes: 'I said that in your work is *intensity*, and said you got your intensity through a certain personal intensity habitual with you. But I ought to have said that the intensity by the time it reaches its expression is no longer *personal*, entering into the world of art, the personal ego is dropped away—for I think personal art is bad art, at any rate second rate.' He goes on to praise Turner's painting above the work of the Impressionists.

A NOTE RECOMMENDING SONIC
TERMS FOR POETICS

'Image' is a single word but an image is not a determinate entity. There is no way of deciding precisely where an image begins or where it ends; and there is no definitive criterion by which we can say what is an image in poetry and what is not. Yet the word continues to be used with a misleading air of precision.

A visual image is always in a context, in a field of vision and raised out of that field; but in Poetic the image never emerges from its field—it is always fused into its context. If this were not so, the poetic image might (as the term suggests) be primarily visual; but language cannot renounce its allegiance to sound. We may determine the point beyond which there is no metaphorical resonance, but we can never distinguish what has caused the resonance and consequently cannot distinguish the precise confines of the resonant image. The visual analogy is not only inadequate for understanding poetry: it is altogether inappropriate. For the relation between word and event in poetry is much more obscure and indirect than the relation between image and 'thing' in painting. We are driven back to where we started and where we are, after all, most at home—in the inaccessible but familiar darkness of the apprehending self.

> *Those masterful images because complete*
> *Grew in pure mind, but out of what began?*
> *A mound of refuse or the sweepings of a street,*
> *Old kettles, old bottles, and a broken can,*
> *Old iron, old bones, old rags, that raving slut*
> *Who keeps the till. Now that my ladder's gone,*
> *I must lie down where all the ladders start,*
> *In the foul rag-and-bone shop of the heart.*

I should like to abandon the term 'image' altogether. As long as one uses it, it is difficult to avoid the misleading definition Mr Day Lewis offers: a poetic image (he says, with some reservations) is 'a word-picture with emotion or passion'. Now a resonant metaphor is not static in the way a picture is; neither can it be 'taken in at a single glance'. For the poetic image is not so bounded with a wiry line; and a whole poem is not bounded by a discrete frame, but by an ocean of reverberant silence. Sound, rhythm, the fluent unfolding and elapsing movement of time, the fusion by collision and reverberation—these, much more than visual clarity, are the essence of poetry. Even though poetry is not entirely a matter of sound, much of what it says to us is conveyed through sound. I should therefore prefer a sound-word to represent the elemental unit (or principle) of articulation in Poetic. There is no such word in the language, but it may be worth introducing one if only to assert that in poetry—as in all expression intimately related with man's moral experience—there are no distinct and easily distinguishable outlines. I suggest that the word *sone* might be used; the word being coined from the French *son* (sound) on the analogy of the English word 'tone' from French *ton*.[1]

The term *sone* will be very difficult to define if it is to present an adequate figure of metaphorical process. A sone might be described as a group of words so selected and arranged as to come into resonance in the process of metaphor; the sone being the irreducible dynamic unit in poetry. But a poem cannot necessarily be constructed out of a series of these sonic units as though they were bricks. No addition or multiplicity of sones can by itself constitute a poem. Some sones are fertile: some are barren. The barren sone is the brilliant metaphor which fails to bring its larger context into resonance; the fertile sone when fully developed and resonant is the whole poem, yet within it in some cases we may distinguish internal sones, some of them visual enough in character to be termed images.[2]

So difficult is it to stop thinking of poetry in terms of images that one wonders whether it is worth the effort. The analogy of vision is not troublesome in an account of imagination, the process by which the data of sense are accumulated and constellated; for those data— whether of sight, sound, touch, taste, or smell—can all be thought of as intrusions upon the consciousness from without and we readily take as the type of such sensations those which we can most readily abstract, namely visual images. But when we consider actual poems and the way they are brought to completion by the poet and are recreated by a reader, we are no longer considering simple perceptual

[1] The adjective *sonic* is already current though usually in technical contexts.

[2] In the fully developed fertile sone, internal sones may bear to the whole poem the same sort of relation that a melodic or rhythmic theme bears to a musical movement. But when we consider that the sone (as here described) has no exact counterpart in music—unless it be 'tonality'—we recognize the intimate fusion of all internal elements in the fully realized poem.

sensations but extremely intricate and dainty transmutations into and out of language: we are dealing with linguistic events which, though they arise from and somehow terminate in sensory experience, are not themselves sensory. As long as they are linguistic events, the element of 'meaning' must enter; and since utterances can only convey meaning as they unfold themselves in time, the element of time must enter. As soon as time is admitted into the scheme, rhythm can develop and with it that internal fusion essential to poetic language which we have called 'resonance'. None of these features properly belongs to a picture as such, or to what we normally regard as an image. Only when the attention is shifted from the picture to the person-viewing-the-picture do the elements of rhythm and internal congruence enter. The eye travels around within the picture to reconstruct the rhythm, and in its passage apprehends the congruence of internal relations. Once we recognize that the specifically poetic character of a picture does not reside simply in the picture as a static entity, the analogy of the visual image in poetry loses its charm. The terms 'sone', 'sonic', 'reverberant', 'resonance', should serve as constant reminders that the typical effects of poetry are syntheses to be grasped directly. The method of subdivision and schematic reconstruction does not apply because the margins of the poetic elements are never unquestionably distinct. Criticism, aesthetics, and poetics can profitably recognize that poetry is no more accessible than music, and that Poetic cannot operate unless the ear is engaged.

IX

Symbol and Myth

All symbolic art should arise out of a real belief.—W. B. YEATS

WHEN metaphor is considered as the irreducible distinctive unit for Poetic, and as the means by which language comes into resonance through connections other than logical, the borders between one sense and another and between thought and sense become confused. This disorientation is essential if we are to get rid of the notion that there ever is or can be a 'sense datum' which can serve as external test for the value or integrity of a work of art. The term 'poetic image' seems to suggest some test of visual clarity; yet by examining metaphorical images we have found that they refer more directly to sound than to sight, that their outlines are nebulous, that their influence diffuses itself in complicated ways. We have also found that metaphor is the means to express whatever cannot be clearly conveyed in a logical or technical manner.

It is in symbol and myth that the peculiar nature and scope of Poetic are to be seen in full development. These terms involve no discontinuity in the account; for the symbol proves to be a special kind of metaphor and the myth proves to be a cluster of symbols brought into resonance in the process of metaphor. 'True art', Yeats observed, 'is expressive and symbolic, and makes every form, every sound, every colour, every gesture, a signature of some unanalysable essence.' Virginia Woolf finds her attention and vision directed to

164

'that which is beyond and outside our own predicament; to that which is symbolic, and thus perhaps permanent, if there is any permanence in our sleeping, eating, breathing, so animal, so spiritual and tumultuous lives'. The permanence which symbols ensure however is not the permanence or certainty of mathematics. Here again the distinct character of Poetic asserts itself by being rooted in value and being, in the luminous instant of personal apprehension.

It is a disaster then that critics should ever have used the word *symbol* as though a symbol were an indicating mark standing for something other than itself, a sign for unambiguous substitution.[1] Language is now so commonly used in a technical, and even arbitrary, manner that it may be waste of time to quarrel about the application of terms. But one must insist upon reclaiming to their original status the two words 'symbol' and 'myth'; for they belong to the very birthright of poetry.

The word *symbol* is a noun from the Greek verb συμβάλλειν: the word implies throwing together, chance encounter, conflict, union in tension. One nominal form of this verb, ἡ συμβολή, preserves the root sense of encounter and collision; but the noun from which the word 'symbol' derives—τὸ σύμβολον—lost its root meaning by erosion and so shifted towards the sense now current in mathematics and logic. Originally σύμβολα were counters which contracting parties broke and preserved as tokens of identity and mutual good faith. When this contractural figure had decayed, the word σύμβολον had lost the vigour of its root sense and came to mean simply a token, sign or watchword. In Christian usage, however, the word σύμβολα was used with a threefold reference—both of the whole system of belief as embodied in creeds and articles of faith, and of signs and marks to identify Christians to each other,[2] and of certain ritual objects and passages of the liturgy. That the word 'symbol' should have a long history in theology and mysticism helps to recall that poetry and mysticism both spring from the contemplative way of mind, that

[1] Mr Day Lewis writes in *The Poetic Image* that 'An intense image is the opposite of a symbol. A symbol is denotative; it stands for one thing only, as the figure 1 represents one unit. Images in poetry are seldom purely symbolic, for they are affected by the emotional vibrations of their context so that each reader's response to them is apt to be modified by his personal experience.' R. G. Collingwood, in his aesthetic works, had also used the word 'symbol' in this mathematical sense, but without introducing for art a term corresponding with Day Lewis's 'intense image'.

[2] One of the earliest was a fish—the Greek for which (ἰχθύς) forms the initial letters for the phrase 'Jesus Christ, Son of God, Saviour'.

poetry and religion are inseparable in the primitive situation, and that the language of mysticism is poetry.

The root-sense of symbol is admirably suited to the process of metaphor: a clashing together, collision, meeting, dialectic, and—by implication—concentration and focusing. In the sense in which I use the word 'symbol', every metaphorical expression has symbolical character; every charged or resonant image is potentially a symbol and strives towards full symbolic status. But since the process of metaphor adequately covers the general order of poetic articulations, the term symbol may conveniently be reserved for those poetic events which we recognize to be especially valuable, those poetic entities which bring Value most sharply into focus. The adjective Symbolic then refers to the fullest development in Poetic. Symbol may be further limited at the upper end of the scale by using the word *myth* when we speak of whatever in poetry corresponds in religion to a system of beliefs.

Within this general area of reference further discriminations must be made. Symbol—which is always in any case paradoxical and ambivalent—manifests itself in two characters: as the quality of a poetic event, and as the focal image around which the whole event crystallizes and orientates itself. In the first character it is sonic, out-ward-moving, centrifugal, and embracing; in the second character it is (like a visual image), inward-moving, centripetal, and focusing. Most attempts to describe poetic symbolism concentrate upon the second character and represent the symbol as a 'thing'—as an object of contemplation only, without considering how one object can be preferred above another, or how *any* object of contemplation can have any peculiar force unless associated with an event in history or a current literary expression.

A symbol, like a metaphor, does not stand for a 'thing' or for an idea; it is a focus of relationships.[1] And it is a focus for those relationships which we judge to be of highest value. In one aspect,

[1] Wherever in art the operation of simple substitution occurs the cryptographer's term *cypher* is useful. In *The Statesman's Manual* Coleridge—writing about the formulated allegory—gives an admirable account of cyphering as being 'but a translation of abstract notions into a picture-language, which is itself nothing but an abstraction from objects of the senses; . . .' Some poets have been misled by mistaking cyphers for symbols, and not a few critics have beguiled themselves into treating symbols as though they were cyphers. The offspring of this confusion is some clever but barren verse, and some vast structures of ingenious but nugatory fantasy masquerading under the name of 'scientific interpretation'.

symbol is extremely condensed—so minutely focused that a single image, often indicated by a single word, may be distinguished as a symbol. It is in this character that symbol has come to be confused with mathematical cyphers. A symbol however is not simply an image or a single word capable of conveying important truths regardless of its context. If a symbol 'means' anything, it will mean something different in every single context; for the symbol, being a vehicle for the highest values in poetry, is more sensitive to its context than any other kind of image or word.[1] Each context must, in the general manner of Poetic, be self-evident; the force of any particular use of symbol depends not upon the symbol itself so much as upon the context; and the context is controlled and informed by the force of the poet's conviction, the reality of his beliefs. In certain historical periods a poet may take over symbols ready-made and, relying upon current emotive response to those symbols, prepare a context which is elliptical, not self-contained, a context which in another period would need historical or archaeological interpretation. The symbolical context as a focus of belief may be terse or discursive depending upon the nature of the individual poet; and some extremely terse symbolical expressions which are inscrutable to analysis are self-contained, revealing their 'meaning' without any external appeal. Much of Eliot's and Yeats's poetry, and some of Pound's, is of this kind.

Man's constant desire is to *be*; and the goal of his speculative longings is to understand Being. 'I think profound philosophy must come from terror,' Yeats writes. 'An abyss opens under our feet; . . . Whether we will or no we must ask the ancient questions: Is there reality anywhere? Is there a God? Is there a Soul?' Symbols are those objects of contemplation which reveal the primary values in life: the relations between man and the universe, between man and man, between man and God. Single symbols cluster about and point towards various aspects of these primary relations: birth, death, love, fear, fertility, desolation, immortality, suffering. At the very lowest these may be regarded (in George Rylands's phrase) as 'consecrated images'—images, words and names consecrated, not simply by religious usage, but because they recur in the general consciousness; because they persist in that residual storehouse of human memory

---

[1] Yeats, for example, says of his poem *Cap and Bells*: 'The poem has always meant a great deal to me, though, as is the way with symbolic poems, it has not always meant quite the same thing.'

laid up throughout human history and transmitted in social custom, in ritual and literature, and preserved in the culture of education. In their origin, symbols are religious; originally magical, they appear over and over again in a variety of rituals and customs which bear no direct geographical, social, or literary relation to each other.[1] Jung has recently given the name of 'archetypal images' to these antique symbols. Miss Maud Bodkin's summary (*Archetypal Patterns in Poetry* (1934)) is well known: 'The special emotional significance possessed by certain poems—a significance going beyond any definite meaning conveyed—he attributes to the stirring in the reader's mind, within or beneath his conscious response, of unconscious forces which he terms "primordial images", or archetypes. These archetypes he describes as "psychic residue or numberless experiences of the same type", experiences which have happened not to the individual but to his ancestors, and of which the results are inherited in the structure of the brain, *a priori* determinants of individual experience.'[2]

[1] This is not the place to distinguish clearly between the artistic and the religious mind. Both are essentially contemplative; but we should notice that in mystical practice the object of contemplation disappears whereas in poetry it is always preserved. This difference is luminously discussed by H. A. Hodges in a paper entitled 'Art and Religion' (July 1947), from which the following passage is taken. 'With the artist, to see is to express. The religious contemplative may, indeed often does, give literary expression to the earlier stages of his vision and to the incidents of his journey along the road; but the ultimate confrontation he cannot utter, and does not commonly wish to. He is the true iconoclast, who rejoices to see himself stripped bare of images which, being his own, must always involve some danger of idolatry; and it is here, in the recesses of the worshipping soul, and not in the public worship of the Church, that iconoclasm is properly in place.'

[2] Christopher Caudwell combines the notion of primordial memory with the rhythm of symbolic extrication: 'Emotions, generated collectively, persist in solitude so that one man, alone, singing a song, still feels his emotion stirred by collective images. He is already exhibiting that paradox of art—man withdrawing from his fellows into the world of art, only to enter more closely into communion with humanity.' See also Dorothy Emmet, *The Nature of Metaphysical Thinking*, p. 102.

Yeats remarks upon some of the intersections of personal memory and the 'world memory'. 'Any one who has any experience of any mystical state of the soul knows how there float up in the mind profound symbols, whose meaning, if indeed they do not delude one into the dream that they are meaningless, one does not perhaps understand for years. Nor I think has any one who has known that experience with any constancy, failed to find some day in some old book or on some old monument, a strange or intricate image, that had floated up before him, and to grow perhaps dizzy with the sudden conviction that our little memories are but a part of some great memory, that renews the world and men's thoughts age after age, and that our thoughts are not, as we suppose, the deep but a little foam upon the deep.'

Primordial images embody archetypal patterns of experience, and are capable of evoking those patterns. Primordial images (whether or not with Coleridge and Jung we postulate a Collective Unconscious to accommodate them) are not however the only symbols. When Gilbert Murray stated that one 'leaps in response to the effective presentation in poetry of an ancient theme' he was only partly right; for the primordial image is consecrated not merely by antiquity but by value. An image consecrated by use at successive periods acquires a special quality when seen (as it were) disposed in its multitudinous characters and lights down the convergent corridor of history. But the peculiar power of poetry is to obliterate the dimension of time, to bring into a momentary focus all the historical implications of a word or image, so that roots strike into the teeming secrecy of unconsciousness and bring forth clusters of antique memories. No matter what historical basis they may have, archetypal experiences belong to a luminous present and owe their force to their peculiar quality. They are recognized in experience as having that intense value which we usually ascribe only to what is most ancient and abiding. But the value is in the instant of experience itself, and does not depend upon any extrinsic judgment of permanence or antiquity. Yeats again has a memorable observation upon this point. 'It is only by ancient symbols, by symbols that have numberless meanings beside the one or two the writer lays an emphasis upon, or the half-score he knows of, that any highly subjective art can escape from the barrenness and shallowness of a too conscious arrangement, into the abundance and depth of nature. The poet of essences and pure ideas must seek in the half-lights that glimmer from symbol to symbol as if to the ends of the earth, all that the epic and dramatic poet finds of mystery and shadow in the accidental circumstances of life.' 'In uncertain dreams,' Gide notes in his *Journal*, 'are already sketched out vaguely the great figures of eternity.'

When we respond to primordial images and to symbols we have an incredulous sense of recognition—'almost', as Keats said, 'a Remembrance'. This recognition does not arise from the perspective element of time. Rather it is a way of interpreting to ourselves the remarkable sense of wholeness and inevitability when the poem 'enters into one's soul, and does not startle it or amaze it with itself, but with its subject'. We are astonished at the unity of consciousness and at the unity of human experience, and find a body for that astonishment in a sense of recognition. The 'rightness' and Value of the experience is interpreted in terms of the tragic dimension of time, in the same way that Plato and Proclus and Vaughan and Wordsworth extrapolate the vividness and freedom of childhood into the spiritual perfection of a life before birth. All men—poets and readers —are all in some sense men; we have similar responsive organisms, we share similar experiences, we tend to express our experience in similar ways; and when a person suddenly achieves a state of wholeness he recognizes it for what it is, whether or not he remembers that it has happened to him before.

Primordial images constitute a sort of alphabet of human experience. The same clusters of images tend to persist simply because man is constituted as he is and is embedded in a Nature which has not altered substantially within human memory. In moments of ecstasy the attention tends to be fixed upon some natural object or phenomenon which happens to be present. We contemplate these objects as though they were keys to our most vivid and disturbing experience; the objects do not lose their identity but they take on an urgent and inscrutable significance. Some of these correspondences are clear if unanalysable; it is not difficult to think what some of these primordial images would be. The moon, for example, rapidly alters its appearance and moves swiftly through the sky in a very complex manner; it differs even from the planets—the wandering ones—in the speed and intricacy of its movements, and from the stars which remain fixed in relation to each other though the whole vault of the sky may turn in a stately diurnal motion. The moon is also related with the rising and ebbing of the tides, and with rhythmic physical occurrences in human beings. The sea is manifestly both creator and destroyer. A seed placed in the ground rots and puts forth a growth which, springing out of the seed's death, and nourished by sun and water, is not a replica of the seed. And if 'the grave's a fine and private place' so is the womb.

These images, however, can symbolize the quality of an experience only under certain conditions; their inscrutable significance can be grasped only when one is aware of the integrity of nature, the integrity of man, the integrity of consciousness. Within the whole compass of the created world, except for the 'self' at the centre of experience, no 'thing' is of itself more important than another; no image is more apt than another to be a symbol; any relationship whatsoever is legitimate. The artist's function is to recognize, distinguish, and express relationships of value. Some of these relationships are so much part of everybody's experience that when they are clearly embodied they strike with a singular sense of recognition even though they usually pass unrecognized. The poet's history is evoked; the reader's personal history is evoked and stirred: and both being men partake of the history of their race and of their species. Any object whatsoever or any event can become a symbol, whether or not it has ever been applied symbolically before. Between the primordial symbol and the personal symbol there is no difference in kind; for all true symbols evoke primordial resonances. Some consecrated images can resonate in contexts not very fastidiously controlled; but the poet's greatest achievement is to fashion a symbolical context for a personal symbol —that is, to create a new symbol or recreate an old one. For no symbol—not even a primordial symbol—is active unless freshly and vitally apprehended in personal vision. Every symbol must be discovered in its initial vitality and novelty every time it is used: only in such a primal act of discovery and recognition can any image achieve symbolic stature, power, resonance.

A symbol is not a single word or object, like 'moon', 'ocean', 'womb', 'seed'; the single word, the single image requires a context, a poetic situation. In any symbolical situation we usually find embedded a single dominant image or word; once removed from the controlling context this image or word degenerates into an entity for emotive or ideational response. The symbol in its appropriate context is poetic in character; it is always a vehicle for feelings, for complex and valuable states of awareness, and never a vehicle for dogma or for ideas.[1] And since the symbol is a focal point for a relationship between reality and a person it reaches out both towards reality and towards the suffering person. And since these two can never be

[1] *Emblem* is a term standing between *cypher* and *symbol*, but generally having the character of cypher. Emblems are not arbitrary marks standing for persons or things, but rather honorific or heraldic badges which refer to some particular quality of the person or thing. The four Evangelists have four beasts as their emblems; or a king has the emblem of a lion, or an Indian chief the emblem of a wolf, a bear, a fox. An emblem is a suppressed simile, but not a metaphor; the suppressed simile is at best partial, a simple ascription of certain general characteristics. Emblems, though not symbolical, are potentially symbolical. When St John is given the emblem of the eagle, and St Matthew the cock, the simile 'fits' better than the lion fits St Mark or the bull St Luke; but that is because the eagle as emblem of strength and the cock as emblem of dawn are more evocative terms. Criticism would do well to recover the seventeenth-century use of the term *emblem* to indicate words and images which, from recurrent use and a consequent fusion of word and referent, suggest that they have special symbolical possibilities. But since the emblem is used to represent an abstract quality,

identical, a symbol is always ambivalent, revealing itself to the empirical and technical mind as paradox—a paradox quite as embarrassing to the scientific critic as it is to the formal logician. Cyphers have 'meaning': they point to more or less unambiguous (though sometimes secret) concepts which can be exhausted by lexical or archaeological ingenuity. Symbols are not *without* meaning, but their primary function is to evoke and sustain a particular state of awareness which is also of high value. A symbol is, therefore, inexhaustible to both analysis and meditation.[1]

*   *   *

The nature of symbol is not, I think, better described than by Coleridge. His most luminous account appears in *The Statesman's Manual* (1825), and is informed as much by his theological preoccupation as by his direct inquiry into Poetic in *Biographia Literaria* (1815–17). 'A symbol (ὁ ἔστιν ἀεὶ ταυτηγόρικον [which is always self-energizing]) is characterized by the translucence of the special in the individual, or of the general in the special, or of the universal in the general; above all by the translucence of the eternal through and in the temporal. *It always partakes of the reality which it renders intelligible; and while it enunciates the whole, abides itself as a living part in that unity of which it is the representative*' [my italics]. In the same book, he speaks of the imagination as 'that reconciling and mediatory power, which incorporating the reason in images of the sense, and organizing (as it were) the flux of the senses by the permanence and self-circling energies of the reason, gives birth to *a system of symbols, harmonious in themselves, and consubstantial with the truths of which they are the conductors*'. And in an essay on Cervantes he notices that in

or to illustrate a moral fable, it is evidently of the order of cypher and not of symbol. The beast imagery in Shakespeare's *Lear*, for example, seems to me a matter of emblems and not symbols.

[1] If the question 'What does this symbol mean?' can be answered simply and directly, the image in question is not a symbol. To say that in a particular poem 'the moon is a symbol of pity' is a meaningless statement unless further elucidated. To accord with my account of symbol the statement would have to imply something like this: 'Here the poet has charged the image of the moon with a peculiar feeling which is like nothing so much as the feeling of pity; and because I know that pity is a valuable experience I call the image of the moon *in this context* a symbolical usage, and call the word "moon" a symbol as being the focus through which principally the feeling of pity is generated in me.' Even the most experienced shorthand writers sometimes have difficulty in reading back their own notes.

symbolical writing 'it is very possible that the general truth represented may be working unconsciously in the writer's mind during the construction of the symbol'.

These passages may be taken as illuminating texts, for this is not the place to attempt a full-dress account of Coleridge's doctrine of symbol. Several important features of symbol are noticed here. The symbol 'partakes of the reality which it renders intelligible': that is to say, the symbol is an integral element in the event of reality which it illuminates. The symbol does not simply stand for an object present in the event but preserves the feeling *for* an object which in the event had special significance: or as Gide has observed, 'The symbol is the thing around which a book is written.' The symbol has its origin in sensory experience, and by partaking in an event of reality becomes (to extend Coleridge's visual figure) translucent—a lens (as it were) focusing for the poet the Value of the event, and also bringing the event into sharp focus for the reader.

If an image is to become a symbol, an integral part of the reality which it renders intelligible, it must in experience serve a double function. It will assume a focal position as an object of contemplation (whether or not 'actually' present): the poet's attention concentrates in a 'fixed gaze', and an activity supervenes which is not that of observation but of vision in the mystical sense. The object loses its distinct outline as 'thing' and its opaqueness as a 'thing-in-itself'; it becomes translucent, luminous, the focal point through which the complex energy of an event of reality flows in, the lens through which the poet 'sees' a world of spirit beyond. This world he recognizes as his world of here-and-now transfigured. In this heightened mood of vision 'images of memory flow in on the impulse of immediate perception', and in the developing event of reality the focal image, the symbol, sustains and concentrates the whole feeling of the event. If the feeling of the event is to be enucleated and bodied forth with its pristine power and with structural fidelity, the focal symbol alone cannot be a sufficient vehicle: the symbol may be there by accident, and in any case it cannot be a direct substitute for the event. When the process moves from contemplation into the purifying phase of embodiment, the focal symbols gather to themselves—from the perceived present and from the shaping well of memory—other images, thoughts, tunes. If the poet is faithfully to embody his moment of vision he requires not only distinct symbols but 'a system of symbols'. 'All art is sensuous,' Yeats admits; 'but when a man puts only his contemplative nature and his more vague desires into his art, the sensuous images through which it speaks become broken, fleeting, uncertain, or are chosen for their distance from general experience, and all grows unsubstantial and fantastic. When imagination moves in a dim world . . . we go to it for delight indeed but in our weariness. If we are to sojourn there that world must grow consistent with itself, emotion must be related to emotion by a system of ordered images. . . . It must grow to be symbolic, that is, for the soul can only achieve a distinct separated life where many related objects at once distinguish and arouse its energies in its fullness.' Symbols appear in clusters, in ordered patterns, harmoniously disposed. And when Coleridge shifts from a visual to a sonic term we are reminded again of the metaphorical resonance.

*   *   *

The sonic character of symbols, their tendency to appear not singly but in resonant clusters, may conveniently be illustrated with a few passages of poetry. These will also illustrate degrees of resonance and show that the presence of symbolical words is not enough to bring a whole passage into resonance. Consider first a passage in which Shakespeare makes fanciful play with images of conception in *A Midsummer Night's Dream.*

> *Set your heart at rest:*
> *The fairy-land buys not the child of me.*
> *His mother was a vot'ress of my order:*
> *And, in the spiced Indian air, by night,*
> *Full often hath she gossip by my side;*
> *And sat with me on Neptune's yellow sands,*
> *Marking th' embarked traders on the flood;*
> *When we have laught to see the sails conceive*
> *And grow big-bellied with the wanton wind;*
> *Which she, with pretty and with swimming gait*
> *Following,—her womb then rich with my young squire,—*
> *Would imitate, and sail upon the land,*
> *To fetch me trifles, and return again,*
> *As from a voyage, rich with merchandise.*
> *But she, being mortal, of that boy did die; . . .*

The imagery in this passage is in metaphorical but not in symbolic

resonance: the conceit is charming and delicately sustained but strikes
to no deeper level. A speech almost immediately preceding does not
even achieve metaphorical resonance, despite the presence of quite a
number of 'symbol-words'. (Oberon has charged Titania with making Theseus break faith with four other ladies for love of her.)

> These are the forgeries of jealousy:
> And never, since the middle summer's spring,
> Met we . . .
> But with thy brawls thou hast disturb'd our sport.
> Therefore the winds, piping to us in vain,
> As in revenge, have suck'd up from the sea
> Contagious fogs; which falling in the land,
> Hath every pelting river made so proud,
> That they have overborne their continents:
> The ox hath therefore stretch'd his yoke in vain,
> The ploughman lost his sweat; and the green corn
> Hath rotted ere his youth attain'd a beard:
> The fold stands empty in the drowned field,
> And crows are fatted with the murrion flock;
> The nine-men's-morris is fill'd up with mud;
> And the quaint mazes in the wanton green,
> For lack of tread, are undistinguishable:
> The human mortals want their winter cheer;
> No night is now with hymn or carol blest:—
> Therefore the moon, the governess of floods,
> Pale in her anger, washes all the air,
> That rheumatic diseases do abound:
> And through this distemperature we see
> The seasons alter: hoary-headed frosts
> Fall in the fresh lap of the crimson rose;
> And on old Hiems' chin and icy crown
> And odorous chaplet of sweet summer buds
> Is, as in mockery, set: the spring, the summer,
> The chiding autumn, angry winter, change
> Their wonted liveries; and the mazed world,
> By their increase, now knows not which is which:
> And this same progeny of evils comes
> From our debate, from our dissension;
> We are their parents and original.

'The winds, piping to us in vain' strike a responsive chord with John the Baptist's words, 'We have piped unto you, and ye have not danced'; but there is no answering echo, and the decorative catalogue continues, separating the dancing from the piping. A more powerful note is struck by the rotting corn, the double meaning of the word 'beard', and the ironical evocation of Christ's words: 'Except a corn of wheat fall into the ground and die, it abideth alone: but if it die, it bringeth forth much fruit.' For a moment the note is sustained by echoes of the desolate city described in *Ecclesiastes* and in the *Revelation*; but it lapses almost at once into a brilliant confusion which is not rescued by the punning cross-reference of 'maze' and the distant reference to the beard of youth in 'old Hiems' chin'.

If we turn to Yeats's poem *The Second Coming* we hear the true symbolic tone with its primordial undersong.

> *Surely some revelation is at hand;*
> *Surely the Second Coming is at hand.*
> *The Second Coming! Hardly are those words out*
> *When a vast image out of* Spiritus Mundi
> *Troubles my sight: somewhere in sands of the desert*
> *A shape with lion body and the head of a man,*
> *A gaze blank and pitiless as the sun,*
> *Is moving its slow thighs, while all about it*
> *Reel shadows of the indignant desert birds.*
> *The darkness drops again; but now I know*
> *That twenty centuries of stony sleep*
> *Were vexed to nightmare by a rocking cradle,*
> *And what rough beast, its hour come round at last,*
> *Slouches towards Bethlehem to be born?*

Here primitive, pagan and Christian symbols, interfused in a vertiginous perspective of time, are turned to a shocking irony. And in another poem of his the power of symbolic statement is manifested in remarkable degree.

LEDA AND THE SWAN

> *A sudden blow: the great wings beating still*
> *Above the staggering girl, her thighs caressed*
> *By the dark webs, her nape caught in his bill,*
> *He holds her helpless breast upon his breast.*

How can those terrified vague fingers push
The feathered glory from her loosening thighs?
And how can body, laid in that white rush,
But feel the strange heart beating where it lies?

A shudder in the loins engenders there
The broken wall, the burning roof and tower
And Agamemnon dead.
                    Being so caught up,
So mastered by the brute blood of the air,
Did she put on his knowledge with his power
Before the indifferent beak could let her drop? [1]

My purpose here is not *explication de texte* but simply to illustrate a scale of Value in poetry, and to point to the palpable *qualitative* difference between symbolical poetry and poetry that is not symbolical. Every poem, every work of art, expresses and implies a universe, a vision of Being; some of these universes are more extensive and valuable than others.

An individual poet will find certain images more fruitful in contemplation than others; and these by the accretion and overlaying of successive vivid experiences—and often through rigorous criticism —constitute his personal myths. The cluster of images which his experience has purified to a state of translucence and matured to symbolic stature comprise points of entry to his personal universe of value.

Does the extent and value of the universe depend upon the currency of the myth in which that universe is embodied, upon the number of people who (as it were) 'understand the allusions'? I should say not. I should say that the authority of a poem must always

---

[1] Yeats's counter to the romantic view of sexual love recurs several times in his later poems. See for example *The Lady's First Song*:

> *I am in love*
> *And that is my shame.*
> *What hurts the soul*
> *My soul adores,*
> *No better than a beast*
> *Upon all fours.*

Leonardo da Vinci had similarly observed: 'Love in its fury is a thing so ugly that the human race would die out if those engaged in it were to see themselves.' But at the same time Yeats was preoccupied with the notion that 'the tragedy of sexual intercourse is the perpetual virginity of the soul'.

rest within the poem; it does not derive from the weight or number of external references the poem may make. If a poem is to be symbolical the symbols must have come glowing with life into the poet's words as incarnations of his belief, as the body of his vision.

*   *   *

A myth is a direct metaphysical statement beyond science. It embodies in an articulated structure of symbol or narrative a vision of reality. It is a condensed account of man's Being and attempts to represent reality with structural fidelity, to indicate at a single stroke the salient and fundamental relations which for a man constitute reality. A myth in this sense is primitive, communal, and religious in origin; and its only possible mode of expression is Poetic. Myth is not an obscure, oblique, or elaborate way of expressing reality— it is the *only* way. Myth has as its purpose, its source and end, revelation; myth is not make-believe but the most direct and positive assertion of belief that man can discover.[1] Myth is an indispensable principle of unity in individual lives and in the life of society.

'Make-believe is an enervating exercise of fancy not to be confused with imaginative growth. The saner and greater mythologies are not fancies; they are the utterance of the whole soul of man and, as such, inexhaustible to meditation. They are no amusement or diversion to be sought as a relaxation and an escape from the hard realities of life. They are these hard realities in projection, their symbolic recognition, co-ordination and acceptance. Through such mythologies our will is collected, our powers unified, our growth controlled. Through them the infinitely divergent strayings of our being are brought into "balance and reconciliation".'[2]

As with the word 'symbol', this meaning of myth must be asserted as clearly as possible; for the 'ordinary' meaning of myth has no bearing upon Poetic, or upon the attitude of mind from which myth

[1] Jung supports this view in his recent contribution to an *Introduction to a Science of Mythology* (1951): 'The primitive mentality does not invent myths, it *experiences* them. Myths are original revelations of the preconscious psyche, involuntary statements about unconscious psychic happenings, and anything but allegories of physical processes.'

[2] I. A. Richards, *Coleridge on Imagination* (1934, 1951). Cf. Paul Valéry: 'The image of this world is part of a family of images, an infinite group, all the elements of which we possess—but unconsciously—consciousness of possession is the secret of the inventors' (*Note and Digression*, 1919).

prings. The *New English Dictionary* records only a meaning of 1830, defining myth as 'A purely fictitious narrative usually involving supernatural persons, actions, or events, and embodying some popular idea concerning natural or historical phenomena. Often used vaguely to include any narrative having fictitious elements.' And 'mythical' is defined as 'Having no foundation in fact'. Despite the efforts of several critics and aestheticians in this century to restore an older meaning to the word, this is the way most people at present would define myth. And the dominant notion of myth—as fictitious, having no foundation in fact, embodying some 'popular idea'— clearly indicates the dominance of the technical way of mind. Myth, as an articulated image of reality, has nothing to do with 'fact' in the scientific sense; it reveals Being and Value, and is not primarily concerned to record a series of events as they 'actually happened' in historical sequence. The myth becomes most translucent, it would seem, when a mythical narrative can also be shown to be 'a true story'; that is one reason for the vitality and variety of the Christian myth. The primary requirements for vital myth are that it should spring from belief, and that it should embody the *quality* of spiritual events and not merely that it should establish the historicity of certain physical events.

In Homer the words *myth* ($\mu\tilde{v}\theta o\varsigma$) and *logos* ($\lambda\acute{o}\gamma o\varsigma$) are synonyms and mean simply 'what was said'. For some reason Homer preferred the word 'myth' to the word 'logos'; but he does not use it in any special sense. Pindar was evidently the first to distinguish between 'myth' and 'logos', thinking of myth as a false story and logos as true. The two words diverge as soon as history abandoned the rhapsodic celebration of deeds and the affectionate accumulation of 'logoi' (? travellers' tales) and turned to analytical criticism in the attempt to discern dominant forces in social events. 'Logos' came to be applied to 'factual' and critical history such as Thucydides wrote; 'myth' was applied to poetry and to the legendary collections like that of Herodotus. The change was very sudden: Herodotus and Thucydides were born only about twenty years apart. Plato's philosophy supported the dichotomy; but Plato himself knew that he could illuminate the more visionary ranges of philosophy only by using myths; and he assumed that the truth or falsity of a myth depended upon interpretation and not upon the myths themselves. Through the differentiation in historical writing, 'logos' became associated with the faculty of 'reasoning'; but the corresponding faculty at work in myth was neither named nor clearly distinguished. 'Logos', by meaning not only a 'word' or 'story' but also a system of 'true fact' passed into the adjectival form which epitomizes the analytical method—*logic*.[1] For a short period—in the Fourth Gospel and in the Neoplatonic Christian philosophies—the word Logos turned back towards its primitive identity with myth, implying the magically powerful, the supremely creative.

In the beginning was the Word, and the Word was with God, and the Word was God.

The same was in the beginning with God.

All things were made by him; and without him was not any thing made that was made.

In him was life; and the life was the light of men.

And the light shineth in darkness; and the darkness comprehended it not.

If we regard the prototype of human expression as utterance springing from immersion in reality, the starting-point is (to use Maritain's term) the 'magical and potent Name', the means by which man realizes his world and himself.[2] And we may paraphrase St John's opening words as the foundation and starting-point of all Poetic: 'In the beginning was the Myth.' By this we mean, not merely in the beginning of time, in the primordial state of man, but now and always, in the eternal-evanescent present of reality. For whenever the mind falls upon contemplation the myth is at hand to clarify and make sane all action and all utterance which, being moral, responsible, valuable, can properly be called human.[3]

*　　　*　　　*

[1] See also J. A. K. Thomson, *The Art of the Logos* (1935); Perceval Frutiger, *Les Mythes de Platon* (1930); J. Tate, 'Plato and Allegorical Interpretation', *The Classical Quarterly*, vols. XXII and XXIII (1929, 1930).

[2] Cf. Baudelaire's saying: 'Il y a dans le mot, dans le *verbe*, quelque chose de *sacré* qui nous défends d'en faire un jeu de hasard. Manier savamment une langue, c'est pratiquer une espèce de sorcellerie évocatoire.'

[3] When the dictionaries refer to myth as a fictitious, *popular* opinion, they presumably have in mind what is usually called an 'old wives' tale'—popular in the sense of being held by uneducated people—or a 'superstition'. Superstition, however, is not the prerogative of uneducated persons; the difference between myth and superstition is the difference between *belief*, and *hypothesis* or presupposition. To suppose that swinging a dead cat in moonlight will cure warts rests upon a false conception of the scientific hypothesis of cause-and-effect. It is bad science because based upon too little observation and a hasty analysis of the wart-moon-cat situation; but that does not make it

I have spoken so far as though a myth were a symbolical narrative; but this was only for convenience. It seems to me that narrative is an accidental and not an essential feature of myth. Myth is rather a grouping of symbols which brings them into resonance with each other to embody a comprehensive view of reality. The relations which induce the resonance are not explicit and logical but dialectical and in the order of Poetic. Narrative order, on the other hand, is a logical order, even though the narrative take the loosely knit manner of epic—a string of episodes spun around a central heroic figure and related only through that figure. Whether or not 'supernatural' incidents are included does not affect the logicality of narrative structure. Once the myth has taken a narrative form it has started to fall from grace, to move in the direction of 'legend'—a narrative which treats (or purports to treat) of historical events with some 'imaginative' freedom.[1] It is the function of myth to hold symbols in resonance.

a superstition. What makes it a superstition is, not that it is *bad* science, but that it is science at all. Scientific method rests upon a group of hypotheses, the most serious of which from the human point of view is that events are neither moral nor of Value; the observer is supposed to be an impersonal recording instrument. When an attempt is made to interpret every aspect of human experience according to scientific hypothesis, the resulting picture of man, his nature, and his situation is a superstition and *not* a myth; for that account cannot admit (except perhaps as a grudging or flippant afterthought) morality or Value or that individual integrity of which Poetic is the only expression. Such a picture leaves 'nothing to believe in'—a state of spiritual paralysis characteristic of all 'rationalist' periods. It is easy to see how the obscurantist tendency of science when spread abroad in common minds should invert such important terms as myth and symbol: myth (in the correct sense) is represented as superstition or make-believe, symbol as a mathematical operation. Those who have put their money on a superstition will not readily admit the true quality of belief, nor subscribe to the ironical view of Richards that 'poetry is the supreme use of language, man's chief co-ordinating instrument, in the service of the most integral purposes of life'.

It is surprising to find Sir James Frazer, in his Introduction to Apollodorus' *Library* (1921), asserting the popular view of myth. 'By myths I understand mistaken explanations of phenomena, whether of human life or of external nature. Such originate in that instinctive curiosity concerning the causes of things which at a more advanced stage of knowledge seeks satisfaction in philosophy and science, but being founded on ignorance and misapprehension they are always false, for were they true they would cease to be myths. . . . In short, the range of myths is as wide as the world, being coextensive with the curiosity and the ignorance of man.'

[1] Legend as pseudo-history is a movement away from true myth towards the 'ordinary' or vulgar view that the function of imagination is to lead one into what Keats called 'the realms of gold'. This movement is clearly to be seen in Ezra Pound's poem *The Flame,* in which he meditates nostalgically upon Provençal legend. The word 'legend' is almost a late return to the original sense of *logos*—'what is said'.

In the legend the cluster of symbols dissipates and becomes confused (sometimes by accretion, as in Egyptian mythology), and loses
resonance; the emphasis moves from the symbols themselves to the
narrative events and the personalities of the actors in those events
Such a process was at work when the Greek myths were transferred
into the more clear-cut, anthropomorphic, and hierarchical religion
of the Romans. But a hasty generalization must be avoided; the
Homeric poems (the Homeric Hymns are not Homeric) have lost
much symbolic force in their narrative emphasis. Pindar rediscovered Greek myth and symbol in a lyric mode; and the Greek
tragedies, despite their firm narrative structure, restore symbolic force
perhaps mostly through the use of inscrutable gnomic choruses. Yet
many centuries later some process of attrition and confusion fell upon
the Arthurian legend; the primordial symbols were submerged, and
out of the chaos of the legend no distinct myth emerges but only
fragmentary recollections of some emblematic figures and episodes
and the dominating primordial symbols of lance and Graal. Out of
the Homeric legend—and especially in the hands of Joyce and
Pound—arises the figure of Odysseus; but Odysseus, not so much
a symbol as an emblem of distracted twentieth-century man; the
morose and crafty opportunist-adventurer; without belief, but in his
own absent-minded way faithful to a nostalgic self-preoccupied
yearning, the man without a passport, the tragic playboy of the
Western world. In the Christian myth, however, one finds luminous
constellation of primordial symbols combined with a fresh myth of
inexhaustible vitality. The new myth is rooted in history and the
Gospels are told in a loose narrative form; but the emphasis is always
upon Christ's deeds as symbolical, and his sayings as poetical
Through these deeds and sayings a vast web of primordial symbols is
brought into resonance by, and oriented upon, the central symbol of
Christ himself—not the personality, but the *person* of Christ. The
only way the power of the Christian myth can be curtailed is by
removing it from the sphere of Poetic, by regarding it in an attitude
not religious, by substituting for the poetically articulated myth an
ethical system, an abstract philosophy, or a casuistical set of rules—
none of which can induce the contemplative state of awareness from
which alone valuable action can flow.

The precise outlines or limits of a myth can never be determined
every myth is compact of primordial symbols, and every myth
through primordial symbolism is in resonance with every other

myth. This is simply a macroscopic view of our first account of myth as a resonant cluster of symbols. Every myth singly and all myths together comprise what Coleridge called a 'subtle Vulcanian Spider-web Net of Steel—strong as Steel, yet subtle as Ether'. Touch this intricate web, no matter how lightly, and 'instantly the trains of forgotten Thought rise from their living catacombs'; a touch, a breath, a vibration of the air—and it is transmitted directly to some mythic centre and spreads outward in rings of evocation to bring back from the dark fringes of secret experience vivid echoes of forgotten suffering and the joy that is also suffering.

> . . . still the heart doth need a language, still
> Doth the old instinct bring back the old names.

Only thus can the most primitive and the most civilized mentality fuse in the incandescent moment of reality which is all we know of eternity. For

> . . . every powerful life goes on its way
> Too blinded by the sight of the mind's eye,
> Too deafened by the cries out of the heart
> Not to have staggering feet and groping hands.

And every great work of art, and every great discovery, is made by a man groping his way out of a dead end—the dead end of apathy, of unbelief, of terror.[1]

*   *   *

A sane and stable society will supply itself with a coherent structure of symbols for the mythical expression of reality and Value. But a myth can never be a formula for directed action. Whenever myth is turned in a practical direction it decays by losing its inner Poetic coherence, by submitting to the alien coherence of logic. Symbols need constantly to be recreated and clarified if they are to preserve the inner vitality of myth. But myth, being religious, draws its vitality not from communal lip-service but from vivid personal creations and recreations. In an unstable or disintegrating society the communal myth has collapsed and been replaced with a multitude of unrelated superstitions. The artists, the myth-makers, are then deprived of the

[1] Cf. Henri Michaux's statement: 'Tous ceux qui ont fait de grandes choses les ont faites pour sortir d'une difficulté, d'un cul de sac.'

established structure of symbol and are obliged to rediscover and revive ancient symbols and even to create symbols and myths of their own.[1] Symbols, whether ancient and established or not, must constantly be discovered and rediscovered and made personal to the poet if they are not to degenerate into cyphers or emblems. The present disintegration of society presents only a special instance of a general problem for the poet. But the artist has in this century been so isolated from society that the artist's introspective preoccupation with his work has secreted a great deal of valuable detail about the way poetic symbols are created.

In a little angry verse Yeats celebrated his own departure from a tapestried archaeological manner:

> *I made my song a coat*
> *Covered with embroideries*
> *Out of old mythologies*
> *From heel to throat;*
> *But the fools caught it,*
> *Wore it in the world's eyes*
> *As though they'd wrought it.*
> *Song, let them take it,*
> *For there's more enterprise*
> *In walking naked.*

From an adaptation of historic symbols not his own, he turned to discover and shape to his personal vision personal symbols, no matter of what origin so long as they were his own, grasped and set afire by his own experience. The stark, passionate, terrifying metaphysics of *Byzantium* and *The Second Coming* prove upon the pulse that Yeats succeeded in his quest for a personal symbolism. Without

---

[1] This accounts for the private, fragmentary, and archaeological character of much twentieth-century art. In such conditions there is a very wide gulf between the best and second-best artists, because of the almost insuperable difficulty, when society has no eye or ear for symbolical expression, of raising personal vision to the level of vital symbol. Of contemporary esoteric writing Paul Valéry notes in *Note-Book B1910* 'An important part of modern literature is given to communicating—not the final state of impressions, the state of something seized, unravelled, organized, cleared up—but the initial state, that of having still to understand (the encounter still to be met), the problematical state, confused, sentimental, sensorial. Instead of writing formulas it writes data in the form of implicit functions—somewhat as the modern definitions are made by independent postulates and no longer by one single sentence. Much the same as music.'

an extensive mythological gloss, without even the 'vehiculatory gear
and swim-bladders' of *Per Amica Silentia Lunae* and *A Vision*, his
personal symbols—of pern and gyre, swan and heron and hawk, the
winding stair, the tower, Byzantium—convey directly their charges
of feeling, their 'meaning' in Poetic.[1] If this were not so they would
not be symbols. How this came about is more than hinted in his
poem *On a Picture of a Black Centaur by Edmund Dulac*:

> . . . *yet I, being driven half insane*
> *Because of some green wing, gathered old mummy wheat*
> *In the mad abstract dark and ground it grain by grain*
> *And after baked it slowly in an oven; but now*
> *I bring full-flavoured wine out of a barrel found*
> *Where seven Ephesian topers slept and never knew*
> *When Alexander's empire passed, they slept so sound.*

The self-contained, self-evident force of Yeats's mature metaphysical
manner might be regarded as an isolated psychological development, not typical of the symbolic process in poetry. But the same
process is to be seen in the work of other poets. And it can be clearly
demonstrated, where one would perhaps be least disposed to find it,
in the work of Coleridge. In *The Ancient Mariner* he had fashioned a
myth in narrative form, weaving it around a group of symbols, few
of which—and notably the albatross—were consecrated by previous

---

[1] While this chapter was in final revision I have read with great profit T. R. Henn's
The Lonely Tower (1950). From his book I have lifted an epigraph: for I have not read
Albert Béguin's *L'Âme Romantique et Le Rêve*.

I do not suggest that Yeats's poems—or anybody else's—should be read one by one,
out of the context of the whole corpus of his work. But the single poem must contain
within itself the power which, if inscrutable, will send us in search of clarification.
With Yeats the clarification can be found within his own work; with other poets this
not so. (See Rosamund Tuve, *A Reading of George Herbert* (1952), for the importance
of knowing what a poet took for granted.) Yeats himself does not argue for unreflective
impressionism. 'Take some line that is quite simple, that gets its beauty from its place in
story, and see how it flickers with the light of the many symbols that have given the
story its beauty, as a sword-blade may flicker with the light of burning towers.' 'A
poetical passage cannot be understood without a rich memory, and like the older school
of painting appeals to a tradition . . . in rhythm, in vocabulary; for the ear must notice
slight variations upon old cadences and customary words, all that high breeding of
poetical style where there is nothing ostentatious, nothing crude, no breath of parvenu
or journalist.' 'Day after day I have sat in my chair turning a symbol over in my mind,
exploring all its details, defining and again defining its elements, testing my convictions
and those of others by its unity, attempting to substitute particulars for an abstraction
like that of algebra.'

symbolic use.[1] Beyond *The Ancient Mariner* and his better-known poems he sustained, without conscious intent, a coherent structure of personal symbols powerful enough to animate many a passage of his intimate prose as well as his poems. These symbols, some of which touch primordial references, attained symbolic stature by being taken up from direct observation in actual events, made objects of contemplation and vehicles of the contemplative passion ('When a man writes any work of genius, or invents some creative action, is it not', Yeats asks, 'because some knowledge or power has come into his mind from beyond his mind? It is called up by an image, as I think; . . . but our images must be given to us, we cannot choose them deliberately.') Coleridge's personal symbols—the moon, the blue sky, the ocean, trees, fire, the candle flame (if they are to be called by name)—control the power of the Moon-gloss in *The Ancient Mariner*: 'In his loneliness and fixedness he yearneth towards the journeying Moon, and the stars that still sojourn, yet still move onward; and everywhere the blue sky belongs to them, and is their appointed rest and their native country and their own natural homes, which they enter unannounced, as lords that are certainly expected, and yet there is a silent joy at their arrival.' A brief series of extracts from his private Notebooks will illustrate how clearly he recognized and understood symbolic process.

'. . . at first, we are from various causes delighted with *generalities* of nature which can all be expressed in dignified words; but, afterwards, becoming more intimately acquainted with Nature in her detail, we are delighted with *distinct*, vivid ideas most when made distinct.'

'I am not certain whether I should have seen with any emotion the mulberry-tree of Shakespeare . . . if a striking tree, I fear that the pleasure would be diminished rather than increased, that I should have no unity of feeling, and find . . . an intrusion that prevented me from wholly (as a whole man) losing myself in the flexures of its branches and intertwining of its roots.'

'Sometimes when I earnestly look at a beautiful object or landscape it seems as if I were on the *brink* of a fruition still denied—as Vision were an *appetite*.'

'In looking at objects of Nature while I am thinking, as at yonder moon dim-glimmering through the dewy window-pane, I seem

---

[1] I incline to the view that *Dejection: an Ode* is not less impersonal and mythical than *The Ancient Mariner*.

rather to be seeking, as it were *asking* for, a symbolical language for something within me that already and forever exists, than observing anything new. Even when that latter is the case, yet still I have always an obscure feeling as if that new phenomena were the dim awakening of a forgotten or hidden truth of my inner nature. It is still interesting as a word—a symbol. It is Λόγος the Creator, and the Evolver!'

'One of the strangest and most painful peculiarities of my nature . . . I will here record—and my motive, or, rather, impulse, to do this seems an effort to eloign and abalienate it from the dark adyt of my own being by a visual outness, and not the wish for others to see it.'

'What a swarm of thoughts and feelings, endlessly minute fragments, and, as it were, representations of all preceding and embryos of all future thought, lie in one moment! So, in a single drop of water, the microscope discovers what motions, what tumult, what wars, what pursuits, what stratagems, what a circle-dance of death and life, death-hunting life, and life renewed and invigorated by death! The whole world seems here in a many-meaning cypher. What if our existence was but that moment? What an unintelligible, affrightful riddle, what a chaos of limbs and trunk, tailless, headless, nothing begun and nothing ended, would it not be? And yet scarcely more than that other moment of fifty or sixty years, were that all?'

'Our mortal existence, what is it but a stoppage in the blood of life, a brief eddy from wind or concourse of currents in the ever-flowing ocean of pure Activity, who beholds pyramids, yea, Alps and Andes, giant pyramids, the work of fire that raiseth monuments, like a generous victor o'er its own conquest, the tomb-stones of a world destroyed! Yet these, too, float adown the sea of Time, and melt away as mountains of floating ice.'

'Unconsciously I stretched forth my arms as to embrace the sky, and in a trance I had worshipped God in the moon—the spirit, not the form . . . Oh! not only the moon, but the depths of the sky! The moon was the *idea*; but deep sky is, of all visual impressions, the nearest akin to a feeling. It is more a feeling than a sight, or, rather, it is the melting away and entire union of feeling and sight!'

In a note written in the early morning of Wednesday, 2 November 1803, we see the interflux of feeling, growing out of sounds and visual images, flowing across the passivity of rapt attention in a mood of searching agony. The symbols constellate: the complexity of feeling is borne by the interfusion of symbols and their paradoxical ambivalence. In this note, made in the white heat of vision and intended for no eye but his own, we see 'the shaping spirit of Imagination' moving on the face of the waters, the symbols emerging, clarifying, physically embedded in vivid perception yet pointing forward into a central area of spiritual experience.

'The voice of the Greta and the cock-crowing. The voice seems to grow like a flower on or about [? above] the water beyond the bridge, while the cock-crowing is nowhere particular . . . A most remarkable sky! the moon, now waned to a perfect ostrich egg, hangs over our house almost, only so much beyond it, gardenward, that I can see it, holding my head out of the smaller study window. The sky is covered with whitish and with dingy cloudage, thin dingiest scud close under the moon, and one side of it moving, all else moveless . . . Now while I have been writing this and gazing between-whiles (it is forty minutes past two), the break over the road is swallowed up, and the stars gone; the break over the house is narrowed into a rude circle, and on the edge of its circumference one very bright star. See! already the white mass, thinning at its edge, *fights* with its brilliance. See! It has bedimmed it, and now it is gone, and the moon is gone. The cock-crowing too has ceased. The Greta sounds on for ever. But I hear only the ticking of my watch in the pen-place of my writing-desk and the far lower note of the noise of the fire, perpetual, yet seeming uncertain. It is the low voice of quiet change, of destruction doing its work by little and little.'

At a touch of vivid perception upon the 'subtle Vulcanian Spider-web', 'instantly the trains of forgotten Thought rise from their living catacombs': 'images and shattered fragments of memory'; not ideas, not propositions, not abstract notions trooping by in pale personification—Hope, Love, Remorse, Guilt, Aloneness—but the multitudinous cumulus of consciousness suddenly selecting and grouping itself into a state of vital wholeness. This state is an over-whelming awareness, a pure joy which in its intensity is suffering, a suffering which in its integrity is delight. And here the self is made whole and lost in its immersion in reality. The limits between self and other, self and Nature, mind and the laws of its own universe, are obliterated. The struggle to realize and make integral the self, the need to identify the self while yet preserving the reality, are in these circumstances an unslakable thirst. The work of art, the physical secretion of this extricating process, becomes the necessary condition of withdrawal, the means of faith, the buttress against self-betrayal. Out of such a finely intrinsicated web of personal symbols does the myth spring as the body for a moral universe, a personal universe of value.

So profound and urgent is the need for myth, that a myth remains fluid, ready always to accommodate whatever is germinal and clarifying, quick to reject what was become inert or sterile. The true myth never hardens into a crystallized system. The personal myth preserves its integrity in an infinity of variations and resonant combinations; the incandescent centre of emphasis falls now on this symbol, now on that; and with each fresh arrangement, each gracious combination of personal symbols, the flow of evoked images, words, sounds is modulated to serve the compelling integrity of the myth. The myth hangs dove-like over the chaos of memory, calling to what creatures it knows not; and those creatures—though they do not know their names, though they do not understand the language in which the cry is uttered—come forth into the light, answering un-uttered names, dancing in grave style to the compulsion of a tune, 'ditties of no tone' perhaps, a heart-beat, a rhythm. In the process of integral fusion each individual element preserves its identity and is changed, yet 'abides itself as a living part in that unity of which it is the representative'. The primitive and civilized, the communal and the private, the primordial and the personal, the accidental and the permanent, join in a ritual dance gesturing forth the present epiphany, while the poet relives and revives a past in the present from which already a future is taking shape.

A NOTE ON ALLEGORY

Allegory is almost invariably represented as the antithesis of symbol —'a translation', as Coleridge says, 'of abstract notions into a picture-language, which is itself nothing but an abstraction from objects of the senses'. The effort to isolate the transcendent power of symbol has turned too often upon a comparison with the formulated allegory— allegory in decay. The same attitude is expressed by Yeats: 'Symbolism said things which could not be said so perfectly in any other way, and needed but a right instinct for its understanding; while Allegory said things which could be said as well, or better, in another way, and needed a right knowledge for its understanding. The one thing gave dumb things voices, and bodiless things bodies; while the other read a meaning—which had never lacked its voice or its body—into something heard or seen, and loved less for the meaning than for its own sake.' [1] C. S. Lewis's *Allegory of Love* (1936) on the other hand has clarified the nature of true allegory, but only at the expense of confusing the nature of symbol. I wish to advance the view that allegory in its full poetic development is a symbolic mode, and in its formulated state is a species of cyphering.

Allegory is a convention by which the inner drama of conscience and love may be revealed. Different features of the individual soul are personified and, within the conventional setting of a dream, the personifications take on individual identity and act out the inner drama in a discursive (usually epic) narrative. In allegory two levels of attention and action operate simultaneously. Lewis has scotched the standard view that a reader cannot sustain two levels of action at once. 'It is a mischievous error to suppose that in an allegory the author is "really" talking about the thing symbolized, and not at all about the thing that symbolizes; the very essence of the art is to talk about both.'

Allegory in its full development is a highly specialized form of symbolic expression. But because the purpose of allegory is psychological revelation, it arises at best from a mixed poetic intension, and very easily becomes the vehicle for deliberate didacticism. Allegory

[1] Elsewhere, he writes: 'I find that though I love symbolism, which is often the only fitting speech for some mystery of disembodied life, I am for the most part bored by allegory, which is made, as Blake says, by the "daughters of memory", and coldly, with no wizard frenzy.'

reveals by dissection; it separates out prominent psychic elements and personifies them as dramatic 'characters'. And this substitution, which is cyphering or embleming and not symbolization, makes allegory extremely unstable; for it establishes an unpoetic coherence at variance with the integrity of consciousness. This unpoetic strain is further strengthened by two other demands for technical coherence: the narrative, as principal focus of interest, must at least be a coherent narrative; and if the narrative element is allowed to develop fully *as narrative* the personified psychic elements will tend to lose their distinct identity as cyphers by becoming more or less complex in response to the need for a 'life-like' effect in the narrative. True allegory—allegory as a symbolic mode—is therefore a very rare achievement: the list would perhaps only include *The Romance of the Rose, Pilgrim's Progress* (with some reservations), and parts of *The Faerie Queene*. (Symbolical allegory occurs in limited passages of poems which do not attempt to sustain a full narrative allegory; but these too are rare.) In the symbolic allegory we find the characteristic symbolical resonance between the allegorical persons and the faculties of the soul, between the narrative and the inner drama; and the character of this resonance is precisely what Coleridge postulated for symbol. The most prominent feature of symbolic allegory is the distinct self-subsistence of both the 'surface' story and the implied allegorical 'meaning'. As soon as the self-subsistence of the allegory at both levels of interpretation relaxes or ceases, symbolism has degenerated into cyphering.

Symbolical allegory can only appear at a particular phase of personal and social self-consciousness: a burning desire to understand and describe inner conflict must arise at a time when there is no satisfactory direct means of revealing 'inner goings-on'. Such a period will be of short duration; and while it lasts, allegory is the only symbolic means of psychological revelation. For symbolic writing is not an alternative or indirect or calligraphic way of saying something —it is at certain times the *only* way. As a method, allegory is cumbersome and inflexible, and doomed to give place to more direct and economical modes of expression; and this process is hastened by the inherently unsymbolic character of allegorical structure. In the Middle Ages—probably because it proved a powerful instrument for teaching religion and manners—allegory continued as a conventional mould, a debilitated formula long after the internal necessity for the method had disappeared. As soon as the luminous identity between the story and the allegorical meaning is lost, allegory degenerates into a cryptographic cyphering device for concealing a criticism of social, political, and theological issues beneath an innocent surface. Much the greatest quantity of allegory is of this sort; and so it comes about that the degenerate allegory has almost invariably been regarded as the type of allegory and the antithesis of symbol. Many sections of *The Faerie Queene*, though not all, are formulated allegory. And Swift's *Gulliver*, though not strictly an allegory, is as much the degenerate offspring of true allegory as the morality play is.

The work of a perceptive and original writer, however, is not doomed to decline with an outworn mode. Chaucer, steeped in the tradition of symbolic allegory, recognized that allegory had ceased to be a necessary method of expressing his psychological insight. He suddenly breaks off in the middle of writing *Anelide and Arcite*, abandons the elaborate high manner of romance, and turns to write one of the greatest psychological poems ever written—*Troilus and Criseyde*. And this poem (as C. S. Lewis has shown) preserves some of the allegorical cypher-persons, but changed back into real persons. Pandarus is not *really* the Bialacoil of the allegory of love: he is a perplexed, well-meaning man-of-the-world, absent-mindedly vicious. And Criseyde is not a cypher for any quality or any group of qualities; she is not even an emblem of feminine fickleness and wilful infidelity. She is a person of 'slyding corage', muddled, frightened almost to the point of paralysis, capable only of languid, despairing action—a person so credible, alive, and pitiful that Chaucer himself cannot pass judgment upon her even when he goes through the motions of drawing a moral to his tale.

If symbol and allegory, emblem and cypher, can be clearly discriminated, the nature of symbol emerges very clearly. The word 'symbol' is most important as a central critical term and should if possible be protected from vague usage. There is a further consideration. There are signs—especially in the novels of James Joyce and Franz Kafka, to mention only two writers—that we are entering upon, or may even have entered, one of those small areas of history in which symbolical allegory is the only possible mode for original psychological revelation. Psychological theory in this century—in the general mind at any rate—has turned the *psyche* into such an unastonishing little machine that we probably require the refreshment of a stylized mode that will make beforehand few easy assumptions about what is to be revealed.

X

Music and Rhythm

I T is worth recalling Mallarmé's statement that poems are made with words. Anything that tends to undermine or destroy the *verbal* character of words in a poem strikes a blow to the heart of poetry, by destroying the medium of Poetic. If language is exploited as though it were a resource of pure sound, the result cannot be better than a crude sort of music: a penny whistle can make better music. If poetry is not to be regarded as an inferior sort of music, fatally hampered from the start by having to work in an unmusical medium, we need to consider what the distinctive 'music' of poetry is. We are confronted by another dynamic equation; in discovering more about the 'music of poetry' we discover more about the 'music of music'.

When I said that poetry was sonic rather than visual I meant that poetry was most suitably to be apprehended by ear; that the patterns, resonances and rhythms of poetry will scarcely stand forth unless the ear is engaged. It does not follow, however, that poetry is primarily

193

'a matter of sound'. Yet what is usually implied by calling a poem 'musical' is that the 'sound matches the sense', that it is 'harmonious' or 'smooth'. Although words have the qualities of sounds, they are never—*as* words—pure sounds; words always imply some sort of meaning. The music of poetry is not typified by such languid musicalities as Poe's celebrated phrase 'the viol, the violet, and the vine', nor by that glowing chestnut from a forgotten prize ode—'A rose-red city half as old as time'. And as for the 'lyricism' of Shelley, it is his own executioner, a trick of indiscipline to be invoked when the poetry flagged.

> *There the voluptuous nightingales,*
>   *Are awake through all the broad noonday.*
> *When one with bliss or sadness fails,*
>   *And through the windless ivy-boughs,*
>   *Sick with sweet love, droops dying away*
> *On its mate's music-panting bosom;*
> *Another from the swinging blossom,*
>   *Watching to catch the languid close*
>   *Of the last strain, then lifts on high*
>   *The wings of the weak melody,*
> *'Till some new strain of feeling bear*
>   *The song, and all the woods are mute;*
> *When there is heard through the dim air*
> *The rush of wings, and rising there*
>   *Like many a lake-surrounded flute,*
> *Sounds overflow the listener's brain*
> *So sweet, that joy is almost pain.*

Only a jejune conception of music could have informed Swinburne's emasculate and contrived *Hymn to Proserpine*.

> *In the night where thine eyes are as moons are in heaven, the night where thou*
>   *art,*
> *Where the silence is more than all tunes, where sleep overflows from the*
>   *heart,*
> *Where the poppies are sweet as the rose in our world, and the red rose is*
>   *white,*
> *And the wind falls faint as it blows with the fume of the flowers of the night,*
> *And the murmur of spirits that sleep in the shadow of Gods from afar*
> *Grows dim in thine ears and deep as the deep dim soul of a star,*

n the sweet low light of thy face, under heavens untrod by the sun,
et my soul with their souls find place, and forget what is done and undone.[1]

To turn words into imitative noises may require virtuosity but not
ny finely attuned ear.

> *I am the Gutter Dream,*
> *Tune-maker, born of steam,*
> *Tooting joy, tooting hope,*
> *I am the Kallyope,*
> *Car called the Kallyope.*
> *Willy willy willy wah* HOO!
>
> (VACHEL LINDSAY)

At least this springs from a modest purpose: the same cannot be said
or a song in Webster's *Duchess of Malfi*. (Did the singing voice and
ccompanying music redeem this from crude contrivance?)

> *Here by a madman this Song is sung, to a dismal kind of music*
>
> *O, let us howl some heavy note,*
> *Some deadly dogged howl,*
> *Sounding, as from the threatening throat*
> *Of beasts and fatal fowl!*
> *As ravens, screech-owls, bulls, and bears,*
> *We'll bell, and bawl our parts,*

[1] Swinburne at least had the good grace to parody this manner in his *Nephelidia*:

> *From the depth of the dreamy decline of the dawn through a notable nimbus of nebulous noonshine,*
> *Pallid and pink as the palm of the flag-flower that flickers with fear of the flies as they float,*
> *Are the looks of our lovers that lustrously lean from a marvel of mystic miraculous moonshine,*
> *These that we feel in the blood of our blushes that thicken and threaten with throbs through the*
>   *throat? &c. &c.*

The same slack langour afflicts most of Yeats's youthful hexameters:

> *Wrapt in the wave of that music, with weariness more than of earth,*
> *The moil of my centuries filled me; and gone like a sea-covered stone*
> *Were the memories of the whole of my sorrow and the memories of the whole of my mirth,*
> *And a softness came from the starlight and filled me full to the bone.*

This is the sort of verse of which Yeats said: 'I have felt in certain early works of my
own which I have long abandoned, and here and there in the work of others of my
generation, a slight, sentimental sensuality which is disagreeable and does not exist in
the work of Donne, let us say, because he, being permitted to say what he pleased, was
never tempted to linger, or rather to pretend that we can linger, between spirit and
sense.'

Till irksome noise have cloyed your ears,
   And corrosived your hearts.
At last, whenas our quire wants breath,
   Our bodies being blest,
We'll sing, like swans, to welcome death,
   And die in love and rest.

Pater maintained that all the arts 'aspire towards the condition of music'. The remark is coloured (I suspect) by the nostalgic notion that music is the most 'spiritual' of the arts—an error that leaves music conveniently unexamined in order to avoid the incorrigible *impurity* of language.[1] Such a view condones—as with Shelley, Swinburne, and Poe—a nerveless hieratic verse which is no more music than it is poetry. Words refuse to behave as though they were simply musical noises. The eerie refrain in 'The Fire Sermon'—

   Weialala leia
   Wallala leialala—

argues however that effects of pure sound *can* serve the highest interests of poetry. And we notice that sustained poetic passion has a way of gesturing itself forth in orchestrated vowel sounds and the percussions and meltings of consonants. Wordsworth, for example, can establish a setting for 'sounds of undistinguishable motion' in which move

   Huge and mighty forms, that do not live
   Like living men—

'enormous shapes', Yeats calls them, 'who still were old when the great sea was young'.

   Dust as we are, the immortal spirit grows
   Like harmony in music; there is a dark
   Inscrutable workmanship that reconciles
   Discordant elements, makes them cling together
   In one society. How strange that all

[1] Hanslick's *Vom Musikalisch-Schoenen* follows Schopenhauer in separating music from the other arts; music, he maintains, is 'pure tone' and is not written with intent to arouse emotion in the listener. Hanslick is much concerned to detach music from any kind of 'representation' or programme; and that is where the strength of his position lies. The view is briefly outlined in Einstein's *Music in the Romantic Era* (1947) pp. 349–52. Valéry (as I noted earlier) considered music to be the most 'spiritual' of the arts—and so does Maritain.

The terrors, pains, and early miseries,
Regrets, vexations, lassitudes interfused
Within my mind, should e'er have borne a part,
And that a needful part, in making up
The calm existence that is mine when I
Am worthy of myself! Praise to the end!
Thanks to the means which Nature deigned to employ;
Whether her fearless visitings, or those
That came with soft alarm, like hurtless light
Opening the peaceful clouds; or she may use
Severer interventions, ministry
More palpable, as best might suit her aim.[1]

or all that this is a profoundly original effect, it inclines to a certain
Miltonic monotony; the sound nearly—but not quite—undermines
the verbal quality of the words. To grasp the sonic resources of
poetry, greater variety than this is required. The clue is in sight when
we compare the appalling levity of Adam's after-dinner speech in
Paradise Lost with the ritual dignity of his untainted conscience.

Eve, now I see thou art exact of taste,
And elegant, of Sapience no small part,
Since to each meaning savour we apply,
And Palate call judicious; I the praise
Yield thee, so well this day thou hast purvey'd.
Much pleasure we have lost, while we abstain'd
From this delightful Fruit, nor known till now

---

[1] Compare an unashamedly Miltonic section of the Prospectus to *The Excursion.*

For I must tread on shadowy ground, must sink
Deep—and, aloft ascending, breathe in worlds
To which the heaven of heavens is but a veil.
All strength—all terror, single or in bands,
That ever was put forth in personal form—
Jehovah—with his thunder, and the choir
Of shouting Angels, and the empyreal thrones—
I pass them unalarmed. Not Chaos, not
The darkest pit of lowest Erebus,
Nor aught of blinder vacancy, scooped out
By help of dreams—can breed such fear and awe
As fall upon us often when we look
Into our Minds, into the Mind of Man—
My haunt, and the main region of my song.

True relish, tasting; if such pleasure be
In things to us forbidden, it might be wish'd,
For this one Tree had bin forbidden ten.
But come, so well refresh'd, now let us play,
As meet is, after such delicious Fare;
For never did thy Beauties since the day
I saw thee first and wedded thee, adorn'd
With all perfections, so enflame my sense
With ardor to enjoy thee, fairer now
Then ever, bountie of this vertuous Tree.

An even more instructive passage is Enobarbus' description
Cleopatra. It opens like a tone-poem, harmonious, full of a
alliteration and assonance, the sounds matching the languoro
sense.

The barge she sat in, like a burnisht throne,
Burnt on the water: the poop was beaten gold;
Purple the sails, and so perfumed that
The winds were love-sick with them; the oars were silver,
Which to the tune of flutes kept stroke, and made
The water which they beat to follow faster,
As amorous of their strokes. For her own person,
It beggar'd all description: she did lie
In her pavilion—cloth-of-gold of tissue—
O'er-picturing that Venus where we see
The fancy outwork nature: on each side her
Stood pretty dimpled boys, like smiling Cupids,
With divers-colour'd fans, whose wind did seem
To glow the delicate cheeks which they did cool,
And what they undid did.

This is 'fine' writing with a vengeance, but monotonous, mere
'beautiful', not touching the deepest springs of poetic music. B
Shakespeare has only tuned his orchestra: there is more to com
'O rare for Antony,' cries Agrippa; and Enobarbus continues o
like a man in a trance.

Her gentlewomen, like the Nereides,
So many mermaids, tended her i' the eyes,
And made their bends adornings: at the helm
A seeming mermaid steers: the silken tackle

Swell with the touches of those flower-soft hands,
That yarely frame the office. From the barge
A strange invisible perfume hits the sense
Of the adjacent wharfs.

With this extravagant figure a new dimension enters; the intensity rises, the flaws of irony and impudence increase in sharpness until the complex person of Cleopatra is sketched forth.

ENOBARBUS   *The city cast*
Her people out upon her; and Antony,
Enthroned i' the market-place, did sit alone,
Whistling to the air, which, but for vacancy,
Had gone to gaze on Cleopatra too,
And made a gap in nature.

AGRIPPA   *Rare Egyptain!*

ENOBARBUS   *Upon her landing, Antony sent to her,*
Invited her to supper: she replied,
It should be better he became her guest;
Which she entreated: our courteous Antony,
Whom ne'er the word of 'No' woman heard speak,
Being barber'd ten times o'er, goes to the feast,
And for his ordinary pays his heart
For what his eyes eat only.

AGRIPPA   *Royal wench!*
She made great Caesar lay his sword to bed:
He plough'd her, and she cropt.

ENOBARBUS   *I saw her once*
Hop forty paces through the public street;
And having lost her breath, she spoke, and panted,
That she did make defect perfection,
And, breathless, power breathe forth.

MAECENAS   *Now Antony must leave her utterly.*

ENOBARBUS   *Never; he will not:*
Age cannot wither her, nor custom stale
Her infinite variety: other women cloy
The appetites they feed; but she makes hungry
Where most she satisfies: for vilest things

Become themselves in her; that the holy priests
Bless her when she is riggish.

A few words are added to get the actors off the stage, and the scene closes. Enobarbus is not a poet; he is a blunt soldier, despising cultivated ways. Not by accident is this account of Cleopatra placed in his mouth; if the ironic complexities of her 'infinite variety' are to come forth, something is required beyond grandiloquent verse. There is needed the sharp edge of racy speech and unerring insight. There is needed a return to Philo's savage mockery:

> *[Antony] is become the bellows and the fan*
> *To cool a gipsy's lust. Look where they come:*
> *Take but good note, and you shall see in him*
> *The triple pillar of the world transform'd*
> *Into a strumpet's fool.*

Enobarbus is Antony's intimate: already in his description of her, there is a foretaste of Antony's spiteful words of loathing:

> *I found you as a morsel cold upon*
> *Dead Caesar's trencher; nay, you were a fragment*
> *Of Cneius Pompey's; besides what hotter hours,*
> *Unregister'd in vulgar fame, you have*
> *Luxuriously pickt out: for, I am sure,*
> *Though you can guess what temperance should be,*
> *You know not what it is.*

The impudent angularity of the verse—as in Donne's fourth *Elegy*—opens chinks in the hieratic surfaces of poetry, through which flows the passionate vigour of compulsive expression.[1] Over and over

---

[1] Cf. the section in *The Waste Land* deliberately modelled upon Shakespeare's original. The woman's boudoir is described at length with voluptuous exactitude. By an unexpected modulation the verse takes an ominous turn, recovers for an instant, disintegrates into shapeless apathy, then crackles with empty desperation. After twenty lines of descriptive blank verse, the poem reads:

> *Above the antique mantel was displayed*
> *As though a window gave upon the sylvan scene*
> *The change of Philomel, by the barbarous king*
> *So rudely forced; yet there the nightingale*
> *Filled all the desert with inviolable voice*
> *And still she cried, and still the world pursues,*
> *'Jug Jug' to dirty ears.*

gain we hear it in Yeats's late verse:

> Civilization is hooped together, brought
> Under a rule, under the semblance of peace
> By manifold illusion; but man's life is thought,
> And he, despite his terror, cannot cease
> Ravening through century after century,
> Ravening, raging, and uprooting that he may come
> Into the desolation of reality:
> Egypt and Greece, good-bye, and good-bye, Rome!

The effects here are fundamentally musical. This is the music that sustains rhythm and prevents verse from degenerating into an absent-minded chant or a mechanical monotone. The words remain verbal throughout, and their sounds serve a purpose other than the exploitation of sound. In these passages the verse is literally (to use Valéry's term) 'musicalized': it gains an astonishing capacity for swift modulation, unprepared allusion, sudden shock, instant peace.

> Could I revive within me
> Her symphony and song,
> To such a deep delight 'twould win me,
> That with music loud and long,
> I would build that dome in air,
> That sunny dome! those caves of ice!
> And all who heard should see them there,
> And all should cry, Beware! Beware!
> His flashing eyes, his floating hair!
> Weave a circle round him thrice,

> And other withered stumps of time
> Were told upon the walls; staring forms
> Leaned out, leaning, hushing the room enclosed.
> Footsteps shuffled on the stair.
> Under the firelight, under the brush, her hair
> Spread out in fiery points
> Glowed into words, then would be savagely still.
>
> 'My nerves are bad to-night. Yes, bad. Stay with me.
> 'Speak to me. Why do you never speak. Speak.
> 'What are you thinking of? What thinking? What?
> 'I never know what you are thinking. Think.'
>
> I think we are in rats' alley
> Where the dead men lost their bones.

And close your eyes with holy dread,
For he on honey-dew hath fed,
And drunk the milk of Paradise.

Alliteration, assonance, the imitative shaping of consonant sound
all subserve the need in poetry for a resonant setting. Language is no
normally capable of such abrupt transitions; emphasis, mood, and
intension can be altered only after just preparation. When verse i
musicalized it is as though an additional dimension had been added
to the language; an envelope of harmonics and harmonies spread
outward to embrace the whole poem; resonance has been achieved.

★   ★   ★

In the passages chosen for illustration it is clear that the 'music' i
as much a matter of pace and rhythm as it is of 'sound'. Melody is
musical term with no counterpart in poetry. The effects we hav
been noticing may properly be regarded as 'tonality', implying a key
centre from which the music may depart and to which it may return
Now that the classical notion of tonality has been disrupted b
atonal music it is possible to suggest that tonality may not be wholl
a matter of establishing and departing from fixed tonal centres. Wha
tonality does in fact secure in music is points of rest, points of recogni
tion for arrival and departure. In Western music these points hav
until recently been established by the harmonic relationships betwee
the notes in a scale or mode; other systems of tonality may well exis
and may well yet be discovered. The contemporary 12-tone musi
suggests a very much closer relation between tonality and rhythn
than has hitherto been noticed. I wish to consider the possibilit
that poetry is 'musical', not because it imitates or shares certai
resources of sound with music, but because it grows independentl
from the same root as music. That root I take to be a primal rhythmi
awareness in man.

★   ★   ★

Although rhythm is of all poetic elements the least susceptible to
analysis, it indicates most clearly from what level and range of con
sciousness the poem springs. On the one hand, 'the essence of object
called "living" is that they are rhythmic'. In poetry subject and form
are identical; the form is the poem. The rhythm is the form and th

life, because the rhythms of poetry (and of prose) are the rhythms of the feelings and thoughts there embodied. Whitehead has given a brilliant account of rhythm in his *Principles of Natural Knowledge*. 'A rhythm involves a pattern and to that extent is always self-identical. But no rhythm can be a mere pattern; for the rhythmic quality depends equally upon the differences involved in each exhibition of the pattern. The essence of rhythm is the fusion of sameness and novelty; so that the whole never loses the essential unity of the pattern, while the parts exhibit the contrast arising from the novelty of their detail. A mere recurrence kills rhythm as surely as does a mere confusion of differences. A crystal lacks rhythm from excess of pattern, while a fog is unrhythmic in that it exhibits a patternless confusion of detail.' [1] Rhythm is an arched movement which suggests that it can repeat itself; but in fact it never does repeat, for it is the springing up of a single lark in song in a moment that can never recur. A rhythm once created *can* be repeated by rote, though even in music that is scarcely possible; but a rhythm can never repeat itself. Rhythm is the stamp of the undetermined cause, the jet of inner self-determinate form. And rhythm can be classified and measured only in the roughest way; for rhythm is the constant surging and hovering and falling away of feeling, the stumbling urgent pulse which presents in any measurable interval of time a unique pattern. The rhythms of poetry—like every other fundamental feature of poetry—make themselves known only to the attentive and finely attuned ear.

A distinction must immediately be drawn between metre and rhythm. Poetry is a concentrated use of language; formal concentration is achieved by imposing physical limitations to induce shape and articulation. Metre is an abstract recurrent pattern of pulses which controls the length of rhetorical units. Metre like rime rouses the reader's excitement, suspense, anticipation, and imparts a stride once it has revealed the length of its measure. Metre, however, is an abstract pattern: it is never actually present in the poem, for the actual movement varies according to the natural stress and duration of individual words and groups of words. When the actual movement of the stresses in a poem does not vary significantly from the abstract metre,

[1] Herbert Read, in *Annals of Innocence and Experience* (1941; pp. 226–7), describes with what excitement he discovered in 1922 this and other passages in *The Principles of Natural Knowledge*. See also Dorothy Emmet, *Whitehead's Philosophy of Organism*, pp. 112, 599.

it is a sure sign that the poem springs from a shallow level of consciousness or is unduly cerebral and technical. And a poem which reiterates its metre insistently may become so soporific and benumbing that it soon fails to convey even the most prosaic and superficial meaning. Nonetheless, the abstract metre *is* implied by the actual movement of the words and may remain in the back of the mind, like the steady ticking of a metronome; and when the metre is present in this way it tends to throw into relief the non-repetitive movement of the rhythm.

Rhythm is more important to poetry than any other musical feature. Not only does it manifest the perpetual novelty of wholeness, but it is one of the conditions of a poem existing at all. 'The purpose of rhythm is to prolong the moment of contemplation, the moment when we are both asleep and awake, which is the one moment of creation, by hushing us with an alluring monotony, while it holds us waking by variety, to keep us in that state of perhaps real trance, in which the mind liberated from the pressure of the will is unfolded in symbols.' Yeats is here thinking probably more of the reader than of the poet; for the poet, rhythm is inseparable from the poem, the poem being conceived to a great extent *as* rhythm. Yeats again has given a vivid account of rhythm as an integral feature of contemplation; his description leads him naturally to remark upon the timelessness of contemplation and its power to call into the present the currents of recorded history and the symbols which live in *Anima Mundi*. 'But the passions, when we know that they cannot find fulfilment, become vision; and a vision, whether we wake or sleep, prolongs its power by rhythm and pattern, the wheel where the world is butterfly. We need no protection but it does, for if we become interested in ourselves, in our own lives, we pass out of the vision. Whether it is we or the vision that create the pattern, who set the wheel turning, it is hard to say, but certainly we have a hundred ways of keeping it near us: we select our images from past times, we turn from our own age and try to feel Chaucer nearer than the daily paper.' If the poet's contemplative state is sustained by rhythm it is the rhythm of the apprehended reality which commands that state, clamouring to find a body.

*　　　*　　　*

My purpose, however, is not to give an account of poetry in all its physical features, but to sketch out the processes which terminate in poetry and to show how these processes manifest themselves in the physical features of poetry. But so overwhelmingly important is rhythm—both in 'the secret joinery of verse' and when we form critical assessments of poems—that we may consider a little further some of the resources and varieties of rhythm.

Various species of counterpoint arise in poetry from the inter-action of the repetitive metrical structure and the fluent movement of the rhythms, the momentary matchings, divergings, collisions, which dissolve and restore the relation between them.[1] And here, where metrical, tonal and rhythmic qualities are fused, we encounter the fully developed musical expression of the metaphorical process. Musical counterpoint or polyphony is an interweaving of melodic lines, each of which preserves its melodic and metrical identity. In poetry there can be no strict analogy to musical polyphony; for in speech it is scarcely possible for contrasting themes to be uttered simultaneously without confusion. But even in musical polyphony the simultaneous development of themes is a means of embodying complex feeling. The compelling power of musical counterpoint—and probably its essential character—is found in its urgent forward movement, complex texture, and subtle rhythms.

Contrapuntal themes in music, like the elements of metaphor, maintain their distinctness in the interweaving; but in their conflict and interinanimation they produce effects other than harmonic com-binations. The conjunction and separation of the distinct themes produces tonal ambiguities, to which there is no precise parallel in poetry. But the most important effects of counterpoint are rhythmical; for the rhythms reveal more directly the informing passion than do the shapes of the separate themes; and each melodic theme will have some metrical shape. That the central feature of musical counterpoint

[1] Although my use of the term 'counterpoint' in this section does not derive from Hopkins's use, it is interesting to quote the relevant section from the 'Author's Preface' to his *Poems*. 'If . . . the reversal [of stress] is repeated in two feet running, especially so as to include the sensitive second foot, it must be due either to great want of ear or else is a calculated effect, the superinducing or *mounting* of a new rhythm upon the old; and since the new or mounted rhythm is actually heard and at the same time the mind naturally supplies the natural or standard foregoing rhythm, for we do not forget what the rhythm is that by rights we should be hearing, two rhythms are in some manner running at once and we have something answerable to counterpoint in music, which is two or more strains of tune going on together, and this is Counterpoint Rhythm . . . And in fact if you counterpoint throughout, since one only of the counter rhythms is actually heard, the other is really destroyed or cannot come to exist, and what is written is one rhythm only and probably Sprung Rhythm. . . .'

is rhythm rather than theme is shown by the forward impulse of contrapuntal thought. Rhythm arises, not only from interweaving the independent metrical schemes; for this would tend merely to produce a larger-scale metre. It also arises from the disposition of tonal points of rest, ambiguity, and implied resolution.[1] A vertical harmonic music, though powerful in establishing tone and mood, cannot rise to the subtleties of rhythm, emphasis, and transition that are found in counterpoint. In both choral and instrumental music, counterpoint commonly appears at moments of most passionate intensity; not by accident do so many sets of variations end in a fugue, the most compressed and concentrated of all contrapuntal forms. Counterpoint is a mode of vocal writing; even when sophisticated, it preserves something of primitive rhythmic complexity—a complexity which the civilized mentality finds difficult to grasp or to reproduce. The contrapuntal method when manipulated by rote can be as arid as any other technical mode applied without artistic necessity. But to suppose that counterpoint is 'mathematical' and that Bach's fugues—or Hindemith's—could have been written by a calculating machine is a comfortable fallacy enjoyed by unmusical sophisticates in all periods.[2]

*　　　*　　　*

The salient features of musical counterpoint are its subtle and com-

---

[1] Since atonal writing has now secured the independence of all thematic material, any melodic line can theoretically be combined with any other. Most contemporary counterpoint is remarkably fussy, arhythmic, and arbitrary. But a few exponents of the 12-tone scale—notably Bartok and Hindemith—have discovered means of achieving genuine cadence, repose and movement as a basis for contrapuntal rhythm, by constructing themes (Hindemith particularly) according to firm acoustic principles of tonal relation.

[2] The dissemination of Bach's music through Europe in the latter part of the nineteenth century, and the faithful recovery of vocal and instrumental folk-music, saved romantic music from the sterile verticality of exclusively harmonic thinking. The harmonic principle of tonality reached a terminus in Beethoven and before long had sunk into the shimmering suspensions of Debussy and his followers. The rebirth of English music towards the end of the century arose from a characteristically English feeling for the singing voice; the recovery of much excellent Tudor and Elizabethan writing led composers to explore the polyphonic resources of the modern orchestra. Much of the early effort in atonal music and music written in new or neglected modes was shapeless and suffered from an incorrigible shortwindedness. This has now been redeemed by the rise of counterpoint in the 12-tone scale.

plex rhythms, its forward impulse, and the concentration of its patternings. Poetic counterpoint requires to bring into conflict distinct systems to produce similar effects within the verbal medium. For this purpose the English language and English prosody are admirably suited. Fundamentally, English is a stressed language and will not lend itself to quantitative (or periodic) measures as a sole system of scansion. But in the course of its development out of Anglo-Saxon it has by admixture with other languages undergone important changes in vocabulary, pronunciation, and syntax. The most important influences have come from two powerful and diverse sources: the classical languages, Latin and Greek; and the Romanic languages, especially French and Italian. Linguistic influences have modulated English versification by affecting profoundly the sounds as well as the character of spoken words. But the changes in English prosody have occurred not by attrition but by a continuous assimilation and adjustment of foreign principles. Different systems of versification have remained distinct because, by happy accident, they have been embodied in poetry of a high order before their character had been obscured. In the fourteenth century, when (as far as we know) most of his contemporaries were using a debased form of alliterative stress-scansion, Chaucer wrote his work (with significant variations) in the syllabic systems of the Romanic languages. The art of English versification had practically to be rediscovered in the sixteenth century, owing to a lacuna in English composition and the great changes in pronunciation since Chaucer's death. In the struggle for expression which flowered in the Elizabethan and Jacobean ages, English prosody was again germinated by French models, and through French by Italian. Even more important perhaps was the negative struggle to adapt the quantitative classical prosody. The final rejection of that single principle rediscovers and perpetuates the peculiar poetic genius of English as a stressed language. Yet quantitative prosody had subtly fertilized English prosody with the principle of duration as a basis for rhetorical scansion. This principle is prominent not only in Donne's poetry and in Coleridge's *Christabel* and in Gerard Manley Hopkins's sprung rhythm, but emerges as controlling factor whenever English verse turns towards the spoken word and the original scheme of stress found in Anglo-Saxon verse.[1]

[1] Milton's prosody in *Samson Agonistes* anticipates the later and more conscious search for organic forms in poetry. But so much of the *Samson* is in blank verse and in lines which—though of uneven length—are on the iambic pattern, that Milton does

All matters of prosody, and so of counterpoint and rhythm, are ultimately referable only to the ear rather than to any theoretical system; the stress and duration of words in a line of poetry will be precisely those of good speech when allowance is made for the poet's concentrated and deliberate use of words. English prosody has been taught so persistently on the model of classical (quantitative) and Romance (syllabic) scansion that a reader of English verse will almost inevitably establish in his mind an abstract syllabic metre as soon as the metrical shape of the poem begins to make itself clear. It is in the clash between the abstract and actual movements that the rudimentary species of poetic counterpoint occur. For example, an iambic pentameter line will theoretically comprise ten syllables, five of which will be stressed and five unstressed. In actually speaking the

not advance beyond the flexibility of Shakespeare's late plays. Even his boldest effects had already been explored (as Milton was undoubtedly aware) by Shakespeare.

> *O dark, dark, dark, amid the blaze of noon,*
> *Irrecoverably dark, total Eclipse*
> *Without all hope of day!*

(For all the hard things T. S. Eliot has said about Milton this passage echoed in his memory. In *Samson Agonistes* Milton continues, three lines later:

> *The Sun to me is dark*
> *And silent as the Moon,*
> *When she deserts the night*
> *Hid in her vacant interlunar cave.*

And at the opening of the third section of *East Coker* Eliot writes:

> *O dark dark dark. They all go into the dark,*
> *The vacant interstellar spaces, . . .*)

Hopkins's sprung rhythms, and heavy alliteration (another distinctively Anglo-Saxon feature), were evolved spontaneously by him to supply his needs in poetic expression, and were controlled by fastidious reference to the complex principles of classical prosody. Two extracts from his letters establish this clearly. 'To my ear no alliteration is more marked or more beautiful [than alliteration in vowels], and I used to take it for granted as an obvious fact that every initial letter led to every other before ever I knew that anything of the sort was practised in Anglo Saxon verse.' 'Sprung rhythm, once you hear it, is so eminently natural a thing and so effective a thing that if [earlier poets] had known it they would have used it. . . . So far as I know—I am enquiring and presently I shall be able to speak more decidedly—it existed in full force in Anglo Saxon and in great beauty; in a degraded and doggerel shape in *Piers Plough-man* . . . ; Greene was the last who employed it at all consciously and he never continuously; then it disappeared—for one cadence in it here and there is not sprung rhythm and one swallow does not make a spring.' (*Letters*, III, 183; I, 156.)

line, however, the stressed syllables will not be of equal force, and there will be considerable variety among the unstressed syllables, for some will stand midway between the stressed and unstressed. Even though the metre may imply five (or five and a half) uniformly iambic feet, the spoken line may produce as few as three—very occasionally two—strongly stressed syllables or as many as seven, and occasionally eight. The octave of Shakespeare's *Sonnet 55* will serve as an illustration. (The strong natural stresses are marked with an accent, the doubtful or half-stresses with a cross.)

Not marble, nor the gilded monuments	(3 or 4)
Of princes, shall outlive this powerful rime,	(4)
But you shall shine more bright in these contents	(5)
Than unswept stone, besmeared with sluttish time.	(5)
When wasteful war shall statues overturn,	(5)
And broils root out the work of masonry,	(4)
Nor Mars his sword nor war's quick fire shall burn	(6)
The living record of your memory.	(3 or 4)
'Gainst death and all-oblivious enmity	(4 or 5)
Shall you pace forth; your praise shall still find room	(6 or 7)
Even in the eyes of all posterity	(4)
That wear this world out to the ending doom.	(5 or 6)

The first two lines impart a strong forward movement, a rapid anacrustic effect. The stable core of 5-stress lines, each of which approaches closely to the abstract pattern, disintegrates under the force of heightening feeling; and after two 3-stress lines which differ markedly from each other, the crisis is reached in the solemn emphatic tread of the long tenth line; the octave closes cadentially on a 5-stress line which shows a single important variation from the abstract metre.[1]

This may be called *metrical* counterpoint; in which two distinct

[1] It is interesting to notice with what freedom and urgency Milton strides into the first lines of any book of *Paradise Lost*, and how firmly he closes most of the books with an emphatically final and exact 5-stress line.

metrical systems—the abstract and the actual—are related within the unit of single lines. In Hopkins's view, Milton is the greatest master of this species of counterpoint; but it is to be seen in the work of any mature poet, more particularly in blank verse, the sonnet, and where the ends of lines are clearly defined.

> *Thus was I, sleeping, by a brother's hand*
> *Of life, of crown, of queen, at once dispatcht:*
> *Cut off even in the blossoms of my sin,*
> *Unhousell'd, disappointed, unaneled;*
> *No reckoning made, but sent to my account*
> *With all my imperfections on my head:*
> *O, horrible! O, horrible! most horrible!*
>
> (SHAKESPEARE)

> *Faustus, these books, thy wit, and our experience*
> *Shall make all nations to canonize us. . . .*
> *Like lions shall they guard us when we please;*
> *Like Almaine rutters with their horseman's staves,*
> *Or Lapland giants, trotting by our sides;*
> *Sometimes like women, or unwedded maids,*
> *Shadowing more beauty in their airy brows*
> *Than has the white breasts of the queen of love:*
> *From Venice shall they drag huge argosies,*
> *And from America the golden fleece*
> *That yearly stuffs old Philip's treasury;*
> *If learned Faustus will be resolute.*
>
> (MARLOWE)

> *You may discern the shape of loveliness*
> *More perfect in her tears than in her smiles:*
> *She will muse for hours together; and her silence,*
> *Methinks, expresseth more than if she spake.*
>
> (WEBSTER)

The variations of stress in metrical counterpoint not only control the pace and emphasis of the lines, but hint at and sometimes overflow into a broader rhythmic movement—'the harsh and abrupt crossing of the rhythmical [and metrical] by the rhetorical pattern' that Grierson noticed in Donne's *Satyres*.

> *Thinke he which made your waxen garden, and*
> *Transported it from Italy to stand*

With us, at London, flouts our Presence, for
Just such gay painted things, which no sappe, nor
Test have in them, ours are; And naturall
Some of the stocks are, their fruits, bastard all.

Since rhythm is non-repetitive and unclassifiable, and since any rhythm may pass fluently from one order to another, few distinct species of rhythmic counterpoint can to any purpose be distinguished. Any stanzaic form implies metrical counterpoint by reiterating the stanza as a rhetorical unit larger than a line. *Terza rima* is a particularly interesting instance of this counterpoint. As used by Dante, each triad is a long rhetorical unit, conceived as a single expression which embraces the line-unit, the triads being held together by the interlocked rime-scheme *aba, bcb, cdc,* &c. Shelley, in the excitement of his *Ode to the West Wind,* breaks out of this structure—which in any case he never mastered—to construct a new sonnet form which (as far as I am informed) has not been further explored. But a passage in Eliot's *Little Gidding* suggests that even in this classical form the triad-unit and rime-scheme are not essential features. Here a cadenced *terza rima* is fashioned into long dream-like paragraphs in which alternate feminine and masculine endings serve for rime.

In the uncertain hour before the morning
Near the ending of interminable night
At the recurrent end of the unending
After the dark dove with the flickering tongue
Had passed below the horizon of his homing
While the dead leaves still rattled on like tin
Over the asphalt where no other sound was
Between three districts whence the smoke arose
I met one walking, loitering and hurried
As if blown towards me like the metal leaves
Before the urban dawn wind unresisting.

When the line loses its recurrent identity (particularly by abandoning couplet-riming and persistent end-stopping), sweeping rhythms may gather up and cut across the metrical pattern to inundate the line-ends. Rhetorical units longer and shorter than the lines may be established and then abandoned, the rhythm surging forward in a compelling arched wave, resonant and ominous, which will gather into its scope many lines, a whole sonnet, a huge paragraph.

This powerful contrapuntal rhythm is often encountered in Milton, Wordsworth, Donne; but it does not rely necessarily upon the unbroken surge of the pentameter or the sustained weight of Miltonic paragraphing. Here it is again in George Herbert—staccato, nervous, resentful.

> I struck the board, and cried, No more;
> I will abroad.
> What? shall I ever sigh and pine?
> My lines and life are free; free as the road,
> Loose as the wind, as large as store.
> Shall I be still in suit?
> Have I no harvest but a thorn
> To let me blood, and not restore
> What I have lost with cordial fruit?
> Sure there was wine,
> Before my sighs did dry it: there was corn,
> Before my tears did drown it.
> Is the year only lost to me?
> Have I no bays to crown it?
> No flowers, no garlands gay? all blasted?
> All wasted?
> Not so, my heart: but there is fruit,
> And thou hast hands.
> Recover all thy sigh-blown age
> On double pleasures: leave thy cold dispute
> Of what is fit, and not: forsake thy cage,
> Thy rope of sands,
> Which petty thoughts have made, and made to thee
> Good cable, to enforce and draw,
> And be thy law,
> While thou didst wink and wouldst not see,
> Away; take heed:
> I will abroad.
> Call in thy death's-head there: tie up thy fears.
> He that forbears
> To suit and serve his need,
> Deserves his load.
> But as I raved and grew more fierce and wild
> At every word,

MUSIC AND RHYTHM

Methought I heard one calling, Child:
And I replied, My Lord.

*   *   *

The purpose of this section has been to indicate in what ways rhythm, as the most immediate manifestation of vitality in poetry, shares the resonant character of metaphor and symbol.[1] As for the *musical* quality of poetic counterpoint, it begins to be clear that counterpoint is a rhythmic resource which poetry and music both exploit. If contrapuntal rhythms are as vital as I have suggested, it is unlikely that poets would borrow the device second-hand from music. Indeed poetic counterpoint is least rhythmic and powerful when it is most 'musical'. The key to poetic counterpoint is passionate contemplative speech—'blood, imagination, intellect running together'. It is when a poet utters forth his words with the cadence of actual vigorous speech that his poetry is most rhythmic and most bespeaks vitality. When he treats words as homogeneous sounds—as though they were musical tones varying only in pitch and *timbre,* to be patterned in terms of time and emphasis—his verse may become sonic, harmonious, smooth, but it will probably also be slack and enervating. Consider the harmonious musicality of an early Yeats poem:

A weariness comes from those dreamers, dew-dabbled, the lily and rose;
Ah, dream not of them, my beloved, the flame of the meteor that goes,
Or the flame of the blue star that lingers hung low in the fall of the dew:
For I would we were changed to white birds on the wandering foam:
*   I and you!*

[1] Two other instances of what (in a very general way) might be called counterpoint occur in poetry. (*a*) Two systems of symbols—one personal and one primordial—may be brought into conjunction. This perhaps, like the antiphonal devices of a repeated refrain or of two independent verbal themes interwoven, is dialectical rather than contrapuntal: it is primarily a matter of tensions and incipient rhythms rather than of fully developed rhythmic complexity. Eliot himself calls this 'counterpoint', thinking evidently only of the polyphonic and not of the rhythmic character of counterpoint. (In the closing pages of *The Music of Poetry* (1942) he considers theoretically how such polyphonic devices might be extended.) (*b*) The mode of combining simultaneous strands of meaning has been most fully and eruditely explored by Joyce in *Finnegan's Wake.* His system of biplanal and triplanal punning is controlled by allusions to selected texts—Homer, Giordano Bruno, Giambattista Vico. Being unmetrical, it bears to poetic counterpoint (I suppose) the same sort of relation that symbolic allegory bears to myth.

I am haunted by numberless islands, and many a Danaan shore,
Where Time would surely forget us, and Sorrow come near us no more;
Soon far from the rose and the lily and fret of the flames would we be,
Were we only white birds, my beloved, buoyed out on the foam of the sea!

And compare it with a passage from his epitaph poem.

You that Mitchel's prayer have heard,
'Send war in our time, O Lord!'
Know that when all words are said
And a man is fighting mad,
Something drops from eyes long blind,
He completes his partial mind,
For an instant stands at ease,
Laughs aloud, his heart at peace.
Even the wisest man grows tense
With some sort of violence
Before he can accomplish fate,
Know his work or choose his mate.[1]

In this second passage he is speaking the way Aileil spoke out of his sleep thirty years before:

not with his own voice or a man's voice
But with the burning, live, unshaken voice
Of those that, it may be, can never age.

*   *   *

In the concentrating process of composition all technical devices whatsoever tend to merge in the single impulse towards self-determinate form. No element loses its distinct identity, yet each interinanimates every other. 'All sounds, all colours, all forms, either because of their preordained energies or because of long association, evoke indefinable and yet precise emotions, or, as I prefer to think, call down among us certain disembodied powers, whose footsteps over our hearts we

---

[1] *The White Birds* and *Under Ben Bulben*. It is interesting to compare the second Book of *The Wanderings of Oisin* (1889) with the opening pages of *The Old Age of Queen Maeve* (1903). The difference is not simply in the firmer sense of form, but in the broken melodic line of the peasant voice—John Synge's version of peasant speech. I suspect that Yeats's ear was always coarse (compared say with Coleridge or Arnold); but he made virtue of this disability by finding how to impart a hoarse irony through vigorous rhythm and rough texture. His riming however is admirably subtle.

call emotions; and when sound and colour and form are in a musical relation, a beautiful relation to one another, they become as it were one sound, one colour, one form, and evoke an emotion that is made out of their distincte vocations and yet is one emotion.' But when poetic energy flags the resonance disintegrates, single elements assume obtrusive prominence, the texture of the verse turns coarse, banal, or monotonously smooth.[1] Consequently the texture of a poem—the whole inter-rove complex of sound, move-ment, feeling, and meaning—when submitted to the sensitive judg-ment of the ear, bespeaks the level of awareness and the breadth of integration from which the poem springs. In practice, critical atten-tion may at first be concentrated exclusively upon rhythm. Consider this passage from Wordsworth's 1805 *Prelude*:

> *To a lodge that stood*
> *Deep in a Forest, with leave given, at the age*
> *Of four and twenty summers he retir'd;*
> *And thither took with him his Infant Babe,*
> *And one Domestic for their common needs,*
> *An aged woman. It consoled him here*
> *To attend upon the Orphan and perform*
> *The office of a Nurse to his young Child*
> *Which after a short time by some mistake*
> *Or indiscretion of the Father, died.*

In *Vaudracour and Julia* (1820) 'The office of a Nurse to his young Child' is altered to 'Obsequious service to the precious Child' as token that the passage was revised; but the rest—incredibly—remains untouched. It is a mechanical ending tacked on to a heavily dis-guised account of an incident too secret and personal openly to publish to the world, and the passage insists upon moving 'like the forced gait of a shuffling nag'. So does the passage where he tells how his heart leaped up at first sight of London.

> *Never shall I forget the hour*
> *The moment rather say when having thridded*

[1] Verse of this sort readily supports ingenious analytical theories of poetry. Freud's generalizations upon poetry and art, for example, are completely vitiated by his failure to tell poetry from what was not poetry. Verse of a low order submits without com-plaint to analysis and will yield a number of formulae—both stylistic and psychological. But Freud (and most of his followers) never seem to have understood that what he said about artists was derived from questionable evidence.

The labyrinth of suburban Villages,
At length I did unto myself first seem
To enter the great City. On the roof
Of an itinerant Vehicle I sate
With vulgar Men about me, vulgar forms
Of houses, pavement, streets, of men and things,
Mean shapes on every side; but, at the time,
When to myself it fairly might be said,
The very moment that I seem'd to know
The threshold now is overpass'd, Great God!
That aught external to the living mind
Should have such mighty sway! yet so it was
A weight of Ages did at once descend
Upon my heart; no thought embodied, no
Distinct remembrances; but weight and power,
Power growing with the weight: alas! I feel
That I am trifling: 'twas a moment's pause.
All that took place within me, came and went
As in a moment, and I only now
Remember that it was a thing divine.

Or consider a couple of stanzas—at random—from William Cullen Bryant's poem *To the Fringed Gentian*: not hamstrung like the Wordsworth lines, but flat, lifeless and flat.

Thou blossom bright with autumn dew,
And colored with the heaven's own blue,
That openest when the quiet light
Succeeds the keen and frosty night.

Thou comest not when violets lean
O'er wandering brooks and springs unseen,
Or columbines, in purple dressed,
Nod o'er the ground-bird's hidden nest.

Or take a quatrain from that sad poem of Tennyson's—*In Memoriam*:

I hold it true, what'er befall;
I feel it, when I sorrow most;
'Tis better to have loved and lost
Than never to have loved at all.

Despite the Spartan consolation of the closing lines, this strikes dully upon the ear; we seem to attend upon a hypochondriac's sick-bed and watch the patient indulge the regimen he has prescribed for himself—

> The sad mechanic exercise,
> Like dull narcotics numbing pain.

And if a poet should apply his technique with conscious designs upon the reader and turn away from disinterested concentration upon the poem that is coming to birth, a coarse texture also results. The poem's integration is thwarted by the intrusion of any specific practical impulse, or any desire to impose a predetermined form from without; for, as E. M. Forster has said, a work of art is 'the only material object in the universe which may possess internal harmony. All the others have been pressed into shape from outside, and when their mould is removed they collapse. The work of art stands by itself, and nothing else does.' Edgar Allan Poe, whose work for a time was influential beyond his poetical capacity or his critical insight, offers a wealth of imprecisions and crudities—even if we do not descend to the facile janglings of his *Bells* or the inconsequent bone-rattling of *The Raven*.[1]

> At midnight, in the month of June,
> I stand beneath the mystic moon.
> An opiate vapour, dewy, dim,
> Exhales from out her golden rim,
> And softly dripping, drop by drop,
> Upon the quiet mountain-top,
> Steals drowsily and musically
> Into the universal valley.
> The rosemary nods upon the grave;
> The lily lolls upon the wave;
> Wrapping the fog about its breast,
> The ruin moulders into rest;

[1] Paul Valéry writes of Poe in 'Situation de Baudelaire', *Variété II* (1930): ' . . . la gloire universelle d'Egar Poe n'est faible ou contestée que dans son pays d'origine et en Angleterre.' Valéry makes no modest claim for Poe's achievement, on the grounds that by contact with Poe's work Baudelaire's 'talent on est transformé, sa destinée en est magnifiquement changée'. Poe's importance as catalyst in Baudelaire's development has little or no bearing upon his magnitude as poet and critic. His theory was a relatively crude restatement of Coleridge's theory, and his verse seldom if ever rises above the level of oddity and contrivance.

> *Looking like Lethe, see! the lake*
> *A conscious slumber seems to take,*
> *And would not, for the world, awake.*
> *All Beauty sleeps!—and lo! where lies*
> *(Her casement open to the skies)*
> *Irene, with her Destinies!*
>
> ('THE SLEEPER')

Or consider the intrusion of a too-conscious struggle for the bizarre in Webster's *Duchess of Malfi*.

> *What would it pleasure me to have my throat cut*
> *With diamonds? or to be smothered*
> *With cassia? or to be shot to death with pearls?*
> *I know death hath ten thousand several doors*
> *For men to take their exits; and 'tis found*
> *They go on such strange geometrical hinges,*
> *You may open them both ways: . . .*

'Thou art a box of worm-seed, at best but a salvatory of green mummy. What's this flesh? a little cruded milk, fantastical puff-paste. Our bodies are weaker than those paper-prisons boys use to keep flies in; more contemptible, since ours is to preserve earth-worms. Didst thou ever see a lark in a cage? Such is the soul in the body: this world is like her little turf of grass, and the heaven o'er our heads, like her looking-glass, only gives us a miserable knowledge of the small compass of our prison.'

Here are no trumpet notes; we can distinctly see a hand turning a crank. 'Poetry should be great and unobtrusive,' Keats cried; 'If Poetry come not as naturally as Leaves to a tree it had better not come at all.' There is asperity in these words: he hated 'poetry that has a palpable design upon us', and on this occasion was refusing 'to be bullied [by Wordsworth] into a certain Philosophy engendered in the whims of an Egoist'. Whether, in a particular instance, coarseness of texture arises from shallowness of feeling or an inappropriate attitude to the materials cannot always be determined: the two defects often go together.

If the technical 'devices' of a poem grow directly out of the poem's inner need they will be so closely woven into the fabric of the poem that you could not say whether they comprised the poem or were ancillary to it. When that inner need is satisfied—sustained, nourished, contemplated until it has found its body—the tone, the tune, is unmistakable: it is Tom Piper's whistle and we cannot choose but hear. Listen to Shakespeare and to Donne.

> *The odds is gone*
> *And there is nothing left remarkable*
> *Beneath the visiting moon.*

· · · · · ·

> *These miracles we did; but now alas,*
> *All measure, and all language, I should pass,*
> *Should I tell what a miracle she was.*

We hear this tone even in the symbol-haunted liturgical movement of some of Coleridge's prose: 'And even when all men have seemed to desert us and the friend of our heart has passed on, with one glance from his "cold disliking eye"—yet even then the blue heaven spreads it out and bends over us, and the little tree still shelters us under its plumage as a second cope, a domestic firmament, and the low creeping gale will sigh in the heath-plant and soothe us by the sound of sympathy till the lulled grief lose itself in fixed gaze on the purple heath-blossom, till the present beauty becomes a vision of beauty.' But was not Matthew Arnold wrong to find the quintessence of poetry in short fragments and phrases? Rhythm and tone need room and impetus to establish themselves—more room than a phrase, for the next phrase may destroy it. Suddenly it will burst into full orchestration—the sound, the rhythm, the symbolic resonance, the swift eagle-stooping from image to image, the sword-flash of intelligence, the tone unfolding itself in ineluctable rightness of rhythm. Between what is genuinely Poetic and what is simply 'good poetry' there is an absolute difference. This is the quality of true Poetic.

FELIX RANDAL

> *Felix Randal the farrier, O he is dead then? my duty all ended,*
> *Who have watched his mould of man, big-boned and hardy-handsome*
> *Pining, pining, till time when reason rambled in it and some*
> *Fatal four disorders, fleshed there, all contended?*
>
> *Sickness broke him. Impatient he cursed at first, but mended*
> *Being anointed and all; though a heavenlier heart began some*
> *Months earlier, since I had our sweet reprieve and ransom*
> *Tendered to him. Ah well, God rest him all road ever he offended!*

This seeing the sick endears them to us, us too it endears.
My tongue had taught thee comfort, touch had quenched thy tears,
Thy tears that touched my heart, child, Felix, poor Felix Randal;

How far from then forethought of, all thy more boisterous years,
When thou at the random grim forge, powerful amidst peers,
Didst fettle for the great grey drayhorse his bright and battering sandal! [1]

(G. M. HOPKINS)

MARINA

What seas what shores what grey rocks and what islands
What water lapping the bow
And scent of pine and woodthrush singing through the fog
What images return
O my daughter.

Those who sharpen the tooth of the dog, meaning
Death
Those who glitter with the glory of the hummingbird, meaning
Death
Those who sit in the stye of contentment, meaning
Death
Those who suffer the ecstasy of the animals, meaning
Death

Are become unsubstantial, reduced by a wind,
A breath of pine, and the woodsong fog
By this grace dissolved in place

What is this face, less clear and clearer
The pulse in the arm, less strong and stronger—
Given or lent? more distant than stars and nearer than the eye

Whispers and small laughter between leaves and hurrying feet
Under sleep, where all the waters meet.

Bowsprit cracked with ice and paint cracked with heat.
I made this, I have forgotten
And remember.
The rigging weak and the canvas rotten
Between one June and another September.

[1] The collocation of 'cursed at first', however, is distressingly contrived—as is the phrase 'my heart stirred for a bird' in the otherwise flawless *Windhover*. Hopkins himself was fully aware of the dangers of 'overgreat contrivance . . . to the annulling in the end of the right effect'; yet he did not always circumvent those rocks.

Made this unknowing, half conscious, unknown, my own.
The garboard strake leaks, the seams need caulking.
This form, this face, this life
Living to live in a world of time beyond me; let me
Resign my life for this life, my speech for that unspoken,
The awakened, lips parted, the hope, the new ships.

What seas what shores what granite islands towards my timbers
And woodthrush calling through the fog
My daughter.

(T. S. ELIOT)

THE COLD HEAVEN

Suddenly I saw the cold and rook-delighting heaven
That seemed as though ice burned and was but the more ice,
And thereupon imagination and heart were driven
So wild that every casual thought of that and this
Vanished, and left but memories, that should be out of season
With the hot blood of youth, of love crossed long ago;
And I took all the blame out of all sense and reason,
Until I cried and trembled and rocked to and fro,
Riddled with light. Ah! when the ghost begins to quicken,
Confusion of the death-bed over, is it sent
Out naked on the roads, as the books say, and stricken
By the injustice of the skies for punishment?

(W. B. YEATS)

Here the sound subserves and intensifies the verbal quality of the words; the spoken rhythm not only gives muscle, nerve, and momentum, but almost *is* the poem. Here we feel the whiplash of originality, and the inevitability of form. Suddenly the intimate impersonal moment is embodied, and sustained in a single arched flight of utterance, at once colloquial and hieratic.

XI

Poetry and Criticism

The knowledge of reality is always in some measure a secret knowledge. It is a kind of death.
WILLIAM BUTLER YEATS

Works of art are of an infinite loneliness and with nothing so little to be reached as with criticism.
RAINER MARIA RILKE

THE view of poetry implied in my previous chapters may conveniently be summarized.

1. Poetry realizes, bodies forth, incarnates experience of a special kind. This experience I have called 'paradeigmatic' because it is self-evident and bears within itself a recognition of intrinsic Value. The recognition of Value is also a grasp of reality carrying with it the conviction of genuine knowing; this knowing is pre-logical and requires no external tests to establish itself. This state of knowing manifests itself simultaneously in other modes; as perceptual vividness and intricate feeling.

2. Paradeigmatic experience presents itself as an extensive disturbance of consciousness, as a complex and distinct state of heightened awareness; and this seeks to discharge itself in such a way as faithfully to preserve the structure, intricacy and distinctness of the associated feeling. In the process of symbolic extrication, the state of feeling is transmuted into a patterned artefact; this transmutation plays an indispensable part in clarifying the event of reality, the state of feeling, and the poet's self. The poem in this way makes accessible to contemplation some aspect of reality.

3. Poetry is catharsis, integration, and discovery. Catharsis occurs

when the paradeigmatic feeling has been successfully realized; it presents itself as a stasis, a 'momentary peace', as the termination of an activity which has achieved integration at several levels of consciousness. Poetry is not escape but 'inscape'; it is at once a discovery and fashioning of some aspect of reality and of the self. The event of reality is not fully and clearly known until it has achieved the physical body of a poem.

4. Poetry is neither 'self-expression', nor spontaneous neural response to stimulus. It occurs in a person capable of complex response and integration. Poetry is self-transcending and represents the feeling of being immersed in reality. The poem is fashioned as an indispensable condition of the poet's extricating himself from that immersion and returning to the 'ordinary' world. When the poem is complete, it has been (as it were) secreted; it has been extruded, is separated from the author, and no longer belongs to him. The poem happened and was made through him; but since the process both 'remakes' the poet and is a condition of survival, the author's name merely indicates a point at which time and poetic process intersect. If there are several such intersections for one poet, we are able to infer from them something of that poet's nature—as a poet.

5. The formal features of poems arise from the concentrating effort of that self-circling activity which makes language symbolic; and poetic process, being comprehensive and integrative in every one of its phases, imparts the globe-like singleness which is 'form'. The event of reality reveals itself most directly when the feeling for that reality is clarified and sustained rhythmically. The self-contained unity of the poem arises from rhythmic synthesis.

6. Poetry 'expresses' reality and 'reality' is a personally apprehended system of relations. Every poem is a monad which does not rely upon any other for its Value. A poem may become clearer when read in the context of other works by the same poet: but the symbolic 'meaning' is contained within the single poem. All symbolic meanings are complex and paradoxical, and reveal themselves gradually but never completely. The Value of poetry derives from its origin in reality and not from any conceptual or symbolic structure outside itself; it rests upon a primitive mode of apprehension and a prelogical mode of knowing. Intellectual activity interpenetrates the prelogical mode to criticize the process of poetic embodiment; but intellect is not the poet's sovereign faculty. Poetic process is characteristically perceptual and physical, a matter of feeling rather than of thought or

ideas. Intellect and intelligence are important in refining and enriching the possibilities of perceptual experience, but play a minor role in the process itself. Poetry cannot arise from any activity predominantly conceptual.

7. The materials that accumulate, fuse, and constellate in imagination—in the image-making process—are 'matters of fact' vividly perceived and endowed with their aesthetic character in the poet's primal act of perception.

8. Poetry is metaphysical; its primary function is directly to 'body forth' reality and Being. No other mode of human expression can fulfil this function.

9. The rhythmic character of poems and the intricacy of their textures manifest with sensitive exactness the poet's *intension*. Intension is the person's passionate orientation towards some aspect of Value. A poem, being an 'entity of direct appeal', is judged by being recreated. The worth of a poem cannot be determined from the history of its genesis; neither can it be scientifically assessed as though it were a substantial 'thing'. For the physical poem can never be separated from the dynamic triad poet-poem-reader.

10. The speculative foundations of criticism will be a critique of Value and a critique of intension.

*   *   *

How does this view affect our view of the function and principles of criticism? The question may be clarified by examining a statement of Sir Maurice Bowra's in *The Heritage of Symbolism* (1947).

'No one, not even Aristotle, has found a satisfactory definition of poetry. We all think that we know what it is, but soon find that our idea of it is not shared by our contemporaries, let alone by the great critics of the past. Each definition seems both to include and to exclude too much. The fact is that the theory and practice of poetry differ from age to age. It lives by change and is constantly renewed by the introduction of new standards and new technique. What satisfied one period cannot satisfy another. On a long view the conception of poetry seems to oscillate between two extremes, between instruction and magic.'

I do not understand the passion for attempting to *define* poetry. Do some people hope to smuggle in psychological case-histories for judgments of value, or stumble upon some water-tight technique of interpretation, or discover the magic formula for writing poetry? Poetry smiles at all such fond hopes. A poem simply *is*; or if we wish to take a leaf from Miss Stein's rose 'A poem is a poem is a poem is a poem'. Being multi-dimensional, a good poem has to be discovered for what it is; it must be encountered in the mode of Poetic. Whether or not it is important to be able to define poetry, it is of paramount importance to be able to *recognize* poetry. We recognize a poem when we encounter it in an appropriate attitude. An appropriate attitude is one that brings the poem to life for what it is; and only from the successive encounters with poems do we learn to adjust our attitude to any particular poem. For the adjustment of attitude arises with the recognition; the recognition is a self-fashioning to the poem.

There are, however, more serious reasons for disagreeing with Sir Maurice's statement. The 'definitions' offered at various periods do not reflect differences in poetry itself: they represent differences in the individual and social consciousness, in the range of the poet's awareness and the reader's conscience. *Poetry* is an unfortunate collective term; it confuses the activity which terminates in a poem—Poetic, Poesy, ποίησις—with the sum of physical objects that may be called poems, ποιήματα.[1] When 'poetry' is taken for a deductive generalization about all poems, historical changes in taste acquire a confusing prominence. Poetry (Poetic, the process) does indeed 'live by change' —but not by changes in poetic standards and technique. It lives by that constant principle of change in human life which insists that Value can only arise when a person engages in a luminous present. Poetry does not change; but it can manifest itself in modes more or less fully developed. Once a reader is capable of placing himself in the poetic attitude, contemplative, passively concentrated, so that he can read poems *as* poems, he does not make any adjustment for various historical changes in 'standards' and 'technique'. There is one standard and only one: the nature of Poetic itself, as self-determinate, self-evident. There is one technique in poetry and only one: whatever technique is required perfectly to embody this particular vision,

---

[1] The distinction between Poesy (the constructive power) and Poetry (all poems generally, or the practice of poetry) was never firmly established in the eighteenth and early nineteenth century; and the tendency in neo-classical verse to personify Poesy as a sort of Muse has prevented it from becoming anything but an elegant variant of Poetry. It is probably too late now to try to naturalize the word Poesy, despite its excellently pure Greek origin. Actually there is little need for a new term; it is not difficult to reserve Poetry for the process and 'poems' for the collective term. The distinction between the two concepts is, however, an illuminating one for criticism.

whatever technique has achieved this particular perfect poem. The particular technique must be discovered for each single poem. Perfect technique is the poet's successive discoveries of Poetic at each crisis in his struggle to be real.

> *Nor is there singing school, but studying*
> *Monuments of its own magnificence.*[1]

It is not technical tricks that a poet learns from his mighty predecessors—any writer of advertising copy can imitate those—but the way of mind of the person engaged in vision, in contemplation, in reality. The quest is always the same—to touch upon the true nature of poetry: it may help to think of courting a fickle Muse, but either way it is a hard school. Some poets are better learners than others; some don't know what to look for, and find some paltry thing they came expecting to find; some can respond only in a restricted way and their work will inevitably bear the stamp of that limitation.[2] The 'great' poets have something in common beyond the vague generality of 'greatness'; they all put forth the same power, a capacity for luminous statement which places them beyond mere personality, individual opinion, or society.

> *The truly great*
> *Have all one age, and from one visible space*
> *Shed influence! They, both in power and act,*
> *Are permanent, and Time is not with them,*
> *Save as it worketh for them, they in it.*

Changes in the individual consciousness, changes in the culture

---

[1] Pope, with Horace and Boileau, thrust into a corner by his own argument, finds that the only imitable 'Nature' is Homer and other monuments of classical magnificence. Wordsworth, not ignorant of these forerunners, notes less argumentatively how the poet in peculiar measure may

> *Receive enduring touches of deep joy*
> *From the great Nature that exists in works*
> *Of mighty Poets.*
>
> (*Prelude* V, 615–19)

[2] The following sombre observations appear in John Hayward's introduction to *Poems 1951*—the Penguin edition of the prize-winning entries for the Festival of Britain Competition. 'What was striking in by far the largest number of poems submitted [2,093 entries were received from all parts of the Commonwealth] was the lack of what may be called any literary ancestry, of any evidence, explicit or implicit, that their authors had any knowledge of the English poetic tradition. Many of them, so it seemed, could rarely have read any poetry worth the name, or, if they had, were entirely unaffected by it.'

226

in which a person grows, demand that the nature of Poetic should be discovered and rediscovered, and affirmed and re-affirmed for each person to whom 'creativity' is a matter of life and death. Those discoveries and affirmations are not properly definitions; they are not translations from one way of speaking to another. They are spy-glasses through which we can see that country which alone gives access to the reality we all seek. But the spy-glass does not show the way through that country; for reality does not lie 'beyond'—it is all around us, always present, perhaps too present. That country is the interface: there is nothing 'beyond' it, there are no farther worlds to conquer. A few may trespass there by accident of birthright, by listening absent-mindedly to a tune which conceals its origin and meaning; they will not be turned out, but they will probably wander out again as accidentally as they wandered in. This is no country for anger or possessiveness; and only those who love, those who are in some sense innocent, can see any reason for remaining: for 'Innocence is the highest achievement of the human intellect'.

Good poems are not subject to changes in taste or fashion except in the hands of those who are not poets. By 'good poems' I do not mean what has sometimes been called 'pure poetry'. There is no *pure* poetry; poetry is as much physical as spiritual, as much sound as meaning, as much thinking as feeling; the earth always clings to the potatoes that contemplation secretes in the soil of awareness. The claim for 'purity' goes with debilitated poems and with those fragmented persons who are desperate to contrive their own salvation. The claim is usually preferred quite naïvely as a new discovery—as though all good poems were not 'terrible crystals', as though any poem made in a state of grace did not burn 'with a pure gem-like flame'. For Yeats, the sphinx was a symbol so baffling and fruitful that it made him shudder as though he 'stared into an abyss full of eagles'. The sphinx, which has a man's face and a woman's breasts, and below the waist is animal, is usually taken for Orphic inscrutable wisdom. Is it not rather the symbol of that poetry which can in some manner make wisdom viable? When 'passion bursts into thought without renouncing its uterine darkness' poetry is born. Then the terror is loosed; for the scales drop from the eyes. Transfiguration is not the way of the world; it is not (shall we say?) endearing.

> . . . *were we led all that way for*
> *Birth or Death? There was a Birth, certainly,*

We had evidence and no doubt. I had seen birth and death,
But had thought they were different; this Birth was
Hard and bitter agony for us, like Death, our death.
We returned to our places, these Kingdoms,
But no longer at ease here, in the old dispensation,
With an alien people clutching their gods.

*　　　　*　　　　*

Again, Bowra suggests that 'the conception of poetry seems to oscillate between two extremes, between instruction and magic'. Whose conception? The poet's? The reader's? Does this refer to what poetry does in fact do? or to the effect a poet intends his poems to have? or to the effect that a reader demands? By 'instruction' he means presumably 'teaching', 'fulfilling a didactic purpose'. But the contemplative character of poetry is destroyed by the intrusion of any practical motive—even by such a high-minded motive as teaching. To be contemplative, poetry must be unashamedly disinterested.

But before assuming a facile notion of 'instruction' we might be well advised to consider what Dante's informing attitude was—or Milton's—or even Dryden's. Poetry does in fact instruct: it instructs the poet as well as the reader. Even Samuel Johnson's portentous statement that 'The end of poetry is to instruct by pleasing' can legitimately support the view that 'instruction' is integrative and gnomic and not simply paedagogic and didactic. A poem may instruct a reader in the sense that it may integrate him and deal him 'an immortal wound'; but it does so (as it were) incidentally. In the process of composition—no matter what opinions a poet may hold before or after that event—the poet cannot have any conscious desire to instruct, to teach, or even to integrate. Nor is it the poet's direct purpose to communicate, although in fact a poem can scarcely be said to exist unless it is capable of communicating. A deliberate desire to fulfil any particular purpose, except that of making the poem as well as it can make itself, will damage the integrity of the poem.

It is scarcely necessary to point out that 'instruction' and 'magic' are not antithetical terms. In rejecting 'instruction' as a 'conception' of poetry we are doing nothing more momentous than we do when we reject the view that poetry is 'communication'; for we are not obliged to accept 'magic' simply because we have rejected 'instruction'. But on the whole it is better to connect poetry with magic than with any-thing else. In an earlier chapter I have shown that the springs of poetry are contemplative, primitive, prelogical; and that poetry arises from the same attitude of mind that conceives magic. But magic is not merely superstition; nor is the primitive merely barbaric. It is the contemplative mind which brings into one comprehensive sweep all phases of mind and experience, memory and will, purpose and vision. Whatever emerges from that way of mind—whether it be a work of art, or more perfectly a way of living and acting, a state of being—exhibits a power and coherence which makes even the most brilliant achievements of the technical mind seem pitifully fragment-ary, even irrelevant. This power and coherence might just as well be called 'magic' as something else—provided we do not imagine that we know, before we have experienced it, what 'magic' is.

Poetic does not change any more than technical thinking changes. But poems change their physical features from author to author and from period to period—and in a more limited way from poem to poem within the work of an individual poet. What does vary is the content of the individual poet's memory, the range of his awareness, and more especially his view of reality. Each view of reality will be individual; but in every society, in any historical period, one typical view of reality will predominate and will be generally regarded as 'standard'. The dominant view of reality will have an important effect upon the poet: it will offer him beliefs which he can whole-heartedly accept, or it will clarify his revolt against it. For the poet must use language, the instrument of social communication; and he will be (in some sense) a social being or at least a member of society. At times reality has been generally envisaged as a universe of solid external 'things', connected together by more or less easily recogniz-able 'natural laws'. The Western world has laboured under the 'rationalist' assumption continuously for some three centuries, and now shows only rudimentary signs of groping its way out of that twilight. But no important poet has ever allowed such a view to dominate his work. Even though some poets as 'ordinary' men have subscribed to this view, their best poems betray them. The qualities that make Pope a great poet are not his 'rationality' or his fulminative common sense, but the excitement exquisitely patterned and incised, the tenderness implied by his fierceness, the breath-taking assurance of a keen though limited intelligence wedded to a delicate because limited sensibility.

From time to time efforts have been made to shift poetry into the technical sphere—or to dismiss it—by canonizing pairs of antithetical terms—objective and subjective, romantic and classical, realist and idealist. The next move is to divide all poetry into two camps, to champion one and be condescending to the other. But these pairs of terms are pseudo-antitheses, projecting the contrast between the technical and contemplative mind. None of these is a strict antithesis: in each case one term is more comprehensive than the other and in its activity embraces the other. Certainly they do not indicate differences in poetic process. The way of poetry is contemplative, disinterested, and synthetic: it has no other way.

★   ★   ★

Any piece of writing which does not spring out of the poetic process is not a poem; and conversely, anything which is not a poem will show clearly in its body that it has not sprung from Poetic. There is an extensive shadow-land in which are mingled poems scarcely realized and highly wrought but vain struggles towards poetry; here the critic has his feet in a treacherous way. Society may require for nourishment second- and third-rate art and quantities of what looks like art but isn't; but the critic's main activity belongs—at present—outside that shadow-land, unless he may wish to resort there for special exercise.[1] The distinction between poems and not-poems cuts across all the technical distinctions that have ever been contrived. Behind that distinction lies the radical difference between synthesis and analysis, between experience and abstraction, between total and partial assertion, between wisdom and common sense, between the real and the actual, between belief and hypothesis. The principal task for the theoretical critic at present is to discern those differences, to assert as luminously as possible the nature of Poetic, and to find some adequate means of inculcating Poetic. The object is not to supplant Logic with Poetic: we need both. But since Poetic falls outside the grasp of Logic, and Logic falls within the scope of Poetic,

---

[1] One cannot help supposing that the poet's task is greatly clarified by the existence of special modes for expressing vulgar emotionalism—the lyrics of so-called 'dance-music', most films, and the glossy magazines. Certainly no poet of any stature need start by supposing that he is expected to express 'emotion' for mass consumption. If Yeats, for example, had started writing in the 'twenties as Eliot did, would he have found his own astringent tone any earlier? Would he have come earlier upon that impervious 'irony' that Eliot so sedulously cultivated from the start?

it is unlikely that civilization will check its progress towards apathy until Logic has been placed solidly within the perspective of Poetic.

It is interesting to consider the pseudo-antithesis between objective and subjective—sometimes falsely identified with the pseudo-antithesis between classical and romantic. The distinction generally rests on the assumption that we can genuinely know what 'things-in-themselves' are, and overlooks the fact that all we can know is the relations between a responsive person and distinguishable features of an unknowable physical context. It is also generally represented that the typical attitude of the scientist is 'objective', and that the 'objective' (or 'classical') artist is somehow peculiarly faithful to 'things-as-they-are'. The scientist's professional attitude, however, is not objective it is merely non-subjective.[1] The scientific methodology requires that an observer behave like a mechanical recording instrument, that he eliminate all inner response except conceptual abstraction. In practice this cannot be achieved. When the inner responses of feeling are suppressed the integrity of consciousness is truncated, perception is a formulated monochrome of limited vividness. A one-sided response develops to preclude integration. Within such a scheme, a moral and valuable reality is inconceivable and the scientific ideal of true 'objectivity'—a state of integral awareness oriented upon the 'outside' world—is impossible. Scientific genius is rare because true objectivity is rare: it is possible only when the rules of scientific method are broken.[2]

Poetry, on the other hand, is always an integrated activity; and since wholeness (theoretically at least) may occur in any person, it is in this respect that Poetic may enter any life and any profession. Jacques Maritain has pointed out that 'through the harmonies it constructs, poetry handles and makes use of mystery like an unknown force. . . . Poetry in this sense is clearly not the privilege of poets.

---

[1] Professor Barker Fairley makes this point clearly in his *Study of Goethe* (1947). It is also implied—though not specifically examined—in Paul Valéry's *Introduction to the Method of Leonardo Da Vinci* (1894). And even Coleridge, despite his fondness for the terms 'omjective' and 'sumjective', records the distinction.

[2] 'Method' ($\mu\epsilon\theta\delta\delta\varsigma$) is simply a way of getting somewhere, of arriving, of getting into or through or out of a complication. 'Methodology' presumably should mean a 'science of method'; but is tacitly taken to mean 'the science of the method of science', and is used as a synonym of 'method' or an elegant substitute for that deplorable word 'techniques'. The function of methodology, however, would appear to be, not to enjoin a single method (at present the 'scientific' one), but to examine all possible methods and consider their interrelations, limits, and capacities.

It forces every lock, lies in wait for you where you least expect it.' The 'objectivity' ascribed to the 'classical' poet must be an integral vision arising in a state of total awareness; otherwise 'objective' poetry would not be poetry at all. Without total awareness there can be no paradeigmatic experience, no event of reality, no Value, no poem: nor could there ever have been a *Principia Mathematica* or a Theory of Relativity. Within the possible range of poetic activity, the terms 'objective' and 'subjective' can only refer to a consistent emphasis upon the 'inner' or the 'outer' world, upon the sense of 'withness' or of 'otherness'; if both these points of emphasis can terminate in poems, both attitudes must be contemplative and both must be capable (when fully developed) of bodying forth reality.[1]

If this distinction is carried into another art—the art of painting—it becomes even clearer; it will also help to resolve some of the false analogies commonly drawn between poetry and painting. The philistine assumes that a painting must always be 'about' something, that it represents more or less faithfully distinguishable objects in the 'outside world', and that because those objects are accessible to anybody's eyes it is quite easy to say how 'accurately' any object has been depicted and so to judge the excellence of the picture. Painters call this attitude 'literary'. 'Literal' would perhaps be a better term; for the philistine assumes that painting is only capable of 'depicting' and that poetry is only capable of 'describing'. Actually the art of painting, like the art of poetry, is a means of embodying states of feeling, visions of reality. In discovering a body for his feeling the painter may or may not select forms and colours from the 'outside' world. Yet if he does choose recognizable forms he will require to make them multi-dimensional, and to the common-sense eye they will appear to be more or less distorted and unfaithful. And so there arises the facile distinction between 'objective' painting which depicts objects or dramatic situations faithfully, and 'subjective' painting which does not accurately (photographically) represent its subject-matter. And the 'subjective' painting is supposed to arise from a wilful or pathological distortion in the painter which makes

[1] Herbert Read seems to be saying much the same thing when he writes in *Contemporary British Art* (1951): ' . . . for a painter to ignore the discoveries of a Cézanne or a Picasso is equivalent to a scientist ignoring the discoveries of an Einstein or a Freud. But what is gained by seclusion, from intensive contemplation, and from obstinate independence is, objectively, an intensity of vision and, subjectively, a visionary intensity.'

him 'see things differently'. The philistine can never understand that a painter is not obliged to record what he 'sees' upon the retina of his eye. Art criticism has suffered severely from the accident that painters are seldom competent writers; and competent writers engaged in art criticism have not always understood either the media or the problem of the plastic arts. Most art criticism is incorrigibly 'literary' and strengthens rather than eradicates the misconstructions that common sense is inclined to place upon paintings. The philistine's view—as usual—is an inversion. Painting that grows from a vivid grasp of reality is regarded as 'personal interpretation' or 'representation', an arbitrary and probably irresponsible perversion of 'fact'. Yet the relevant distinction, within the various views of reality, would be between formal and naturalistic. And if we were to regard two paintings of equal artistic merit, one formal and one naturalistic, there is a strict sense in which the formal is 'objective' and the naturalistic 'subjective'. For the formal impulse arises from recognizing impermanence and change and reflects the desire for stability: while the naturalistic impulse grows out of an unquestioning acceptance of the surface of things. The naturalistic painter accepts what T. E. Hulme called the 'messiness' of the particular impermanent object, while the formal painter seeks to reveal the universality and stability of the individual object.[1]

Plenty of pictures are painted without artistic impulse or necessity: many verses are written which are not poems. The distinction between artistic pictures and inartistic pictures is not the distinction between formal and naturalistic, any more than the distinction between poems and not-poems is the distinction between subjective and objective, or classical and romantic.

*   *   *

Where then do we find the consistency and solidity in poetry that can make reliable judgment possible? Language is—in one sense at least—an abstraction; but a poem is not an abstraction, it is not a structure of concepts. It is a physical entity made in language, but untranslatable. In its physical character it must be physically apprehended if it is to be grasped at all as a poem; and the bridge between

---

[1] This distinction is developed at some length by Herbert Read in *The Philosophy of Modern Art* (1952): it was first enunciated by Wilhelm Worringer and was diffused in English through T. E. Hulme's posthumous *Speculations*.

the physical and 'spiritual' in poetry is feeling. The poem, the physical entity, contains within itself a psychic potential, a capacity for inducing response of certain distinct kinds; it is a latent complex of feeling which can give access to the reality from which it originally sprang. If a poem is treated as though it were an abstraction simply, or as a physical object sharing the character of all other physical objects (which are also abstractions), the psychic potential in the poem cannot be released.

Somebody has described the artistic gift as 'a natural susceptibility to moments of strange excitement, in which the colours freshen upon our threadbare world, and the routine of things about us is broken by a novel and happier synthesis. These are moments into which other minds may be made to enter, but which they cannot originate.' The reader, the re-creator of a poem, does not assume towards the poem the same relationship as the poet. The poet, having established a particular relation between himself and something else (unknowable in itself), discovers and makes known to himself that relation, that reality, by transmuting into language his feeling for that relation. Once the poem is completed it has become a distinct monad; its connection with the poet's personality and his *mésaventures biographiques* is broken; having been externalized as part of the process of self-purification the poem is no longer a possession or an extension of the poet. The experience which the poem embodies is not an experience that can be grasped otherwise than through the poet as through a medium, a medium which is conscious, intricately organized, capable of integration, capable of modulating or arresting the experience at any stage of its development. The poem as the physical incarnation of that experience is the only means of recovering that individual experience; and that experience can only be re-created when the reader can regard the poem, not as a 'piece of stuff', but as containing within itself the power to regenerate a particular experience. But that experience is not a detached entity; it is a relation, in the same way that the reality from which the poem sprang was a relation. The 'experience' offered in a poem is not then a 'piece of detached reality' but the poet's feeling *of* and *for* a valuable relation. The nature of the poet as medium is indelibly preserved within the poem; the poet, that is, not as 'personality' but as purified and fully developed self, the essential self that nobody in the world may ever have seen except through the poem. In his poem, the poet goes naked before the world; elsewhere, like another person, he is only accidentally and fitfully luminous, only occasionally 'himself'; and like any other person he is more persistently opaque than luminous.

The poem then stands in the same relation to the reader as the poet stands to reality; but there the parallel ceases. For the poet made the poem as a means of purifying himself and clarifying his reality: the reader, if he can release the self-contained feeling embodied in the poem, allows to grow within himself the *final* feeling of reality which the poet has struggled to discover. What the reader experiences is not a repetition of the process of construction, but the state in which that process terminates. The poem stands at a vanishing-point; it is the one infinitesimal step between the brilliant energy of vision and the stillness of integrity.

When one seeks strenuously to 'understand' a poem, there is a temptation to direct attention upon the poem as a physical entity and to suppose that, like any other physical object, it will yield its secrets to systematic analysis. Certainly the reader-critic can never afford to neglect anything 'to do with the poem', and he must keep his attention very steadily upon the poem; but he does so in the same way the poet contemplates his symbols and for the same reason. A poem is inexhaustible to analysis because it terminates in a 'vision of reality'. Reality is a matter of relationships; we cannot refer a particular poem simply to 'reality', because reality is not a determinate entity. Reality is the great unknown and unknowable. We are constantly in quest of it, yet we can never fully know it and certainly we cannot possess it; the best we can hope for is to preserve our capacity for encountering reality in some of its aspects. Whatever judgments of reality we may make rest upon judgments of value. There are, strictly speaking, degrees of reality to correspond with degrees of value; for reality and value are inseparable.

Critical judgments then are internal; referable only to the internal nature of the poem when it is wholly and directly grasped, and to the internal nature of the reader when he is grasping the poem integrally. There is no external test, there is no quantitative test for the value of a poem; there is no way of being certain except through the 'holiness of the heart's affections', through one's own integrity and a conviction of the poem's integrity. There are direct routes of approach to poetry, and plenty of escape-roads; but there are no short-cuts. Whether we like it or not, poetry constantly strives towards a wholeness in which all technical distinctions interfuse and are obliterated. That is why there never can be a scientific criticism of art.

The case for criticism would be obscure—if not untenable—if it did not find its prototype in poetry itself. What in the first place is 'given' to the poet is not a text for illustration, but a germ to be brought to undistorted maturity. (Even the atheist Valéry says: 'Le premier vers est un don du ciel.') The fertilizing and exploratory influence which the poet exerts in discovering his meaning, his theme—and incidentally himself—is criticism. The poet suffers; at the same time he watches himself suffer with (as we say) critical detachment. He indulges in ecstasy; he stands outside himself. That ecstasy is not unconnected with love, a certain hospitable nicety of attention, an intimate concern for the welfare of what is being fashioned and uttered forth. And as Donne says of physical love: 'This ecstasy doth unperplex . . . and tell us what we love.' Criticism, as it occurs in poetic practice, is not simply a corrective scrutiny supervening upon the flow of 'inspiration'. It is nothing less than the poet's primary means of discovering to himself what he is saying; and it is also the means of fertilizing his germ, and his partial expressions, to stature and clarity. Criticism, as discovering and fertilizing, proceeds most fruitfully (it would seem) when the poet is concentrating upon the humblest and most minute details of versification, rhythm, rime, choice of words; when he is interposing those adroit checks upon sheer exuberance which will envince the form. The 'sense of fact' which Eliot (following Rémy de Gourmont) enjoins upon the critic is the poet's sense of what in any instance is relevant. Only in this way will the critic find his point of entry, the particular detail or technical feature which, on analysis, will enrich and vivify the poem. For a poem is not constructed out of 'facts', in the usual sense of that term; in the fusion of Poetic the poem becomes an integral fact which is its own and only warrant and final explanation. The critic's primary task is to become a good reader; and the reader's task is to be at once tentative, searching, ruthless, personal. Virginia Woolf, discussing the writer's task, has stated this admirably. 'One must put aside antipathies and jealousies and not interrupt. One must have patience and infinite care and let the light sound, whether of spiders' delicate feet on a leaf or the chuckle of water in some irrelevant drainpipe, unfold too. Nothing is to be rejected in fear or horror. The poet who has written this page . . . has withdrawn. There are no commas or semicolons. The lines do not run in convenient lengths. Much is sheer nonsense. One must be sceptical, but throw caution to the winds and when the door opens accept absolutely. Also sometimes weep; also cut away ruthlessly with a slice of the blade soot, bark, hard accretions of all sorts. And so . . . let down one's net deeper and deeper and gently draw in and bring to the surface what he said and she said and make poetry.'

The critic in his perfection will require something beyond extraordinary sensibility and intelligence; namely, superhuman humility. For his task is a very humble one: to bring himself naked into the presence of works of art; and if he have the gift, then to bring others; generating, by shifts infinitely subtle and tactful, the atmosphere of 'togetherness', of rapt attention, in which alone poems will yield their presence. To arrange works of art in order of comparative merit might not be an unprofitable occupation for the dog-watches, but a private matter not to be thrust upon the unwary in the hope of cheap revelations. Yet the critic's position is always unstable and vulnerable. He can never be done with correcting the uncritical; he is subject to the usual vanities and ambitions of mankind; he is victim to the gales of opinion, the deflections of corrective and didactic purpose, the temptations of promotion and enthusiasm, the attractions of spheres more specific and accessible. Is there perhaps some cure for the fragmentariness and partialities of criticism?

The standard answer to this question is aesthetics or a philosophy of criticism. Criticism is indeed the starting-point for aesthetics. But aesthetics is not simply a theoretical correlation of critical observations and dicta. Springing from a direct grasp of particular works of art, aesthetics is a direct inquiry into the modes of artistic expression. The Greek root of the word may profitably be recalled by saying that aesthetics is reflection upon modes of feeling. But we are no nearer to a solution; for the particular mode of inquiry will be determined by the subject of inquiry. We cannot assume that a professional philosopher is any better qualified to establish that mode of inquiry than a poet or critic is. For aesthetics there is required the same sort of attitude that has been ascribed to the artist and the critic: an impulsive contemplative attitude, profoundly different from 'curiosity', more comprehensive than refined connoisseurship; a restless centre of emphasis guided by a sensitive flair for relevance; a subtle tact in discovering and gently unfolding self-revealing processes. Aristotle offered a fruitful glimpse of this attitude when he observed that 'poetry is a more serious and philosophical thing than history'. By 'serious' he evidently means in this context something like 'morally profound'; he may also mean required for spiritual nourishment. This would enjoin upon the critic then a *serious* attitude, a posture of responsible delight, devoid equally of dilettante levity and morose earnestness. By philosophical he simply means 'passionately concerned with wisdom (or truth)'. Judging from his own practice and from his hints towards dialectical inquiry (long ago ignored in formal logic) he does not imply a system of abstracted generalizations moving towards universal categories. The word 'philosophical' seems to me to enjoin a capacity for what Gabriel Marcel calls 'reflection'. 'Reflection occurs when, life coming up against a certain obstacle, or again, being checked by a certain break in the continuity of experience, it becomes necessary to pass from one level to another, and to recover on this higher plane the unity which had been lost on the lower one. Reflection appears in this case as a promoter of life, it is ascendant and recuperatory, in that it is secondary reflection as opposed to primary reflection which is still only decomposing or analytic.' [1] Any merely technical or analytical inquiry will founder (if upon nothing else) upon the logical discontinuities of poetry. The sense of fact will need reorienting; for a fact—far from being a thing-in-itself—is a proposition about an event, and 'the truth of a fact, of any fact, is conferred on it by the mind that grasps it, by the understanding self'. Fact, sensitive apprehension, and the sense of relevance are then inseparable. And Truth no longer appears as a set of acquisitions, bits of information to be picked up and carried about, but as a value: 'it is only under this aspect that truth can become "something *at stake*" '—something worth dying for.

The risks involved in such an undertaking are evident.

> *In order to arrive at what you do not know*
> *You must go by the way which is the way of ignorance.*

The critic, or the aesthetician, must indeed be wary; he must be always on guard against himself—against his own prejudices, his own *clichés* of thought and perception, his own use of language. He must constantly refresh his images and analogies; words, phrases, and theories must be abandoned as soon as they begin to clot the blood-

---

[1] *The Mystery of Being* (1950–1) (Gifford Lectures for 1949 and 1950), I, x (summary). Two important corollaries should be noticed. 'Reflection is never exercised on things that are not worth the trouble of reflecting about'; and 'it seems to me essential that we should grasp the fact that reflection is still part of life, that it is one of the ways in which life manifests itself, or, more profoundly, that it is in a sense one of life's ways of rising from one level to another'.

stream of reflection. The number who can sustain this order of reflection is necessarily small; they will, as Marcel says of the audience
at his lectures, be 'distinguished less by a certain aptitude [technical
and scholastic] . . . than by the level at which they make their
demands on life and set their standards'. The difference between
criticism and aesthetics will be a difference merely in the sustained
quality of reflection; and the critic will be susceptible to aesthetic
reflections, not because aestheticians will be more competent to
frame them but because both reflect at the same level. At the root
of both activities is the reader, the apprehending person, sensitively
engaged with the actual poem.

> Out of the slimy mud of words, out of the sleet and hail
> of verbal imprecisions,
> Approximate thoughts and feelings, words that have taken
> the place of thoughts and feelings,
> There spring the perfect order of speech, and the beauty
> of incantation.

To that order and incantation the reader's ear attunes itself until the
whole person responds, called to a compulsive tune which shapes
him to the clarity and richness of reality. But that will be, not so
much the blinding flash of illumination as a dark incandescence—
partaking of the black fire of Milton's hell, and Yeats's 'complexities
of mire or blood', and the 'ancient pulse of germ and birth' that
Hardy sings. Any tags or charms that can invoke this reflection or
call us to that light are legitimate; and anything that brings a reader
to a state of alert humility is useful. Beyond that the reader must work
out his own salvation.

Acknowledgements

FOR permission to print copyright material, I am indebted to the following: Messrs A. & P. Watt for selections from *The Collected Poems of W. B. Yeats* and for a number of extracts from Yeats's prose writings; Faber & Faber Ltd and Mr T. S. Eliot for selections from his *Collected Poems, Four Quartets, Selected Essays,* and critical writings; Jonathan Cape Ltd for a section of James Joyce's *A Portrait of the Artist as a Young Man*; the Oxford University Press for selections from the Poems, Letters, and Notebooks of Gerard Manley Hopkins; the University Press, Cambridge, for extracts from Sir Charles Sherrington's *Man on his Nature*; Sheed & Ward for extracts from Jacques Maritain's *Art and Scholasticism,* and Editions Poetry (Mandeville Publications) for extracts from his *Art and Poetry*; Mr D. B. Wyndham Lewis for a paragraph from his *François Villon*; Faber & Faber Ltd and Mr Martin Johnson for a selection from his *Science and the Meanings of Truth*; Macmillan & Co Ltd for a few lines from a poem by Vachel Lindsay, and for part of a poem by Thomas Sturge Moore. Seven lines of the *Testament of Beauty* by Robert Bridges are printed by permission of the Clarendon Press, Oxford.

Index

Abstract thinking, 136–7 (Valéry); words, 122, 143–4, 154

Abstraction, 31, 35–6, 42–3, 47, 117; the eye as organ of, 102, 155–6; language as, 233; a poem not an, 233–4; and reality, 32–3; as a way of mind, 36, 36 *n*1, 46–8, 106, 128, 131; Yeats on, 119

Action, 22, 29–30, 29*n*, 35–6, 46–7, 68–9, 102, 130; the artist and, 47, 94, 107, 117, 140; suffering and, 68, 116

Aesthetics, xiv, xvii, 66, 237–9

Alexander, Samuel, *Beauty and Other Forms of Value,* xvii, 41*n*, 99*n*, 93

Allegory, 190–2

Ambiguity, 132, 206

Analysis, abstraction and, 36; Aristotle on, xx, 137; method and, xix-xx, 124

and synthesis, (Joyce) 18, 112–13, 230

Anschauung (intuition), Kant's meaning of, 53 *n*2

Aquinas, St Thomas, xiv, 17–19, 135

Aristotle, xiv, 224; *Poetics,* xxii, 12, 131, 142 *n*1; on analysis, xx, 137; on dialectic, xxi-xxii; on logic, 36, 56, 131; on metaphor, 142–3, 145*n*, 157; on poetry, 13, 237–8

Arnold, Matthew, 214*n*; on art as 'criticism of life', xxxii; on excellence, 138*n*; on testing poetry, 219

Art, Artist; *see also* Poet, Poetry

Art, xxviii, xxix, 2–4; nature of, 8–10; physical nature of, 11–12, 17–18, 45, 48, 97, 223–4, 233–4, (Coleridge) 55–6, (Joyce) 18–20, (Yeats) 21–6; theory of, crucial problem for, 48, 57–8, 96, 101; universality of, (Joyce) 18–19, 133–5; untranslat-

ability of, 2–4, 120; *see also* Definition

emotion and (Yeats), 22; and escape, 24, 72–3, 106–7, 108, 223, (Eliot) 69*n*, (Yeats) 47; as *impure*, 55–6; as non-propositional, xvii, 3–4, 106; personality and, 67–9, 234–5, (Eliot) 69*n*, (Yeats) 23, 83; and society, 21*n*; as universal language (Ruskin), 1–10

Artist, the, 41; autobiographies of, 15–16; detachment of, 25, 117, 117*n*, (Goethe) xxxii, (Joyce) 20, (Marcel) 74–5*n*, (Woolf) 236–7, (Yeats) 23, 38*n*; function of, 170–1; nature of (Bergson), 27

as androgynous, xxxiii-xxxiv; as 'creator', xxix-xxxvii, 93; as critic, xiii, 236–7; as medium, xxx, (Yeats) 29*n*, (Maritain) 38*n*; 223, 234–5; and society, xxx, 21*n*, 101–2, 117, 183–4, 229, 230

Artistic experience, character of, xvii-xviii, xxix-xxx, 10, 41, 234–5, and *passim;* facts of, xv, xxv-xxvi, xxxvii; knowledge and, xxiv-xxv; perception and, 96–7; and philosophy, xvi

Assertions, total and partial, xx, 42–3; J. L. Stocks and D. Emmet on, 32–3

Association, in dream, 24; 'free', 91–2; and memory, 79, 79*n*; Coleridge on, 81; Eliot on, 79–80, 79*n*; Lowes on, 64–5; Whitehead on, 101, 102; *see also* Fancy, Imagination, Memory

Auditory Imagination (Eliot), 157

Bach, J. S., xxii, 41*n*, 206, 206*n*

Bacon, Francis, 5

243

INDEX

Bartlett, Phyllis (*Poems in Process*), 15n
Bartok, Béla, 206 n1
Baudelaire, Charles, 31n, 91, 145; Valéry on, 217n
Beauty, xiii, xxxi, xxxiv, 4, 125n; Alexander on, xvii; Eliot on, 83; Joyce on, 17–18; Read on, xvii; Valéry on, 82n; Yeats on, 22, 22n
Beethoven, Ludwig van, xxii, 14, 41n, 206 n2
Béguin, Albert, *L'Âme Romantique et Le Rêve*, 139, 185n
Being, xxvi, xxxvi, 9, 167, 177, 179, 224; existence and, xviii, 43n; 'Unity of' (Yeats), 21; *see also* Self-being
Belief, 9, 164, 180–1n; and myth, 178, 179
Bergson, Henri, xiv, 34n, 113; *Les Deux Sources de la Morale et de la Réligion*, 116; *Introduction to Metaphysics*, 33n
Berkeley, George, and Johnson, 39–40
Blake, William, on allegory, 190n; verse of, quoted, 158 (*The Sick Rose*)
Bodkin, Maud, *Archetypal Patterns in Poetry*, 65, 66, 168; *Studies of Type-Images*, 31n
Boethius, 44
Boileau-Despréaux, Nicolas, 226 n1
Bowles, W. L., 91
Bowra, Maurice, *The Heritage of Symbolism*, 224–5, 228
Bradley, A. C., *Ideals of Religion*, 32n, 39
Brahms, Joannes, 14
Bridges, Robert, 1, 147
Browning, E. B. B., 153
Bruno, Giordano, 20, 213
Bryant, William Cullen, 216
Bunyan, John, *Pilgrim's Progress*, 191
Burgh, W. G. de, 138, 138n
Burgh, W. G. de, Mrs, 138n

Carlyle, Thomas, 185
Cassirer, Ernst, 128n
Catalysis, analogy of, 87–9
Catharsis, 108, 222–3
Caudwell, Christopher, 168 n2
Causal Efficacy (Whitehead), 99–103
Cézanne, Paul, 232n
Change and poetry, 225–8, 229

Chaucer, Geoffrey, 144n, 192, 204, 207; verse of, quoted, 14
Christian symbols, 176; myth, 179, 182
Clark, Kenneth, *Landscape into Art*, 124–5, 125n
Cochin, Augustin, 113
'Cognitive Ring', 102
Coleridge, S. T., x, xiii, xiv, 7, 13, 16, 49, 49n, 88, 91, 94, 119, 124, 142, 149, 158, 169, 214n, 219
    Biographia Literaria, 61, 172; quoted, xxix, 46, 51–3, 58, 59 n2, 59–60, 79, 88, 142, 149, 158; *The Friend* quoted, 51, 80–1; *Lectures on Shakespeare* quoted, 60; *Notebooks* quoted, vii, xxiv, 62–3, 71, 73, 74n, 75, 81, 95, 183, 186–8; *The Statesman's Manual* quoted, 52, 166n, 172
    The Ancient Mariner, 14, 68, 83, 140 n1, 185–6; quoted, 156; *Christabel*, 207; *Dejection*, 186n; *Kubla Khan*, 14, 64, 65n; quoted, 201–2; *Remorse* quoted, 183; *To W. Wordsworth* quoted, 226
    his interest in psychology and metaphysics, 46; his personal symbols, 185–9
    on allegory, 166n, 190; on association, 81, 183, 188; on communion with life, xxiv; on dreams, 71; and empathy, 73; on feeling, 80–1; on Imagination and Fancy, xxix, 50–3, 58–63, 103, 118, 154; on intensity and extensity, 135n; on Kant, 58n; 'logic of poetry', 142; on passion, 88, 158; and Poe, 217n; on the poet, vii, 51–2; on poetry, 13; on rest and motion, 193; on self-being, 74n; on symbol, 52, 172–4; as word-maker, 62–3
Collective Unconscious, 169
Collingwood, R. G., xvin; *Outlines of a Philosophy of Art*, 48n; *The Principles of Art*, 165n
Communication, 3–4, 5–6, 125–6, 129, 228
Concern, 6, 9, 43, 68, 97; D. Emmet on, 98; value and, 39–41

INDEX